sustainable
gardening

INTRODUCTION

When we go into the garden, we naturally tend to see things on a small, rather immediate scale; plants that need feeding, watering or other care; a path to be swept or weeds to be removed. While our thoughts may wander far and wide, our horticultural activities are not evidently 'global' in their importance. Our actions in the garden however, while small, do contribute to the overall state of health of the planet. In recent years, ecologists have moved towards the view that the earth is in essence a single, self-regulating system with physical, chemical, biological, and human components. The interactions between these parts are complex and far reaching and it is becoming increasingly apparent that human activities frequently and significantly influence it – not always for the good. We hear much about greenhouse gas emissions and climate change, but to this we must also add changes to the earth's land surface, oceans, and coasts through agriculture and development, as well as the changes that result from this to naturally occurring chemical and biological cycles. Indeed, the mass of humanity now present on the planet means that our collective activities are equal to some of the great forces of nature in their extent and impact.

The immensity of the problem ultimately seems to dwarf our own actions, but it is important that you understand that the magnitude of change is due to many individuals, all of whom have only a limited effect in their own right. Indeed, the only way to effect change is to change the activities of individuals. When you move towards sustainable practices in your garden, in a tiny way you are applying the

Sustainable gardens can be ornamental and, with a little prior planning, can be designed to contribute towards the wellbeing of the environment.

brakes to the problem, and while the effect is arguably limited, you no longer contribute to the problem. Indeed, in a small way, you start to become a part of the solution and any such positive action, while small in its own right, is worthwhile and often proves a rewarding and enjoyable experience.

What is a Sustainable Garden?

The term 'sustainable gardening' is hardly a new concept. Invariably, like so much in life, there is very little that we can do in the garden that has not already been done in one form or another. Sustainable gardening, like so many styles of gardening, mostly involves a range of well-established methods that have been employed

in gardens for centuries. At its core it employs good, sensible 'tried and tested' horticultural practices. It should not be seen as a fundamentally new way of gardening then, but as a revised look at the way that we design, make and maintain our gardens.

The basis of the philosophy that underlies sustainable gardening stems from the fact that the planet is getting to be a more and more crowded place, with scarcely a day passing when there isn't some new concern raised about our collective impact upon the environment. We care about it of course, but it often seems remote – too remote; with so very much being out of our own personal control. In short, just thinking about it can be enough to bring on feelings of stress!

These and other worries or pressures of everyday life are why we retreat to the garden; our own little havens of 'good clean living'. It comes as a shock to many gardeners then, when they discover that some activities they carry out in the garden actually contribute to the planet's ever-increasing environmental burden. A quick examination of the cost of this verdant retreat can turn up some surprises. The ever-increasing use of synthetic garden chemicals throughout the twentieth century, the ease and availability of powered garden implements, heated greenhouses, bonfires, plants and equipment transported around the globe by road, air and sea; all of these are part of the environmental cost of our gardens. Even though most of us have been quite innocently involved in this, we have nonetheless been complicit. All is not lost however, and gardeners are in an almost unique position to turn this situation around.

While sustainable gardening is essentially based on simple, well-proven horticultural techniques, it also represents a fundamental shift in the way that we view the impact of our activities in the garden. Acting sustainably necessarily involves taking a worldview while looking for a local solution. Sustainable practices are undertaken in the sure knowledge that even the smallest positive act can have an effect. Understanding the essentials of the planet's ecology and how this can be used to adapt existing practice within a garden is at its core. Having said this though, a detailed understanding of science is not essential. In short, anyone can become a sustainable gardener.

At its simplest, sustainable gardening aims to work with nature in achieving its objectives. In doing this, it will help to harness the potential of gardens to enhance and contribute to the wellbeing of the environment. In order to do this then, gardeners must re-assess the way they garden. This need not compromise the end result of a healthy, attractive outdoor living space. By learning to work with and not against nature – essentially understanding nature's rhythm – you can begin to garden within the natural capacity of your surroundings and still enjoy great results.

Most of the ideas are ideal for even novice gardeners to get to grips with, involving simple solutions such as cutting down on artificial additions such as fertilizers and pesticides and attempting instead to promote natural nutrient cycles. At its core is the aim to reduce, reuse and recycle all waste, as well as promote energy efficiency and resource conservation.

Of course, gardeners will still want to buy things and so advice is also given on making green choices in terms of what to look for when items are bought to ensure that they have as low an environmental impact as possible. Buying plants for example can be fun, but growing the seed is even better and has fewer environmental consequences in the long term.

Sustainable gardening also means paying greater attention to the environment within the garden, and what this really offers in respect of a place for plants to grow. Understanding this can help in the choice of plants, enabling the gardener to concentrate upon those that will thrive there with the least effort. A properly chosen plant will not need the pampering that is so often the expensive and environmentally demanding result of inappropriate or ill-considered selection. The cost of watering or providing artificial food for a plant can have environmental as well as monetary consequences. Choosing a plant that is fit enough to grow in your conditions avoids all of this and, in the long run, contributes to the wellbeing of the environment.

Ultimately however, the changes that you introduce into the way that you garden should never be seen as an excuse to compromise the beauty that results from a well-kept garden. The role of careful design and attention to detail are as important in a sustainable garden as in any other. Finally, the sustainable garden that you create becomes a fusion of your own needs and tastes – possibly in a style that is uniquely your own – achieving this in a way that is sensitive to the needs of the local and wider environment and fundamentally to every living person and thing around you. In short, there is no reason why your garden should not be the envy of other gardeners.

Will a Sustainable Garden Look Different from Other Gardens?

A garden maintained on a sustainable basis is, quite simply, a garden. As such it will be similar in most respects to other gardens, and its look will be dictated in many ways by what you want the garden to be – for example a vegetable patch, floral display or entertaining area. Ultimately then, sustainable gardens can be as diverse from one to another as other more conventional garden types, and can encompass a full range of garden types and styles. The general principles and practices of garden design and many familiar gardening techniques are all applicable to sustainable gardening practices, and so there is no reason why your garden should look vastly different simply because it has enhanced its green credentials.

The main thing to remember is that there is no room to compromise your standards. Good horticultural practice should be the ultimate aim in any garden setting. However, in certain respects your expectations may need to be modified, and this usually involves slight differences in the detail of the garden's appearance, while preserving its overall appearance. Examples of this include letting the lawn grow a little longer – it makes it more drought resistant and greener in dry weather – or it may mean adding or expanding elements such as composting areas or water storage butts. You might also want to consider though, that the higher you set your expectations, the more effort will be needed not only to achieve it but also to maintain it. The best choice for the style and content of a garden may well depend therefore on exactly what time and effort you can (or are willing) to put into it yourself.

The best way, then, to view a sustainable approach to gardening is not to see it as a process of limitation but to see it as an opportunity. By careful application of proven horticultural principles, clever design, a thorough assessment of your own requirements and a comprehensive evaluation of the potential of your garden to meet your needs, you can easily produce a range of garden styles. These, while possibly inspired by traditional concepts, can be new or hybrid styles that, while not being entirely unique, nonetheless borrow from and blend a range of existing styles. In this way you can innovate and ultimately create a garden space that reflects your own preference in terms of lifestyle, outlook and, perhaps even more fundamentally, your own personality.

A garden constructed and maintained along environmentally sensitive lines can still be as colourful and eye-catching as any other garden.

What are the Benefits of Sustainable Gardening?

Perhaps the most important benefit of a sustainable approach to gardening is that it allows gardeners to contribute positively towards the care of the planet. While it is no panacea, it is extremely positive and its results can be just as impressive as so-called conventional, less sustainable practices. It also helps to develop a world view and a sense of satisfaction that local action – action to which gardeners can contribute – is not adding to a global problem but is in fact a part of the solution.

Essentially, sustainable gardening allows gardeners to use what they have to make and produce as much as they can. Even modestly-sized gardens can produce

Even where space is limited, containers of various types offer you the chance to grow and enjoy a surprisingly wide range of garden plants.

impressive amounts of food or act as natural oases for wildlife. In addition, they can become a focal point for green ideals and may inspire other activities in their wake. They can become a place of fun and enjoyment for children and adults alike and, if neighbours share a common interest, sustainable gardening can even contribute strongly to a sense of community.

Most importantly perhaps, gardeners have the ability to add a vital element to the sustainability mix – the human being; the species responsible for much of the problem but also a vital part of any solution. Home gardeners are almost uniquely placed, as they tend the land for enjoyment. Keeping sustainable gardening enjoyable then, and not burdensome or dull is vital. Fortunately, the techniques involved in sustainable gardening can greatly reduce the maintenance burden of a garden; it uses methods that are both cost and time saving, while enabling gardeners to carry on growing what they like and enjoy. Essentially a sustainable garden benefits the environment in a way that is economical, productive and above all great fun and deeply satisfying.

THE LIFE CYCLE OF A GARDEN

Like nature itself, a garden is made up of certain constituent parts. These are essentially divided up into two parts; those that are or have been living – the 'biotic' or organic matter- and those that are non-living – the 'abiotic' or inorganic parts. In order to survive, living things depend upon many non-living elements, which in turn are often affected or changed by the living components themselves.

In simple terms, the non-living parts are things like water, the atmosphere, soil and rocks, as well as the range of chemical elements that form part of these. Living things of course include the plants and animals that we see in the garden, but also include a whole host of micro-organisms which, while being invisible, are fundamentally important nonetheless. In order to start to develop a full understanding of what is happening in your garden then, you must understand what these components are, as well as what their role and importance ultimately is.

The Living Elements of a Garden

Plants

All land plants, whether they are giant forest trees, or the briefest living annual weeds, follow the same pattern of life. Their lifespan, size, apparent durabil-

ity and survival strategies vary considerably, but in the final analysis they have much in common. The majority of plants in nature, and for that matter in a garden, are flowering plants and for that reason, these are the main subject of interest to the gardener and the main focus of this book. Flowering plants all begin their life as seeds; in essence tiny, baby plants that have been left in a state of suspended animation with enough food to support them in the first few days of their new life. In order to grow, these seeds must be 'viable' – that is to say still alive. It is a popular misconception with inexperienced gardeners that seeds are non-living. Of course they are not, and as with all living things, they have a definite lifespan. Despite this apparent limitation though, many types of seeds can be stored or lay dormant in the soil for considerable periods, even for decades, just waiting for the opportunity to commence growth.

Eventually the seed is triggered into germinating (commencing the cycle of growth and development) by the right combination of moisture, temperature and a suitable soil or growing medium, and is totally reliant on its 'on board stored energy' until it pushes its growing tip above the soil. Once above ground, the shoots grow up towards the light and soon produce leaves that unfold and begin to harvest light energy – much like solar panels. From this harvested energy, the plant produces food, using carbon dioxide and water (both inorganic molecules) to manufacture simple sugars (complex organic molecules) that are used to power further growth and development of the plant. As the stems grow upward, the plant also extends its roots down into the surrounding soil aiding its stability and allowing the growing plant to harvest both water and minerals that are vital for growth.

OPPOSITE PAGE: *Malus x zumi* **'Golden Hornet'**
**is well-named on account of its abundant fruit
that follow on from the blossom.**

Changes in internal chemistry trigger the production of blooms like this dazzling sunflower, as plants reach a mature phase and reproduction starts.

Once a plant reaches the stage referred to as a mature phase of growth, changes in its internal chemistry enable it to begin flowering. Exactly when this happens will of course depend upon the species but in many plants – except for those with the very briefest of life cycles – the plant continues to grow while it produces flower buds. These buds eventually develop into flowers, which are pollinated either by the wind, or more likely by pollinators such as bees, moths, or other animals.

Once the flower has been pollinated, the flowers will usually fade quickly before they turn into fruit as the fertilized ovary swells and the new seed develops. This seed will continue to develop within the fruit until the seed embryo is fully mature and the seed is capable of growing into a new plant. This may be very quick in the case of most small herbs but certain shrubs and trees can take two or more seasons for the seed to fully develop. Plants may take just one season to flower or may live for many years before flowering occurs. Once flow-

ering begins, certain species flower repeatedly for many seasons, some lasting decades or even centuries, and while there is a tremendous amount of variability in all of this, broadly speaking there are three types of life cycle seen in plants.

Annuals

Annuals are plants that, generally speaking, live for a growing season or less. In all cases their life cycle is completed within a year, in which time the plant grows, flowers, sets fruit containing seed, and dies. Many common flowering plants – and a good number of common weed species – adopt this strategy as it has the advantage of allowing them to colonize areas quickly and make the best of suitable growing conditions.

Biennials

Biennials are plants that need two growing seasons to complete their life cycle. As a rule, biennials germinate and grow foliage in the first year before resting over the winter period or in times of harsh weather. In the second year the plant enters a mature phase in which it flowers, sets fruit, and then dies. In this way it is similar to an annual as it flowers once before dying. A few flowering plants may grow just foliage for several years before finally flowering and dying and these plants are said to be 'monocarpic' (meaning one flowering).

Perennials

Perennials are all the remaining plant types that live for three or more years; growing, flowering, and producing fruit repeatedly. Some species may take a number of years to grow to flowering size but all of them are characterized by a more permanent existence. Within this group they are further subdivided into those that develop permanent woody growth above ground (shrubs and trees) and those that have soft, non-woody growth and tend to die back to ground level at the end of each season (herbaceous plants).

Animals

Animals are an extremely variable group but all share one defining characteristic; they must derive their food by eating something else. Unlike plants that produce food, animals are consumers and must either eat plants or other animals to get their energy.

They also share the characteristic of being complex, 'multicellular' organisms; many of which are able to move around freely in search of food. They vary considerably in size from those that are microscopic and therefore invisible to our naked eye, to familiar creatures such as birds, mammals and many common garden insects.

Other Life

Aside from living things classed strictly as animal or plant, many others exist which are less evident but equally important. Among these is the vast array of mostly soil dwelling unicellular animal-like protists, bacteria and fungi. Despite the appearance of some fungi, this latter group are not plants but share many things in common with both plants and animals. They have similar proteins to animals and must get their food by digesting organic matter and so are considered a kingdom in their own right. Many of these soil-dwelling organisms play a vital role in recycling living matter and ultimately liberate nutrients back into the soil. There are also however a number of their ranks that cause plant diseases, and these are of course something that we will come back to later in this book.

TOP RIGHT: **Many animals either live in or visit gardens, and while many go unnoticed, others such as this vivid male Emperor dragonfly can be truly breathtaking.**

RIGHT: **This fungus, growing on a rotting stump, is an essential part of the breakdown process, whereby dead plant material is recycled into plant nutrients.**

BOTTOM RIGHT: **Toadstools are a familiar sight in many gardens and are often viewed suspiciously by gardeners, despite fulfilling a vital role in nutrient cycling and soil health.**

Environmental Cycles

Nature could be described as a constant and somewhat rhythmical cycle involving the days and years that mark the passing of time, along with other cycles which mark the constant movement of the basic chemical elements that constitute all matter on earth – including the cycle of life itself.

Technically speaking, the constituent chemical elements that together combine to form the stuff of life itself are constantly being broken down, recycled and rebuilt into new life, in a series of processes that scientists refer to as 'biogeochemical cycles'. Gardeners however are mostly concerned with how this affects plant growth and they usually describe the whole process more simply as nutrient cycling.

Around thirty of the hundred or so elements in the earth's crust are essential to life and their importance means that they are often in short supply. Initially they come from inorganic sources such as rocks (through weathering) or the atmosphere and once incorporated into living things many can only usually be released through biological processes, including decomposition. Fortunately, some of the most important substances such as oxygen, carbon, nitrogen and water, are abundant and are freely cycled through natural processes.

The Water Cycle

The water cycle is often referred to as an elemental cycle. This means simply that the amount of water that there is on the planet remains more or less constant, although it may be combined in other substances or held within the bodies of living organisms. The cycle of rain, evaporation, flowing rivers and use by living things is continuous and extremely important to gardeners.

The Nitrogen Cycle

The nitrogen cycle is also an elemental cycle that involves the most abundant element in the air around us. Nitrogen, especially, is essential to life and plant growth. It constitutes around seventy eight per cent of the air but is unobtainable to plants in this form. It must be captured and processed by bacteria that live in a healthy soil before it is available to plants. In a healthy ecosystem, there is enough of this to support plant growth. Humans have known its usefulness for many years, and as a consequence, a huge amount of artificially captured (industrial) nitrogen has been applied to the soil for several decades. This has led to an imbalance and in some cases natural habitats have suffered as a result. An understanding of how to keep the soil healthy is often the best way to ensure good growth and maintain a natural balance both within and beyond your own garden.

The Carbon Cycle

The carbon cycle is central to life itself. All life on earth is based upon carbon and the chemistry of the carbon atom and its derived substances is called 'organic chemistry'. Carbon has many sources, some living, and much more from the dead remains of organisms. When carbon is released into the air the origin is called a source. All living things release some carbon and are sources but there are other sources such as volcanoes, and human activities such as burning wood, fossil fuels or other industry. When carbon becomes part of a living organism, or is locked up in sediments or rocks, it is said to have entered a sink.

The balance between carbon liberated from sources and that entering sinks is extremely important for the health of the planet and affects the global temperature. In the garden the cycle of carbon is an essential part of a healthy habitat and one that you have the power to help balance.

The Oxygen Cycle

The oxygen cycle describes the movement of oxygen within and between its three main reservoirs – the atmosphere, living things, and the earth's surface – rocks, lakes, rivers and oceans. The main driving force for this cycle is plant life; more specifically its production of food through photosynthesis. When plants make food they release a lot of oxygen (which is good news for all of us) and it is for this reason alone that the atmosphere on the earth contains around twenty one per cent of this gas. We – and all other living things – breathe oxygen in and use it to release the energy contained in food. In this way, the carbon and oxygen cycles combine and balance.

Why it is Important for Gardeners to Work with Environmental Cycles

Nutrient cycles then, are a matter of balance. They have an important impact upon our daily lives and of course upon our gardens. Even though they operate on a global scale, we can modify and adapt some of them, although ultimately the best way is to ensure that our actions fit in with them. While gardeners frequently have an innate appreciation of both seasonality and our dependence upon the other forms of life that share our living space, the real trick is to understand exactly how all natural cycles affect plants and their growth and how to best use them when designing and maintaining a garden.

Harnessing Nutrient Cycles

Nutrients are cycled naturally by many processes and while many of these operate at a global level, the gardener can tap into them using relatively simple techniques. Cultivation is an ancient technique that helps the cycling of nutrients. Freshly dug ground receives oxygen that encourages soil organisms and helps them to break down organic matter. It also benefits many micro-organisms that process inorganic elements into a useful form for plants as these too need oxygen to breathe.

Many organisms are involved in nutrient cycling and keeping a healthy habitat, free of pesticides and the imbalances that can be caused by the excessive use of artificial fertilizers, is the best way to manage these cycles for the benefit of not only your own garden but also the wider environment.

CARBON DIOXIDE (CO_2) – FAST FACTS

What is Carbon Dioxide?
Carbon dioxide (CO_2) is a colourless, odourless gas consisting of molecules of two oxygen atoms and one carbon atom. Carbon dioxide is produced when any form of carbon or almost any carbon compound is burned in an excess of oxygen.

CO_2 is poisonous in high concentrations, but comprises only a fraction of the Earth's atmosphere. This total fluctuates slightly with the changing seasons, mostly on account of seasonal plant growth in the Northern Hemisphere.

What are the Sources of Carbon Dioxide in the Garden?
Carbon Dioxide (or CO_2) is created naturally by animals' breathing (respiration) and by the decay of plant and animal matter. These processes are natural sources of carbon dioxide in the atmosphere and account for about thirty eight per cent of all global CO_2 emissions.

Carbon dioxide is also released by the burning of fossil fuels (coal, oil and gas). These may be used directly in the case of power tools, or indirectly for transport, power and electricity, and the production of manufactured items such as plastics, packaging or cement.

What are the Sinks of Carbon Dioxide?
A 'sink' is a method by which a gas can be removed from the atmosphere. Carbon dioxide has several sinks within the atmosphere, but the most important of these in a garden are trees and plants.

Soil organic matter is also an important sink, which temporarily locks up the carbon held in dead plant matter.

What Can Be Done to Reduce the Amount of Carbon Dioxide in the Atmosphere?
By having plants in your garden, and reducing the amount of hard landscape materials, the amount of CO_2 that can be absorbed will increase. In addition, by reducing the amount of inputs from external sources, recycling plant material on-site as compost, cutting out the use of power tools and implements and reducing your reliance upon manufactured items means that your garden is contributing less to the net production of carbon on a wider scale.

Although digging is essentially an artificial, 'human' activity in the garden, it nonetheless harnesses natural cycles and increases fertility as a result.

Daily and Seasonal Cycles

The simplest and most obvious cycle in a garden is that of the passage of a day, marked by periods of dark and light, which in turn affect all the life within the garden. A certain amount of light may trigger flowering in plants, while lengthening nights may trigger the commencement of dormancy. It is the easiest natural cycle for us to measure, observe and understand. Of course, the gradual passage of the seasons is something that humans have long sought to measure, with some of the most ancient artefacts left by our forebears thought to be elaborate

methods of doing this. The positions of the sun and the lunar cycle have both been used and many argue that these are still important factors in determining our success as gardeners. Calendars make things easy for us in modern times although an experienced gardener may well take their cue from the natural signals that they see all around them in order to assure success. Try talking to other gardeners in your area and compare notes as to what times of the year they do things, and how successful this has proved to be. Over time you will build a picture of what is the best timing for your own circumstances.

Timing of Planting

Much has been written about when is the best time to sow or plant in your garden. The accuracy of this depends really upon where you are and the prevailing conditions you find there. Weather and seasonality can play a major role in how success-ful your garden will be and the timing of when you attempt to establish plants is often crucial.

Many plants are best moved and planted in the dor-mant season (which is winter in temperate regions) when they have more chance of establishing roots at the onset of the growing season. Even with this though there is no set time for all plants. Tender specimens, planted too early in the winter, may perish but other specimens, planted near the end of the cold season, may not root sufficiently before the spring and suffer from water shortage in the hotter months.

Sunlight and Energy Flow

When ancient peoples worshipped the sun, they were in effect recognizing one inalienable truth. Life, in order for it to continue, needs a source of energy to power it. On the earth, this is mostly provided by the sun. Of course sunlight itself cannot be eaten as food, but certain organisms, principally green plants, have evolved a way of capturing it and turning it into energy-rich molecules of sugar via a process called photosynthesis. This food provides the basis of almost all life on earth and as a result, plants are described in an ecological sense as 'producers'.

The vast majority of the remaining living species on the planet are not able to produce their own food and so must rely instead upon eating another organism to get this. Such organisms are called 'consumers'. Some consumers eat the plants directly and are called 'herbivores' – or 'pests' by frustrated gardeners. Others gain their food more indirectly by eating another consumer and are called 'carnivores'. When a creature eats a combination of producers and consumers it is called an 'omnivore' as it eats many things. Humans are one such creature said to be 'omnivorous'. Yet others depend upon eating material from organisms that have died. These are said to be 'decomposers'. Through these strategies organisms are able to obtain the energy they need to live.

Energy Use and Loss

The First Law of Thermodynamics states that 'energy cannot be created or destroyed, it merely changes form'. To contextualize this in a garden setting, remember that the energy of the sun is used to power the life and growth of plants. In doing this, the energy changes its form. The energy contained in the sunlight is changed into energy rich food (sugar) that in turn is used to power the processes used to assemble living tissue. Despite its seemingly miraculous nature though, the process is actually rather inefficient, with around ninety per cent of the original sunlight energy being lost during the conversion.

The remaining ten per cent of the energy that is stored in the food suffers a similar fate each time it is used and so when the food is used to power growth

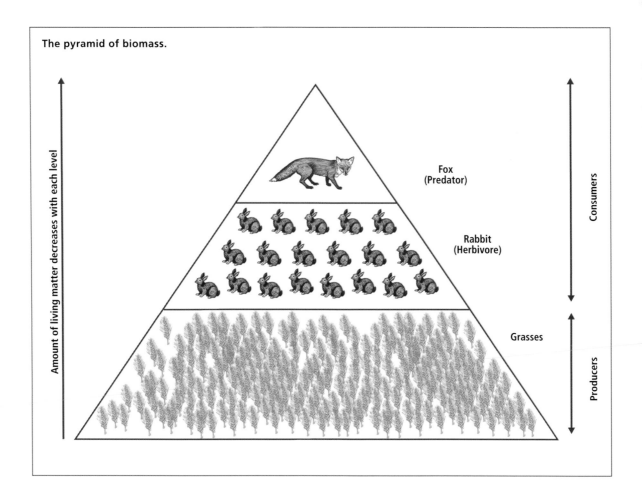

The pyramid of biomass.

Amount of living matter decreases with each level

Fox (Predator)

Rabbit (Herbivore)

Grasses

Consumers

Producers

and development, or if the plant is eaten by an animal, around ninety per cent of the energy may be lost. This then means that there must always be more food produced than consumers as the conversion of food is so inefficient. Scientists use a diagram called the 'Pyramid of Biomass' to explain this. Biomass is the term used to describe the amount of living tissue minus the water content. As an example then, the human body contains about two thirds (by weight) of water. If you weighed 70kg (154lb or 11stone) therefore, your biomass would be just 23.4kg (51.3lb or 3½stone).

If the ten per cent ratio is exceeded, the consumer quickly begins to run short of food and may starve. In this way a balance is achieved and the environment stays healthy, with more producers than consumers.

Food Chains

The concept of a food chain is a simplistic but surprisingly useful way of illustrating the relationship between predators and prey. The chain usually starts with a producer, a plant, before moving on to a primary consumer that eats the plant. In the example shown, the producer is a rose bush and the primary consumer

an aphid. The chain then moves on to show what eats the aphid, in this case a ladybird. Since few things in a garden prey upon ladybirds (they are poisonous), this is the end of the chain and the ladybird is therefore said to be at 'the top of the food chain'. While this is a good way of illustrating the basic principles of predation, the story is rarely as simple as this. Many predators feed on a wide variety of prey meaning that it is not only ladybirds that eat aphids. In addition, it does not take into account smaller consumers such as parasites (diseases) or indeed other factors affecting the size of the populations. In order to consider the complexity of natural systems we would normally construct a food web.

Food Webs

Food webs are useful to help us build an understanding of more complex relationships between predators and prey. Their main drawback is that to be fully accurate they would have to be extremely complex and almost impossible to follow. Nonetheless, they do help to draw attention to a range of complex interdependences that form the basis of natural habitats.

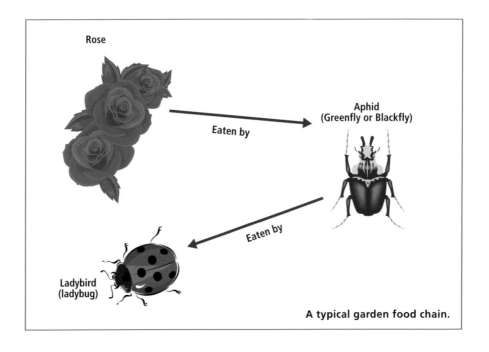

A typical garden food chain.

Predators in the garden

The average garden can play host to a whole range of common species, each of which is a voracious predator in its own right. Many of these offer a useful service in seeking out and eating a range of garden pests that would otherwise damage our garden plants.

Predator	What it eats
Ladybird	Both the adults and young of this common and easily recognizable garden beetle are voracious predators of troublesome garden pests.
Hoverfly	While adults feed mainly upon pollen and are attracted to flowers such as daisy types, larvae are voracious predators of many aphid species.
Frogs and toads	The adults of both frogs and toads are carnivorous and capture a range of mostly invertebrate prey that they entrap using a long sticky tongue.
Shrew	Capturing mainly invertebrate prey and one of the smallest mammals, shrews daily capture and eat two thirds of their own body weight.
Robin	Just one of many birds that eat garden pests, robins are well known for their friendly nature and often pick off grubs around gardeners while they dig and cultivate.

It is not always necessary to be able to construct one of these to understand that the more complex a system is, the more stable it tends to become, as many species help to support one another.

Climate and Weather

According to a popular adage, 'climate is what you expect; weather is what you get'. While this might seem cryptic at first, a simple interpretation might be that you might expect snow or frost in Siberia in the middle of the winter, but you do not necessarily know in advance which particular day it is coming. Weather then, describes the condition of the atmosphere over a short period of time, for example from day-to-day or week-to-week, while climate describes average conditions over a longer period of time.

There are of course many aspects that go to make up the weather: humidity, air temperature and pressure; wind speed and direction; cloud cover (and type of cloud); the amount and form of precipitation (snow, hail, rain and fog). These, or more ordinarily combinations of these, are what is commonly called weather. The weather experienced in a given location is influenced by many factors, including its latitude, elevation, and proximity to water bodies. Even the degree of urban development, which creates 'heat islands,' and the amount of snow cover, which chills an overlying air mass, play important roles.

The climate of an area or country is known through the average weather over a long period of time. If an area has more dry days throughout the year than wet days, it would be described as a dry climate; a place that has more cold days than hot days would render it a cool or perhaps cold climate.

In a sense then, a gardener must be keenly aware of the prevailing climate within their own location, as it is this which will largely limit what they can expect to grow. Having said this however, the weather is often the most immediate threat and gardeners need to take prompt action if sudden or unexpected weather threatens. Plants frequently show remarkable differences in their ability to cope with local weather depending upon where they are planted in the garden, therefore the key to success is as much a matter of understanding your own patch as it is the vagaries of the weather.

Effects of Climate upon Plant Growth

Rainfall

Water is vital for food production and growth in plants and for the plant to sustain itself, and for optimum growth, a steady supply of water is essential. In reality, rainfall is very variable in both its regularity and in quantity, and the best choice of plants are those that deal with the average rainfall for an area.

Humidity

The level of humidity is the quantity of water vapour in the atmosphere at any one time. It is normally referred to as the relative humidity and is measured as a percentage of the saturation point (100 per cent humidity). In places that receive heavy rainfall, relative humidity also tends to be higher. Plants such as ferns thrive in such damp conditions although high relative humidity can have undesirable effects on plants, with plant diseases such as grey mould – Botrytis Cinerea – flourishing in humid conditions.

Light

The light from the sun is a vital constituent of plant food production (photosynthesis) and is vital in producing new growth and sustaining existing growth. The duration of light in a day is known as day length and is characterized by the number of hours; 'short days' having less than twelve hours of daylight while 'long days' have more. Latitude and the season determine day length. Some plants exhibit responses to day length – for example Chrysanthemums produce their flowers in response to short days.

Some plants require full sun while others tolerate even quite deep shade and thrive best away from direct sun, for example ferns and Rhododendrons.

Strong sunlight can damage plants however, with foliage being scorched, especially if water droplets on the leaf 'magnify' the light. Selecting plants suited to the prevailing site conditions is usually the best way to prevent such problems.

Wind

Wind can easily damage plants, especially woody trees and shrubs. The stronger the wind, the more damage is likely to occur and for windy gardens the plants must be chosen in accordance with their ability to resist this. Even quite moderate winds may cause desiccation of leaves in cold or dry conditions although a light wind often has beneficial effects for the plant; cooling the plant's foliage and alleviating a possible stagnant atmosphere that can promote disease.

Temperature

The plant's growth and life processes are all affected by temperature, with all plant species having their own maximum and minimum temperatures at which they can survive. As a general rule the maximum temperature for most plants is around 35°C while the minimum is highly variable. Plants may enter dormancy beyond these thresholds or in more extreme cases may actually die.

Microclimate

In some gardens, such as those in a sheltered site that benefits from the warming effects of the sun, it is often possible to grow plants more ordinarily suited to warmer climates. Soil temperature may also vary, with sandy soils for instance warming up more quickly after a cold season than clay soils; mainly because they are relatively free draining and do not hold as much water. Sites facing, or with a slight incline towards the direction of the sun, will also warm up more quickly than a shady one. Such local variations over the prevailing climate are called microclimates.

A confined or discrete area, such as a small domestic garden may harbour, can offer a range of differing environments to the weather conditions prevailing elsewhere in the locality and gardeners often exploit these microclimates to grow a wide range of plants, some of which would otherwise not have been possible. By careful plant selection, and clever design in accordance with the capabilities afforded by a combination of both climate and microclimate, any garden can easily support the growth of a much greater range of plants than would otherwise have been possible.

Ecology

Ecology is the study of how plants, animals and their environment interact with one another. In this context, the word 'environment' is used to simply mean that which surrounds an organism. This is an extremely complex area of scientific enquiry although at its core are some relatively simple ideas. In order to understand the basic complexities found even in relatively small habitats then, it is necessary to remember three basic principles.

1 Living things do not exist as isolated individuals or groups of individuals. They are part of a huge 'continuum' of life that stretches across the entire surface of the earth.

2 All organisms interact with others of their own species, with other species, and with the physical and chemical environments that surround them.

3 All organisms have an effect on each other and their surroundings. As they interact with both they may actually change the other over time. Trees for instance gradually modify the soil they grow in by the constant dropping of dead leaves that decompose in the soil.

The plants within an environment are grouped together in a number of different ways. A 'species' is a natural group of actually or potentially interbreeding individuals that will not normally interbreed with other related groups. A 'population' describes all the individuals of a given species in a defined area – for instance all the dandelions in a grassland area.

A 'community' refers to the total grouping of the different types of species' populations that tend to occur together in a particular geographical area.

Ultimately, an 'ecosystem' is the community or series of communities and their surrounding environment. This includes both the physical and chemical environment; that is the rocks, water, air and so forth. In an ecosystem, the organisms composing the populations and communities all require energy for survival. That energy comes from the sun in the case of the plants. The plants use the light for photosynthesis, which converts the light energy into basic sugars; the plant uses these as its food and stores them in the form of sugars, starches, and other plant material. Any animals living in that ecosystem derive all of their energy from plant energy stored in their bodies, whether they eat the plants for their energy supply, or eat animals that feed upon plants. In essence then, your garden is an ecosystem, and an understanding of the basics of ecology is an important aspect of understanding how it can be managed in a sustainable way.

Habitats

A habitat, put in simple terms, is a location where a particular species is normally found. It could be said to be a little like a plant or animal's address. A single ecosystem may contain many different habitats in which organisms can live. Shady corners encourage ferns and mosses, whereas sunny spots encourage plants such as poppies or daisies. The suitability of a place for a plant to grow is of course also affected by other factors such as the soil type, the amount of exposure or the average temperature. For a plant to occupy a certain habitat then, it must receive the right combination of factors that it needs to survive.

The major factors that affect plant growth are the correct amount of light, water, the necessary temperature range, nutrients, and a substrate on which to grow – sand, clay, or perhaps even water may be appropriate depending upon the species. All of these factors must be within the range of the plant's tolerance. Even a common plant will disappear from a habitat if an essential environmental factor shifts beyond its range

Daisies are a commonly seen example of a plant that needs to grow in a sunny situation if it is to thrive, the flowers only opening in direct light.

Ferns are plants that generally need moist, shady conditions if they are to grow and thrive, with bright, direct light sometimes proving fatal to them.

of tolerance. The common daisy (*Bellis perennis)* for example, flourishes in full sun but will gradually disappear when surrounding trees and shrubs grow large enough to shade the area. Therefore, understanding a plant's needs will help you to choose those most likely to grow and prosper in your own garden habitat.

Life, Death and Decay

Life, death and decay are a natural and inevitable part of the wider environmental cycle, which gardeners can easily learn to manage to their advantage through actions such as composting. Indeed, composting waste matter ensures that valuable nutrients are not lost from your garden by returning them to the soil in a useful form. This partially decayed organic matter is the food that nutrient-cycling organisms depend upon and this (in combination with air and water) provides them with an ideal environment. The more you minimize waste material leaving your garden and indeed, the more you return to the soil, the more self supporting your garden will be. In short, a sustainable garden is one that is in tune with natural cycles.

Natural Interdependence

Pollination

Pollination, put quite simply, is the process of moving pollen from the anthers (male) to the stigma (female), allowing the flower to develop seeds for reproduction. Some flowers can self-pollinate – when pollen from their own anthers is deposited on the stigma – but for the majority, pollination needs some additional help to move. Wind moves the pollen for some plants – grasses are a prime example of this – whereas others require the assistance of an animal pollinator. These move pollen from the anthers to the stigmas of flowers and often move pollen between different flowers or plants of the same species. There are many animals that are known to be good pollinators of flowers but the commonest ones include bees, butterflies, hummingbirds, moths, some flies, some wasps, and nectar-feeding bats.

TOP: Some fungus such as this Jelly Ear (*Auricularia auricula-judae*) grow on dead wood, still held on an otherwise healthy tree, and do not attack living wood.

TOP RIGHT: Standing deadwood is often home to a range of species that need dry wood as their preferred home and if possible can be left in the garden to help them.

RIGHT: If an old stump is not available, use logs and branch-wood to make an artificial one, which not only acts as a habitat but also can be made into a feature.

BELOW: Old stumps are often home to a wide variety of garden life, and if possible, should be left in place to provide a refuge and home to these creatures.

The bright showy flowers borne by many plants are a vital source of food for insects such as the bumblebee, without which pollination would not occur.

The efficiency of bumblebees in pollinating flowers makes their use as pollinators for tomatoes the cheapest, most environmentally friendly option.

From the plants' point of view, they benefit from pollinators because the movement of pollen allows them to set seed and ultimately begin a new generation. The pollinators however, do not know really do this for the benefit of the plant. For them, pollination is an incidental by-product of their efforts to feed upon or collect nectar and/or pollen from flowers for themselves or their own offspring. In evolutionary terms it is a perfect example of two unrelated species that have gradually adapted mutual dependence, where both benefit from the relationship. Indeed, many plants have become so dependent on one particular pollinator that their flowers have become specifically adapted to favour them. The loss of this animal from that habitat may ultimately result in the extinction of the plant itself!

Once the pollen grain lands upon the stigma, it must reach the ovaries of the flower in order to fuse with the female cell and begin to form a seed. The pollen grain does this by germinating and growing a long thin tube that reaches down the style into the flower's ovaries. The pollen tube provides a pathway for the male chromosomes to reach the egg cell in the ovule. One pollen grain fertilizes one egg cell and together they form the new seed.

Self-pollination and Cross-pollination

While it is possible for some plants to pollinate their own flowers, this is not ideal because the inbreeding limits them genetically. Many plants will have some factor that promotes cross-pollination between individuals of the same species.

'Dioecious' plants (those with separate male and female plants) achieve cross-pollination by their very nature. No self-pollination is possible because an individual plant will only produce either male or female parts.

'Monoecious' plants (those that produce both female and male flower parts on the same plant) avoid self-pollination by having the male or female parts maturing at different times. 'Protandrous' flowers produce pollen first before the stigma is ripe and ready to receive the pollen. The situation is reversed in the case of 'protogynous' flowers where the stigma is ready to receive pollen from different flowers before the stamens of that flower ripen and produce pollen. Physical separation of stamens from stigmas can also help prevent self-pollination in cases where the structures mature at the same time.

Some species are genetically designed so that pollen from the same flower, or from other flowers on the same plant, cannot cause fertilization. This design – known as self-incompatibility – ensures that seed production results only from cross-pollination with a separate plant. Apples are a prime example of this.

Ultimately then, the importance of pollination in respect of the continued existence of plants on earth, means that we must also take steps to protect and encourage the insects and other creatures that provide this service. Bees are arguably the best known of these, although many other (principally insect) species are also important.

Apple blossom is a *protogynous* flower where the stigma is ready to receive pollen from different flowers before its own stamens ripen and produce pollen.

Down Below

The soil is the place where plants become involved with the most complex set of natural interdependencies, in a part of the soil known as the 'rhizosphere'. This is essentially a zone of soil adjacent to plant roots where microbes are affected in some way by the presence of the roots. In addition to microbial changes due to the presence of the roots, the root is also fundamentally affected by the presence of the rhizosphere microbes. This region of the soil is the most ecologically significant in respect of plant growth and health. Indeed, ensuring the health of the microorganisms that inhabit this zone is a key aspect of sustainable gardening.

Plant nutrient uptake through the roots is influenced in a number of ways, and in a healthy soil, microbes benefit appropriate species and may even be involved in the formation of symbiotic associations. Indeed, the greatest population density for soil microbes is usually greatest on the 'rhizoplane' (root surface) with this decreasing sharply only a few millimetres away. Like the roots themselves, the majority of soil organisms require oxygen in order to survive, usually meaning that plant roots (and their associated soil organisms) are limited to a fairly narrow band of the soil. Plants rarely root very deeply, and most of their rooting activity is limited to the narrow layer of soil usually referred to as topsoil; often characterized by its darker colour and different character to the subsoil below.

A single gram (0.04oz) of soil may contain as many as 500,000,000 micro-organisms of between 7,000 and 10,000 different species. This complex community takes a long time to develop, is not static and its population numbers and balance often shift to match a change in conditions; whether slight or extreme, localized or general.

Nutrient Cycling and Release

Technically speaking, the constituent chemical elements that together combine to form the stuff of life itself are constantly being broken down, recycled and 'built-up' into new life, in a series of processes that scientists refer to as biogeochemical cycles. Gardeners however are mostly concerned with how this affects plant growth and it is usually put more simply and referred to as nutrient cycling.

Around thirty of the hundred or so elements in the earth's crust are essential to life and their importance means that they are often in short supply. Initially they come from inorganic sources such as rocks (through weathering) or the atmosphere and once incorporated into living things many can only usually be released through biological processes, including decomposition. Fortunately, some of the most important substances such as oxygen, carbon, nitrogen and water, are abundant and freely cycled through natural processes.

Human Threats to the Environment

Few parts of the world have not been altered, damaged or in some cases destroyed by human intervention as land is taken over to provide homes and agriculture as well as resources from natural areas. Humans have always interacted with their environment and – like many other species – have altered it to be more to their liking and needs. Modern technology, however, has speeded up this process to unprecedented levels and serious damage can be done in a tiny proportion of the time that it would have taken in the past.

There are so many demands on the earth for space – space to build roads and towns, space to grow food, space for people to work and space for them to play. Of course this problem is amplified by the huge increases in population over the last 200 years. Larger populations need ever more resources and often, it is this that has begun to tip the natural balance.

Agricultural development is a major threat to natural biodiversity (the total diversity of life) and native grasslands have (in many developed countries) nearly disappeared beneath an onslaught of ploughing and grazing. Development of water resources for agriculture (and urban use) have also reduced or fragmented many freshwater habitats. Indeed, with more humans on the planet each day, the need for fresh water grows. For some, this is a basic need to survive, raise crops and livestock. Increased development however, often means that water use (per individual) goes up as water is needed for industry, domestic use, sewage and of course industrial scale agriculture to support the population.

Ironically, horticulture itself is not without its problems and the trade in plants for gardens has caused considerable problems. Plants taken away from their native environments can quickly become highly invasive. There are many instances worldwide, and

Construction, essential to support growing populations, claims land that would otherwise help maintain vital natural processes and uses up natural resources.

Farming has always had some form of environmental impact, although until the last 200 years, these were often slow, small scale and limited in impact.

globally, the true cost of damage caused by invasive plant species is recognized as one of the greatest threats to both biodiversity and the economic well-being of the planet. In the United Kingdom for example, more than sixty per cent of invasive plants are 'garden escapees' and there may be as many as 11,000 non-native invasive species in Europe alone. Japanese knotweed is just one example of an ornamental plant introduced to Europe in the mid-nineteenth century and one of the few terrestrial plants to be legislated for in UK law. As gardeners have, albeit inadvertently, caused much (but by no means all) of the problem worldwide, it should be clear then, that we must avoid adding to the problem by the choices we make, particularly when choosing plants for the garden.

Positive Intervention

It is hard not to see things as an inevitable decline when estimates predict that by 2032, more than seventy per cent of the earth's land surface is likely to be destroyed, fragmented or disturbed by cities, roads, mines and other infrastructure of human civilisation (a figure presently at around fifty per cent). While urban development undoubtedly does bring a whole range of problems, most of which are inextricably linked with the ones described above it is not something that we are powerless to stem. In urban settings, the problems become concentrated, and the real danger is that they spread much more widely than the geographic limits of the settlement itself. Dealing with the problems right there is always the best option, and this is in essence much of what sustainable gardening seeks to do. It is only a small contribution but it is something that you can do.

Modern intensified cropping, while giving massive improvements in yield, result in monocultures poor in natural diversity, that demand huge inputs.

ECOLOGICAL TECHNIQUES FOR YOUR SOIL

Understanding Soil

Understanding your garden soil – the parts that make it up and what can live in it – is central to the success of a sustainable approach to gardening. Soils vary widely, both according to the area in which they are found (or originate) and also due to how they are or have been treated in the past. While the study of soils is rather complex, the gardener can, by following a few simple rules, easily start to deal with the land they have and ultimately get good results on almost any land. The first step is of course to find out what type of soil you have in your garden, and from thereon plan which plants and practices will be best suited to that type of land.

What is Soil Made of?

Soil is made up of many things but the majority of soils are made up of small mineral fragments that are derived from the constant physical and chemical action of the weather on rocks. Over time, even the hardest rock is eroded and what remains makes up the mineral soil. These are classed in turn according to their size and the physical properties of their constituent fragments.

- Clay is the smallest type of mineral particle that is found in a soil, being less than 0.002mm, (two micrometers – 2µm) across. As a virtue of being so small, they are influenced by the soil chemistry and tend to bind tightly to one another making the substance very sticky and water retentive. Clay soils are described as being heavy and can be hard to cultivate. On the plus side though, they are very fertile.

- Silt is larger than clay being up to 0.02mm across and as such shares some characteristics with both clay and sand. It is also sticky when wet but does not form the same close bonds and may dry to a quite dusty soil in drought conditions. It is usually derived from rivers and makes for a fertile soil which, if well managed, can be an excellent growing medium for a wide variety of plants.

- Sand is the largest particle being up to 2mm across. While this is still quite a fine particle to our eyes, it is very large in respect of soils and unlike the two smaller factions is very poor at retaining nutrient. This is a combination of the fact that the amount of air that is naturally present tends to rapidly break down any organic matter and also because the particles themselves are unable to hold onto nutrient. As a result, sandy soils tend to be free draining and 'hungry' and need to be managed accordingly.

Soil Texture

Although a few soils are purely sand or purely clay, most are naturally a mixture of two or all three sizes of particle. The amount of each of these mineral constituents present in a soil, dictates to a certain degree what the soil will be like. These are often judged as a relative proportion of the total. The texture of a soil can best be described then as the relative amounts (by weight) of the mineral particles in a soil but not including the organic matter content or water. In most cases though, it is only really important to estimate which of the particles makes up the largest fraction.

Assessing a Soil's Texture by Hand

For the purposes of most gardeners, a simple hand test can give you a good idea of what soil you have. Begin with a small amount of soil about the size of a golf ball. Moisten this and knead it until it is around the consistency of putty and remove any hard lumps

Moistened soil that readily forms a cohesive ball is usually low in sand. If it does not readily crack when pressed, the clay content could be high.

Form a 'ribbon' with the cohesive ball. If this cracks, the soil is loamy sand; if it hangs, then the longer and thinner it can be made, the higher the clay content.

or large stones. Once you have done this, mould the soil into a ball. If it does not readily form a ball and crumbles readily if pressed, then it is sand.

If the ball is firm, try forming it into a ribbon between the thumb and crooked forefinger. If the ribbon breaks easily while you are forming it then it is loamy sand. If it hangs freely, however, then quite simply, the longer and thinner you can make it before it breaks, the more clay your soil has. You may also note that the higher the clay content, the more it glistens when smoothed between the thumb and forefinger.

Soil Structure

The constituents described above are the building blocks of the soil but the property of any garden soil also depends upon how these are arranged. If you imagine the house that you live in, it has been specially constructed using a range of constituent materials. This is its architecture or structure. Soil is much the same. In order to function, it must have areas of open spaces that we call pores; these provide routes for water and air to move through the soil and also the vital spaces that soil life needs to function. In a soil this is called the structure, and a well-structured soil has the right balance of air space to enable drainage of excess water and air movement. Naturally this is achieved by living organisms but gardeners often enhance this by cultivation.

Organic Matter

Organic matter is a normal part of all topsoil, being derived from the dead parts of plants and (to a lesser degree) animals that live in or on the soil. Decaying plant matter is broken down by many soil organisms, especially fungi and bacteria, and is not a constant quantity in the soil as a result. If conditions are right however it can form a substance called humus, which is relatively stable and is excellent at holding onto nutrient, especially when present in sandy or silt soil. It is ultimately all broken down and recycled by decomposers and plants and needs to be replenished on a regular basis.

Why Cultivate Soil?

Cultivating soil is simply a way of giving nature a boost. The real reason for cultivation is to enhance the formation of pore spaces while often providing an ideal opportunity to add organic matter. This free flow of air both in and out of the soil allows oxygen to be replenished while venting toxic gasses that could otherwise build up. The organic matter provides food for micro-organisms that in turn cycle nutrient for plant roots. A steady supply of nutrient, water and oxygen is vital for healthy root growth and this of course ensures strong healthy growth above ground.

Soil pH

Soil pH is a measure of the acidity of a soil. It is an important factor in deciding which plants will grow and thrive and therefore choosing the right plants for your garden. It is expressed on a scale of 1–14, with 1 being highly acidic, 14 being extremely alkaline and 7 being classed as neutral. Most commonly grown garden plants prefer or are tolerant of a specific pH range, that is acid, alkaline or near neutral.

The pH of a soil is important to plant growth as it affects the availability of certain key nutrients. A low pH may cause nitrogen or phosphate deficiency, promote trace element toxicity or deficiency and can cause a more general deterioration of the soil structure. Soils that maintain a pH of around 6.5 however generally have the most nutrients available and are suitable for the widest range of plants.

Most mineral soils have a tendency to become acidic with time, (except for those overlaying chalk) due to a variety of factors. Chief among these is the simple fact that all rainwater naturally contains carbonic acid, sulphuric acid and nitric acid. These are not the result of human activity, but the result of natural chemical reactions in the atmosphere. In addition to this, the breakdown of organic matter in the soil, particularly if it remains wet, causes the release of organic acids (for example acetic acid) that also make the ground more acidic.

If rainfall exceeds evaporation, as it often does, then the excess water drains away through gravity

In nature, leaves and other plant material, deposited during each growing season replenish the soil's natural reserves of organic material.

or surface runoff. This process not only removes the water but also removes nutrients and chemicals based upon calcium – the substance that makes a soil alkaline. This process is called 'leaching', and it gradually causes the soil to become more acidic and lower in nutrients. The degree of leaching varies with the soil type of course; sandy soils tend to leach very quickly, whereas soils with high clay content tend to hold onto their chemicals more strongly, thereby resisting leaching. Other factors that naturally influence soil pH include the locality (how much rainfall and evaporation occurs where your garden is), the soil structure, drainage, organic matter and lime content as well as the vegetation present. Finally of course, the history of the site is important. Gardeners may previously have limed the ground for instance, leading to a localized rise in the pH.

pH Preferences of Some Common Garden Plants

Ornamentals

Plant	pH 4.5	pH 5.25	pH 6.0	pH 6.75	pH 7.5
Carnations			■	■	■
Chrysanthemums		■	■	■	■
Roses		■	■	■	■
Rhododendrons	■	■			
Heather	■	■			
Hydrangea (Blue)	■	■			
Hydrangea (Pink)			■	■	
Coarse Lawn Grasses			■	■	■
Fine Lawn Grasses		■	■	■	■

Edible Crops

Plant	pH 4.5	pH 5.25	pH 6.0	pH 6.75	pH 7.5
Asparagus			■	■	■
Beetroot			■	■	■
Bilberry	■	■			
Bean (Broad)		■	■		
Cranberry	■	■			
Cabbage			■	■	■
Carrot			■	■	
Cauliflower			■	■	■
Garlic			■	■	■
Potato		■	■		
Raspberry			■	■	
Rhubarb		■	■		
Sage		■	■		
Strawberry		■	■		

How Does Soil pH Affect Plant Growth?

Getting the soil pH 'right' has been a goal of gardeners for generations. The golden range of pH 6–7, is of course highly desirable as it enables the maximum range of plants to prosper, including some of our most important food crops. Of course, it is better not to fight too hard against nature in the garden but an understanding of the effect of pH on nutrient availability can help explain why some plants do better than others on your soil.

At lower soil pH, the amount of available nitrogen becomes limited. This is mostly due to the fact that the soil microbes that release the majority of the nitrogen used by plants tends not to thrive as the pH becomes lower. Plants adapted to life in lower pH soils and settings are sometimes specially adapted (carnivorous plants are one example of this) and even among the commoner plants, many exhibit varying tolerances to nitrogen shortage. Phosphate is another nutrient that plants need, which becomes unavailable outside the 6.5–7.5 pH range. Again, adaptations to deal with this do exist and many plants form relationships with soil-borne fungi (Mycorrhiza), which release phosphates to plants in acid conditions.

Certain trace elements such as Copper, Boron and Molybdenum also become less available at low soil pH, with legumes (peas and beans) being particularly prone to molybdenum deficiency. This means that these vegetables will not grow in acid soils, primarily because the Rhizobium bacteria that their roots use to collect nitrogen, do not work in acid soils without Molybdenum. However, it is not always a shortage that proves the problem, and some trace elements, especially Iron, Aluminium and Manganese actually reach toxic levels as pH decreases.

TOP RIGHT: **Fungi are extremely important in the recycling and supply of nutrients to plants. As the pH drops, their importance increases as bacterial numbers fall.**

RIGHT: **Leguminous (pea-flowered) plants such like runner beans house nitrogen-fixing bacteria in their roots and so need more alkaline conditions to thrive.**

Water in the Soil

Wetness is defined as the amount of water relative to the mass of dry soil particles. It is expressed in three ways. A soil can be said to be saturated, when all the 'pores' (air spaces) are filled with water and no further absorption is possible. Most of this water then drains away under gravity – although some always remains – in a similar way that it would for example on a wet sponge. This remaining water is the total water-carrying capacity for a soil and is the maximum available water content – known as 'field capacity'. As further water is lost, through evaporation or uptake by plant roots, soils below field capacity are said to be in deficit. As a rule, most soils are naturally in deficit for much of the growing season. The real trick for the gardener then, is to maintain them as near to field capacity as possible.

The degree of wetness that a soil can achieve depends largely on its porosity. Clay naturally has a huge amount of pore spaces which, as a result of their tiny size, readily hold onto water. Sandy soils also have lots of air space, but it is made up of large voids that drain very easily and it is for this reason that clay soils generally have greater available water content than do sandy soils following natural drainage.

If a soil has been compacted however, the result will be that the water content it can hold onto will decrease, as the pore spaces will have decreased as a consequence. It is important therefore not to do anything that may cause compaction of the soil when working on it. This is rarely a problem when a soil is dry, but wet soils can be very prone to compaction and it is for this reason that you should avoid working on any soil that is very wet or waterlogged.

Plant roots can go deep into the soil to find water and generally speaking, the drier the soils, the deeper down the roots will tend to go. Soils fall into two basic types being either permeable (for example loose sand), or slowly permeable (for example clay soils) with the remainder being somewhere between the two. Although permeable soils are most usually well drained (that is seldom or never waterlogged), in certain situations they can be seasonally or permanently waterlogged to different depths. This is a result of 'groundwater', (permanently saturated soil) the level of which is usually referred to as the water table. Often, the wetness of a soil is more dependent upon the height of this water table, and soils with a high water table (that is near to the soil surface) are described as wet or waterlogged. Soils on river floodplains are often like this.

In contrast, the naturally slower drainage of clay soils means that a fluctuating water table cannot easily rise into them. Conversely, rain water cannot pass down into them and this usually means that a waterlogged surface layer is the result of rain only.

Life

At first glance, a worm, cow, human or a daisy seem to have very little in common. Having said this, they do share a common thread; they are all 'soil organisms'. This may seem a rather strange idea at first but put aside their vastly different shapes and life cycles and the term is basically appropriate – even for the human. This is because creatures that are dependent upon soil for their food or habitat may readily be defined as soil organisms; even if they are not actually soil dwelling. While we do not live within its confines then we are tied to the soil for our very survival.

While our own dependence upon the soil is largely masked by sanitized, mostly urban, modern life, the fact remains that an almost countless multitude of other organisms still inhabit the soil itself; dependent upon it for food, shelter, a place to breed and live. All of these play a vital role in this rich, diverse and often forgotten habitat.

Some soil-dwelling organisms are obvious and well known to gardeners, primarily because they can be seen with the naked eye. Aside from the plants, we recognize certain creatures to be extremely important. Worms for example are usually taken to be a sign of soil fertility although other less well-known soil dwellers, including the fast running ground beetle, help maintain the natural balance by eating a range of would-be garden pests. But for all those that are commonly seen there are many others that are so tiny that they go unnoticed. Size or familiarity is

Estimating the Available Water Content of a Soil

Actual Moisture Availability	Soil	Feel of the Soil	General Appearance of the Soil
Zero (wilting point)	Sand	Dry, loose, single-grained, flows through fingers	Hard, baked, cracked surface; hard clods difficult to break; sometimes has loose crumbs on surface
	Silt	Dry, loose, flows through fingers	
	Loam	Generally as for silt unless high in clay	
	Clay	Dry clods that break down into a powder	
50 per cent or less	Sand	Will not form a ball	Still appears to be dry
	Silt	Somewhat crumbly, but will hold together with pressure	
	Loam	Somewhat pliable	
	Clay	Will form a ball under pressure	
50% to 75%	Sand	Same as sand under 50% or tends to ball under pressure but seldom holds together	May appear dry to some depth
	Silt	Forms a ball, somewhat 'plastic', will sometimes stick slightly with pressure	
	Loam	Forms a ball	
	Clay	Will 'ribbon-out' between thumb and forefinger	
75% to field capacity	Sand	Tends to stick together slightly; sometimes forms a very weak ball under pressure	Generally only appears dry on surface layer
	Silt	Forms weak ball; breaks easily; will not become sticky	
	Loam	Forms a ball and is very pliable; sticks readily if high in clay	
	Clay	Easy to 'ribbon-out' between fingers; feels sticky	
At field capacity (i.e. once excess water has drained away)	Sand	Upon squeezing, no free water appears but moisture is left on hand	Surface may appear moist; moisture seen just below surface
	Silt	Same as sand	
	Loam	Same as sand	
	Clay	Same as sand	
Above field capacity (water-logged)	Sand	Free water appears when soil is 'bounced' in hand	Puddles and free water form on surface
	Silt	Free water will be released with 'kneading	
	Loam	As for silt/clay	
	Clay	Can squeeze out free water	

not a reliable measure when it comes to their value in terms of the overall soil habitat and the key to soil health lies with the countless millions of microscopic creatures. It is these that are the most diverse and arguably the most important of all life in the garden and the good news for gardeners is that they are remarkably easy to look after.

Why Micro-organisms are Important for the Soil

Micro-organisms are extremely important in a garden because they actually enable a steady flow of nutrients to reach your plants. Indeed, microbes are central to most nutrient cycles in soils and are especially important in respect of carbon, sulphur and nitrogen availability for plants, all of which are essential elements in their growth. Other micro-organisms act as a means of removing chemical pollutants that may otherwise build up in the soil. Aside from their obvious importance to plants, microbes also constitute a food source for a vast array of larger soil organisms and consequently form the start of many food chains. This dual role of decomposers and food-source for others means that soil micro-organisms are quite simply the 'driving force' of all life in the garden.

Despite their huge importance though, barely one per cent of the total soil volume is made up of microbes; compare this to the five per cent volume of plant roots and ten per cent dead organic matter and they could seem to be a rather insignificant part. They make up for this in sheer weight of numbers with around ninety million bacteria alone usually dwelling in just 1cm^3 of an average, healthy mineral soil. Bacteria also reproduce rapidly when compared with the larger organisms, meaning that they readily exploit new opportunities, quickly building up numbers where there is food (decaying matter), adequate water and (for most species) oxygen. These 'hotspots' effectively become plant nutrient factories while the food remains, although the need for oxygen mostly limits them to the top 30cm (1ft) of the soil, where they often share intimate association with tree and plant roots. This narrow band of

soil, commonly called topsoil, is familiar to gardeners through its darker colour and often, quite different character to the sub-soil immediately below.

Soil is therefore a complex community of living interdependencies that takes a long time to develop. It is not static and its balance often shifts to match changes in conditions. While it is resilient, if it is not cared for properly it can rapidly lose much of this diversity, causing problems for the larger plants and animals that ultimately depend upon it for their well being.

This need for air (oxygen) and the importance of organic matter have long been understood by gardeners, even if they did not always understand why this helped the soil life itself. Properly timed cultivation has always been seen as a cornerstone of successful gardening, although it is not essentially a matter of looking after the soil itself, or the nutrient balance, but rather the life of the soil itself. Life and not 'dirt' forms the basis of a successful garden and to this end we must treat soil with care and avoid demanding too much from this vital living resource.

Digging

Regular, deep cultivation is the way that gardeners have traditionally used to promote a fertile soil and healthy plant growth. Digging is of course hard work at the outset but the resulting plant growth can be hard to match. Despite this, many successful gardeners never dig their soil at all. Indeed, regular cultivation, while beneficial in some settings is not always vital. Having said that, for soils that have been left for some time or for new garden plots, digging is an excellent way of improving the soil.

When to Dig

If you want to avoid doing more harm than good, then you should always wait until the conditions are right before you start digging. For your own sake, this can mean avoiding working the soil when it is too dry and impenetrable – you may do yourself more harm

What Lives in the Soil?

Much of the life that dwells within the soil is hidden, either by its small size or simply because it is buried there. Microbes are an extremely important part of any soil, being somewhat like the 'eye of the needle' through which all essential life-giving elements must pass at some stage. Despite this all species that depend upon soil have their role to play.

Bacteria, fungi and algae

Unicellular, and almost always invisible unless they are species that form extensive colonies, these collectively form the most common soil organisms. Despite the fact that a few occasionally cause damage to plants, the vast majority are benign or even essential by virtue of their ability to break down and recycle essential nutrients needed to support healthy plant growth.

Earthworms, spiders and insects

While frequently large enough to be seen, they often remain out of sight unless disturbed during cultivation. Many of these creatures are important in the early stages of recycling nutrients and while a few may attack plants, most are important in maintaining the balance within a complex soil food web. Pesticides that target problematic species often wreak havoc at this level.

Plants and trees, birds and man

It is often comparatively easy to see these species but with the exception of the plants themselves, all too easy to imagine that they have no direct link with the soil. In all cases they depend upon the soil either directly or indirectly as a source of essential nutrient; and their actions, whether feeding or otherwise, often have the result in modifying the soil environment in some way or other.

than good. In most cases though, the wrong conditions are when the ground is too wet. Even if the soil is not obviously waterlogged, if it sticks to your tools and boots then it is effectively too wet. Ideally the soil should be moist, with a tendency to crumble when worked. If done properly, digging increases the amount of air space in the soil, which in turn benefits soil-dwelling organisms and plant roots due to the increase in oxygen available. Digging also allows for the addition of organic matter that will feed these vital denizens of the soil and so aids greatly in nutrient cycling.

How to Dig

If you intend adding organic matter to the soil, then you will need to work out how much of this you will need before you start. In most cases, you should aim to add no more than thirty per cent of the volume cultivated. You could always use less than this, of course. A 20m (66ft) plot then, cultivated to one spade depth will need 2.5m³ (88ft³) of manure or compost. Mark out the position of the bed accurately; remove any turf or vegetation, putting it to one side. This can either be buried in the bottom of the trenches as you go (as long as it does not contain perennial weeds) or taken away for composting.

If you have a lot to dig, don't try and do it all at once. Start small, working small areas (say one square metre) whenever you wish – pace yourself and above all, avoid straining your back. Make sure that you have a spade that's right for you and the job you're tackling. Ideally the handle of the spade should be the same height as the top of your hip, and remember than 'T' handled types are generally more comfortable than 'D' handled types if you are using them for long periods of time.

Pace yourself, and avoid trying to lift more than you can handle comfortably. Chances are you'll find that by taking smaller amounts, you can actually dig more for longer periods of time. As you work, try to establish a rhythm and as soon as you feel you've had enough or you find it difficult to straighten up, take a break, or save the rest of the digging for another day. Finally, when doing a lot of heavy digging, be sure to scrape the blade of soil now and then and, if

necessary, use a file to sharpen the end of the spade, following the original bevel of the blade.

Once you have dug a bed, don't walk on it. After all, the whole point is to loosen the topsoil and the subsoil to a depth of two feet so plant roots can grow unrestricted and water can readily percolate through the soil. Walking on the soil packs it down again.

1 Start by digging a trench 30cm (12in) wide and a spade's blade (called a spit) deep across half the width of the bed. Place the excavated soil next to the other half, putting it onto a protective sheet if the surface needs protection.

2 Once empty, loosen the trench base to a depth of the fork's tines, by rocking the fork back and forth. On light free-draining soils the subsoil can be left undisturbed. At this point, spread a 10cm (4in) layer of organic matter over the trench base.

3 (BELOW) Move over one spade's width in the bed, and begin to dig out another trench moving and inverting the excavated soil into the adjacent trench that was just dug. When you get to the end of the bed replace the soil which was set aside.

Light Cultivation

This involves the cultivation of the soil after it has been cultivated by digging or as an alternative when deep digging is not necessary. It is sometimes used to incorporate organic matter into the soil surface, to control weeds or incorporate green manures. The commonest tool used for light digging work is a fork, and a light forking is often the best method to use in areas with permanent plantings of perennial plants or shrubs.

Preparing Different Soils

Clay Soil

Digging can improve drainage. Dig thoroughly, incorporating plenty of well-rotted organic matter and horticultural grit as you go. Digging heavy clay soils before mid-winter will increase the surface area exposed to the weathering effects of frost, which help to break it down by the spring. It is important to avoid walking on the soil until it has had time to drain in spring.

Sandy Soil

Digging is normally unnecessary. Apply a layer of organic matter, such as well-rotted farmyard manure or garden compost to the soil surface in early spring and let the worms do the rest. In certain circumstances, double digging may be necessary if an impervious layer (known as a hardpan) has formed below the surface.

Silty Soil

Digging can be damaging to silty soils that are easily compacted under foot, leading to poor plant growth. Avoid this by keeping off the soil as much as possible, especially when the soil is wet.

The 'No-Dig' Method

No-dig gardening, as the name suggests, is a method of growing plants without cultivating the ground they occupy. While this can seem unnatural to gardeners used to the idea of regular cycles of digging, it is actually the most natural method available. This is because no-dig methods mimic the natural cycle of nature; after all, plants have grown on the earth's surface for over 400 million years without people digging the soil for them!

Essentially no-dig methods rely upon natural soil processes by utilizing the action of soil organisms to produce a good structure and natural nutrient cycling. There are numerous ways that this can be done, but all share reliance upon inputs from the top down. In other words, organic matter is placed on the surface

If space is limited, potatoes can be grown in a no-dig bed by enclosing it in a mesh cage and gradually adding more material as the crop develops.

Even a slightly raised bed helps focus efforts to avoid walking on the growing area. It also provides an anchor point for netting, frost protection, or support.

to be absorbed by the soil itself. Less laborious than digging, the no-dig method does need planning and careful input if it is to be successful. The results are often worth the effort put into the planning stage though, and a properly prepared no-dig bed can be every bit as effective as a conventionally cultivated one.

No-dig methods are extremely useful in situations where water is scarce; primarily because the constant input of organic matter gradually causes the water-holding capacity of the soil to increase, while water loss from runoff and evaporation are reduced by its mulching effect. Plants grown without digging also use water more efficiently, meaning that crops grown in otherwise drought-prone soils, can ultimately give higher yields.

The increased levels of soil organic matter also have a positive effect upon populations of beneficial insects. Predatory beetles and other useful invertebrates help control troublesome pests while earthworms, tiny detritivores and microbes all help liberate vital nutrients for the plant. High levels of organic matter also enhance the chemical stability of the soil in a no-dig system, and this means that once liberated, nutrients are less likely to be lost from the ground through leaching. Finally, less time is required to prepare the soil for planting, and since there is less bare soil there will be fewer opportunities for weeds to get established, as the mulch of organic matter helps suppress them.

No-dig systems are not without their problems however and chief among these are compaction, flooding or poor drainage, particularly if you aim to do this on 'heavy' (clay) land. Soil temperatures under organic mulch can be 5°C (9°F) lower than bare soil and, if combined with wet conditions, can delay crop development, although this can also be seen as an advantage during hot summer conditions.

The key features of no-dig methods are therefore, to keep the soil covered with organic mulch as much of the time as possible, and to avoid walking on the soil used for growing. In the case of vegetable crops, the beds are left permanently in place, and there is no cultivation. This means that a bed system – one that incorporates permanent paths – is essential if digging is to be eliminated. The beds must also be built to a manageable size. This essentially means that all parts of the bed can be reached from the permanent paths. While paths do take up space, using a bed system for edible crops means that you can grow these closer together (you don't need to leave extra space for access) and allows a greater harvest from a smaller area.

Simple raised beds can be made using timber or other suitable materials, and by raising the growing area it is possible to create a deep bed of good quality soil that will warm up more quickly than the surrounding soil. A raised bed also means you don't have to bend down so far to carry out routine tasks and the wooden edging proves extremely useful for attaching supporting hoops, crop covers and cloches. As a rule of thumb, raised beds should be no more than 1.2m (4ft) wide and paths at least 30cm (12in) wide. If you are putting in a number of them, make every other path 60cm (24in) wide so as to allow easy wheelbarrow access. The beds can be of any design, from a simple series of parallel rectangles to a more complex design of interlocking shapes. Whatever design you choose, try to follow the same recommended bed and path widths, remembering that narrow angles and very small beds are more difficult to construct and a less efficient use of space.

Using straw bales as a growing medium not only creates a deep bed of good quality soil, but also heat as it breaks down; this proves useful if captured in a cloche to raise earlier or tenderer crops than the rest of the garden.

Feeding the Soil

Quite a range of potential soil conditioners are available for use in the garden. Some are free – if you do not count the time taken in working and carting them. Others are relatively cheap, and some, usually those bought by the bag, can be quite expensive.

Imported Materials

A traditional favourite among gardeners is farmyard manure, although increasingly these days it comes from stables rather than farms. It is usually cheap or occasionally free for the taking. It should never be used fresh as it has a tendency to acidify the soil as it decomposes and should always be well rotted before use. It can also contain lots of weed seeds, which often come from the bedding used for the animals.

Manure is a by-product of grazing animals and often cheap as a result. Only ever use it if it is obtainable locally and has been well rotted to reduce its acidity.

Having said all of this, it makes an excellent addition to a compost heap; the bacteria it contains providing the perfect natural inoculants, to speed up the composting process.

In sharp contrast to manure, spent mushroom compost is one of the few types of organic matter to have a slightly alkaline effect on the soil. It is a uniform and friable mixture of stable organic materials that is a waste product of the mushroom-growing industry and usually inexpensive. The composting and mushroom-growing processes produce a substance that not only holds onto nutrients more readily than fresh or non-composted organic wastes but also has excellent moisture-holding ability. Spent mushroom compost is slightly alkaline with a pH ranging from 7 to 8, has few (if any) weed seeds, insects or pathogens because the compost is pasteurized before it is removed from the mushroom house. The addition of spent compost to garden soil can result in a higher pH, increased nutrient-holding capacity and better soil structure. One thing to be aware of though occurs when compost is first mixed with soil, as bacteria convert the proteins in the compost to ammonia, which can be toxic to young plants.

Finally, certain by-products of the food industry, such as spent hop waste and cocoa shells, can also be beneficial when added to soils. They are usually poor in nutrients and prove most useful in terms of their ability to improve soil structure but their smell (rancid ale or beer with hops or sickly cocoa) is sometimes enough to put people off.

Home-made Materials

If you have a lot of green waste and want to set it to work right away, you can simply dig a trench or hole a spade's depth 30cm (12in) deep. Put a layer of around 15cm (6in) of fresh green (not woody) material in its base before covering this over with the excavated soil, making a raised mound over the trench. If you do this in late winter it will take perhaps three months to break down, after which you can plant out heavy feeding plants such as peas, beans, courgettes or tomatoes directly on the mound. However, if you want to make use of the green waste elsewhere in the garden you will need to convert it another way.

Planting hungry crops such as this pumpkin over a pit filled with green waste helps to feed them while also warming the soil, thereby speeding up growth.

Larger gardens or places that generate considerable amounts of green waste can use this to produce compost quickly and efficiently on a very large scale.

Making Garden Compost

At one time, all gardeners took great pride in the making of a compost heap, where garden and kitchen waste was converted into a rich organic soil improver. Modern ways and consumerism have led to this becoming something of a 'lost art' to many people, preferring the instant fix of purchasing soil improvers from a garden or DIY centre. Domestic gardens often generate huge amounts of waste which if disposed of as landfill does not rot but ferments, producing large amounts of methane – a harmful greenhouse gas. Not only is this environmentally damaging but is also a pointless waste of one of the best resources your garden can generate. Making your own compost though, could not be simpler. It produces an ideal medium for improving your garden soil and in addition to this will provide food for the vast multitude of soil organisms that benefit your plants and maintain a healthy natural balance in the garden.

Nature is a great recycler of useful products. Many soil-dwelling organisms take advantage of the seasonal bounty that is lavished upon the soil in the form of autumn leaves and other plant debris. These feed on this decaying plant matter and gradually render it into a form that can be re-absorbed by the plants themselves. While a few of these – such as worms – are highly visible, the vast majority of these garden helpers are microscopic. Providing them with a ready source of nutrient can ultimately provide nutrients for plants that are both natural and virtually cost free. This is good news for all gardeners and especially so if you are intending to grow vegetables. Using compost to feed your kitchen garden will mean that they are full of wholesome goodness – just as nature intended.

Composting then, is simply a word that we use to describe how gardeners harness this natural process of decay and nutrient cycling. Simply piling all your organic waste in a heap would ultimately result in compost, although the process may be inefficient and the results variable. Some gardeners take quite a scientific view of their composting and construct heaps that generate heat and rot down very quickly called 'hotpiles.' Alternatively, a more leisurely approach involves allowing the process to continue more slowly, utilizing the activities of larger invertebrates using a method called a 'coldpile'.

Home composting, while smaller and slower than large, commercial operations, can easily produce good quantities of quality soil-enriching humus.

BELOW: If there were space and enough green waste available, a garden would ideally have two or more compost bays to ensure that some is always available.

Even if you take a slower approach it is important to get roughly the right proportions of different materials to make the end product usable in the garden. As with most food preparations – even food for soil organisms – many recipes exist. The gardeners of yesteryear often had their own blends, some of which were closely guarded secrets. There is however, no real secret to the process and the overall recipe is really quite simple. All of the potential ingredients for your compost are generally classed as either 'green' or 'brown'. 'Greens' are materials that are moist and have a high nutrient value. They are usually – but not always – plant materials from the garden. Compared to browns, greens have more nitrogen in them, this element being critical both for plant growth and for the billions of multiplying microbes that cycle other nutrients in the soil. 'Browns' on the other hand are dry and high in carbon. They are usually dry and dead plant materials that are a source of energy for the compost microbes, thereby helping along the process of composting. Because they tend to be dry, browns often need to be moistened before they are put into a

compost heap. For a 'hotpile' aim for equal amounts of both greens and browns, whereas for a 'coldpile' heap roughly three times the amount of browns as greens keeping the compost moist but not too wet while supplying the decomposing organisms with essential nitrogen and carbon.

Good green composting materials include horse, cow, sheep and poultry manures, lawn clippings (thin layers only), fruit and vegetable peel, tea bags, coffee grounds, eggshells, weeds and old garden plants (if not already seeding). Good brown ingredients include autumn leaves, hay, straw, sawdust and shredded prunings.

Whether because of toxins, plant or human diseases or weed problems, there are some things that should never be put into compost heaps. Never compost chemically-treated wood products, diseased plants, dog or cat waste, meat, bones and fatty foods or perennial weed roots that may grow when added back to the soil.

When adding waste materials to the heap, the items should be as small as you can make them. The more surface area exposed, the quicker it will decompose. A chipper or shredder is a big help and hiring one between you and a few of your neighbours will help to keep costs down. Some gardeners recommend adding a small amount of good topsoil to add microorganisms that will kick-start the process. A lesser-known alternative to this is to urinate on the heap, although if you try this one you may be better to do so during the hours of darkness! Compost heaps in containers can be built up with successive layers of 'green' and 'brown' materials separating these with thin layers of soil.

Composting Equipment

At its simplest, a compost heap is made by simply piling up your organic waste somewhere in your garden. Our natural urge for tidiness however means that many of us opt to either build a container for the heap or purchase a pre-made container. A popular design for these is a cone, and these are tidy and compact making them ideal for smaller gardens. They

Plastic commercially produced compost bins are an ideal way of dealing with the waste matter produced by a smaller garden and usually take up little room.

are usually made of plastic and so have a long life and makers often claim that they don't need to be turned although devices are available to let you do this. On the downside though, they only deal with smaller amounts of waste and almost never heat up.

Compost heaps on the other hand are less limited and can deal with large volumes of waste although this simple fact means that they are best suited to large gardens. They can also be made large enough to generate heat although not all will, and this helps the composting process. In any case, heaps work best when turned and the bottom of the pile must have contact with the soil so that beneficial organisms can gain access. If you bag your compost after about a year, it will continue to decompose in the bag and become finer and drier. When you come to bag it up, put anything too coarse back in the heap for further decomposition in the next heap.

If you are adding the right things in roughly the right proportions there shouldn't be any problem with the heap smelling. Most compost heaps that smell are either lacking air or are too wet. In either case, the answer is to aerate the heap by turning and loosening it with a fork (or turning tool if you have a cone) and preferably add some dry materials at the same time.

Where to Put a Compost Heap

Ideally, a compost heap should consist of two bins, one for adding to and maturing, the second containing compost ready for use. If room allows, more could be used. If you want to use the hotpile method, each bin will need to be approximately one cubic metre in volume. Home-made compost bins are usually simply made from old timber, constructed with slatted wooden sides and a door at the front to allow access to the contents. In this way, the bin will allow air circulation throughout. The position of the bins is also important, ideally putting them somewhere warm, sheltered and convenient for trips from the kitchen.

If you want to make a hotpile, then you'll need to make the whole heap in one go. Start the heap with a layer of straw to soak up any 'runoff' then add

Once composting is complete the resulting material should be a dark, crumbly material that is easily broken up and runs freely through the fingers.

some coarse, twiggy material to improve aeration at the base of the heap. Add alternate 15cm (6in) layers of carbon rich brown waste, for example shredded prunings, leaves, newspaper with nitrogen rich green waste, for example farm manures, vegetable peelings, green shoots or grass clippings. Avoid adding meat, fish, bones and pet waste. Keep adding layers until the pile is 1m (39in) high; about three layers each of greens and brown material. Topsoil can also be added as a 2cm (¾in) layer between each cycle of green and brown materials and you should finish the pile with a layer of browns.

Cover the pile if the weather is very dry although this is not necessary under normal circumstances. Check to see that your pile becomes hot within a few days as the activity of bacteria and other micro-organisms soon commence. As they start to break down the material, they heat up the organic matter and the heap may reach up to 70°C. At these high temperatures, most annual weed seed and diseases are destroyed making the compost sterile. However, if in doubt, avoid adding any perennial weeds, diseased or pest-infected material. Turn the pile to expose all the material to the hot centre and decrease composting time. Do this once a week in summer or once a month when cooler. The heat of the composting materials should peak each time you turn the pile, although this peak will be lower with each turn. Always make sure that the material remains moist but avoid over-wetting, as allowing the heap to become wet and soggy encourages anaerobic bacteria that cause the contents to putrefy – in effect become very slimy and smelly.

The compost can be ready for use in as little as eight weeks, though more normally it should take three months during summer, to six months in the winter. Once your compost is complete you should have a dark crumbly material that is easily broken up and runs through your fingers. Sifting the compost is the final stage of the process, with any large pieces of residue being returned back to the new heap. Once made, this compost is the ideal medium to enrich your garden soil naturally. What is more, you will have done this at little or no cost to yourself and perhaps more importantly, at no cost to the environment.

What to compost and what not to compost

You can compost almost anything that was once alive or part of a living organism although not everything you add will make a good addition for a material that you intend to handle. Adding a lot of coarse woody material will significantly slow down the composting process although you can offset this if you shred it first. Be sure to add around three parts green to one part brown and never add any of the items in the 'avoid these' list.

Greens	Browns	Avoid these
Grass cuttings	Straw and hay	Meat or fish scraps
Weeds (avoid weed seeds if possible)	Coffee grounds	Grease or oil
	Dry plant stems and twigs	Cooked food scraps
Urine and manure	Scrunched up paper	Barbeque or coal ashes
Raw fruit and vegetables	Torn up cardboard (e.g. from cereal boxes, egg-boxes, toilet-roll centres etc.)	Dog or cat faeces (best avoided as these can contain dangerous pathogens)
Fresh plants		
Tea leaves		
Seaweed, algae and garden pond cleanings	Pet and human hair (takes a little time)	Plastic or inorganic material
		Treated timber
Wood/peat ashes	Egg shells	

Leaf Mould

Many gardeners swear by leaf mould, believing it to be the finest addition to any soil. The material itself forms naturally under a closed canopy of forest trees and is, as the name suggests, the rotted product of fallen leaves. Anyone who has a ready supply of leaves will find this an easy material to make, with the only real difference between the material you make in a garden, and that naturally found in woodland, is that you make it in a deep pile. It is not a fast operation like hotpile composting, however, as the fungi that break down the leaves tend to be slow workers. Good leaf mould then, takes at least one or (preferably) two years to mature.

To make leaf mould, simply gather wet leaves and put them into a home-made wire mesh container. An alternative to this is to put them into old compost sacks that have had plenty of holes pricked into the sides, tying these at the top before laying them out or piling them in a shady place. A shaded, cool spot in the garden is an essential requirement, ideally under the shade of trees where the leaf mould experiences similar conditions to a woodland and won't be dried out by the sun.

A simple mesh cage supported on the corners by wooden stakes is the easiest way to store fallen, dry leaves as they break down to make leaf mould.

MAKING POTTING MIXES FROM LEAF MOULD

Despite being nothing more than composted leaves, the rich brown/black material that is known as leaf mould can serve as your own 'home grown' seed or potting compost.

To make your seed compost, use fully decomposed leaves (preferably those that have been composting for two years) and sieve this to remove larger particles such as twigs. The resulting material should have a coarse crumbly texture, which is ideal for providing drainage and aeration while being moisture retentive. The fact that it does not contain abundant nutrients means that it is ideal for seed germination, as the seedlings develop a strong root system which will help them remain healthy when threatened with pests and diseases. Make your compost by combining equal parts of sifted leaf mould, sharp sand and sifted garden compost; it is an ideal medium for seedlings or cutting and can really get them off to a flying start. Be aware though that leaf-mould and garden compost are unsterilized products and so may be contaminated with weed seeds or disease-causing spores.

If you want a compost that is well suited for ericaceous plants (heathers, rhododendrons, blueberries and so on), then you can make some additional mould out of shredded conifer leaves and add this to the leaf-mould in equal measures. The low nutrient level means that it is not sufficient in its own right for use in potting mixes and it must have additional grit and slow release fertilizer. Generally speaking, no more than twenty five to thirty per cent of the final volume of the potting mixture should be leaf compost, as it tends to continue to decompose leading to a significant volume reduction of the potting soil over time. Equal parts of well-rotted fine leaf mould, sharp sand and top soil is an ideal medium for potting on or container growing.

You can of use any type of leaf, but leaves from different trees have different qualities that may affect your leaf mould. Conifer needles and leaves of evergreens tend to be rather acidic and mixing green and dry deciduous leaves can cause the heap to heat up like a hotpile. Many gardeners claim that the best quality mould is always made from deciduous oak and beech trees although the inevitable truth is that the best leaves are usually a mix of whatever is falling in or around your garden. Ideally, two permanent pits (or three if you want to make two-year-old mould), should be sited side by side so that one can be emptied and refilled each year.

Worm Compost

Using worms for composting – a process technically called 'vermicomposting' – is probably something that you are partly familiar with if you practise coldpile methods already. In essence, the only real difference is that you employ the worms in a specialized way to quickly recycle green waste. The materials being composted are actually consumed by worms and excreted as casts or 'castings;' a process that binds the nutrients consumed into a plant-usable form while reducing the volume of the original materials. The worms also cover their casts with slow-dissolving, semi-permeable mucus, which is both a time-release mechanism for the cast's nutritional value and the cause of the finished compost's water-retentive capabilities.

A worm colony or 'wormery' can be used to recycle both cooked and uncooked food waste, along with things like shredded newspaper, cardboard tubes, tea bags, egg cartons and so on. In the UK alone, it is estimated that about a third of household waste are food products which could otherwise be composted in a wormery; a staggering total of almost seven million tonnes of food waste and peelings every year.

Before you start to make a wormery though, you will need a supply of worms. There are a number of species that are particularly suitable for composting, most of which are in the genus *Eisenia* (Tiger Worms or 'Red Wigglers'); with *Eisenia foetida* or *Eiseania andrei* arguably being the best, due to

RIGHT: **While it is perfectly feasible to make your own wormery, many designs are available for commercial sale, some of which even come supplied with worms.**

their overall hardiness and generally greater appetite. A third species, *Eisenia hortensis* (the European night-crawler), sometimes sold under the name *Dendrobaena*, is also widely available as they are used by anglers as bait. Before you look for somewhere to buy them though, take a look in your compost bin. If you already have some worms (the small red wriggly ones, not the larger, mineral soil dwelling earthworm *Lumbricus terrestris*) then you already have the ones you need.

Unlike a standard compost heap, raised temperatures and multiple pile-turning are not needed as excessive heat will kill the worms. Indeed, worm

BELOW: **The best worms for composting are** *Eisenia* **(Tiger Worms or Red Wigglers), and** *not* **the larger mineral soil dwelling earthworm** *Lumbricus terrestris.*

colonies are best placed in a shady, cool and moist location to keep the temperature down. Ideally, a box for your worms will have some drainage in its base but be sealed round the sides to keep it moist. Home-made wormeries can easily be made from adapted plastic containers, with old kitchen bins being a favourite choice. Wood is also sometimes used, although some conifers contain resinous oils that may harm worms, and all wooden bins will eventually decay and need to be replaced. Polystyrene (styrofoam) boxes can be particularly useful if you can find large enough ones, due to their ability to regulate an even temperature in the box all year round. Metal containers on the other hand are generally less suitable, as they tend to conduct heat too readily, are prone to rusting, and (in the case of certain alloys) may release heavy metals into the vermicompost itself. Their design of course ultimately depends upon both the available materials and where you intend to keep it.

Bins need holes or mesh (usually in the lid) for aeration, and a spout or holes in the bottom for excess liquid to drain into a tray – ideally for collection as a liquid fertilizer. The base of the box is then filled with 5–10cm (2–4in) bedding material (shredded newspaper is ideal) before the worms and a little partially decomposed vegetable matter are added to this. Leave them for a day or so before adding a couple of handfuls of kitchen green waste; peelings, cabbage hearts and so forth on top of this. New colonies need time to settle in – generally only feed a couple of handfuls a week when you first set it up; over-feeding worms in the early stages results in the green waste starting to rot down before the worms get a chance to eat it. The amount of food can gradually be increased over the next few weeks as the colony increases. If the material inside gets very soggy and wet, then simply shred up some extra newspaper or cardboard and mix this thoroughly right down to the base in order to soak up the excess moisture, as well as helping aerate the compost.

It is advisable to check the pH level every now and then. Thin, white, thread-like pot worms (Enchytraeids) are tiny (just a few millimetres long), occur quite naturally and are harmless – in fact they do the same job

as the larger red Eisenia worms. However, despite this, they thrive at a lower, more acidic pH than is ideal for the larger worms and are not nearly as efficient. Adding calcified seaweed can counter this problem, as can a regular addition of eggshells. After a few months of caring for your worms, you will probably be able to judge the conditions in the box with little more than a glance and amend it accordingly. The worm compost can be used as an additive to potting mixes or as a soil conditioner, whereas the 'worm liquid' that drains off can either be diluted as a liquid plant food or added to your compost heap.

Green Manures

Also known as 'cover crops', green manures are plants that are grown for their ability to improve soil structure; they increase the organic matter content of the soil, smother the soil to prevent weed growth and in some cases raise the available levels of certain nutrients in the soil. They are principally used where soil is likely to be left bare for a while, a situation that leads to a loss of nutrients if it continues for six weeks or more. Green manures help counter this and maintain a more even soil temperature and moisture content. Indeed, some green manures such as alfalfa or bitter lupin send down long roots that are able to tap into resources deeper in the ground. The roots of these deep-rooted types work through the soil, holding it together while they are growing. Once they are dug in, however, they not only help to make it crumbly and friable as they rot, but also release nutrients they harvested from the subsoil. In this respect they could well be described as a form of biological 'deep digging'. Other species such as grazing rye or clover produce a fibrous root system to help build structure in the upper reaches of the soil.

The stems and leaves of green manures also provide cover over the soil surface, protecting it from erosion and preventing capping after heavy rains. It also shades the ground and suppresses weed growth. Despite all this, green manure is a short term fix that after a certain period is dug into the soil, where it breaks down and further improves the soil.

Green manures are useful where soil is to be left bare for a while, helping counter nutrient loss, maintain an even soil temperature and moisture content.

Leguminous Green Manures

Green manures can usually be divided into two types; non-legumes (usually grains) and legumes. The latter of these are highly valued as green manures due to their role as nitrogen-fixers – that is plants that form a symbiotic relationship with certain bacteria known collectively as 'rhizobia'. These rhizobia colonize nodules on the plant's roots and this in turn improves its nitrogen uptake, as the bacteria have the ability to take inert (unreactive) nitrogen from their surroundings and convert it into a more reactive form that the plant can use. Leguminous green manures include clover, vetch, peas, fava beans, bitter lupin and alfalfa. Despite their impressive nitrogen-fixing abilities however, legumes do have the disadvantages of generally adding less organic content, slower autumn growth, and are as a rule not particularly winter hardy.

Of the remaining non-leguminous green manures, winter rye is the most commonly grown, although oats, wheat, oilseed rape and buckwheat are also used. While none of these actually add nitrogen to the soil, they do help maintain the existing levels and they have the additional advantage over legumes of growing faster

or summer crops, on the other hand, grow quickly, although they must be given sufficient time to develop before they are dug in; usually around three weeks for fast growing types such as mustard but two or three months may be needed for slower growing legumes such as bitter lupin or fenugreek. After preparing the soil, plant large-seeded cover crops like bitter lupin in shallow, closely-spaced furrows. Smaller seeds such as mustard, can be broadcast (scattered) over the surface and covered with a light raking, watering if needed until they germinate.

As the time approaches where you want to use the ground the manure is growing in, you should dig it in. As a rule of thumb, allow at least three weeks before you intend to plant to give time for the material to rot down. If the green manure is too tall to dig in easily, you can mow or 'strim' it first.

Fenugreek is a quick growing annual legume, ideal for spring sowings, which not only provides added nitrogen but also can be dug in ten weeks after sowing.

through the autumn thereby giving better weed suppression if soil is to be left unused in the winter. They also tend to break down more slowly than legumes and as a consequence, add more organic matter to the soil.

Green manures intended for winter cover should be planted early enough to give about four weeks of growth before cold weather stops them. Spring

Remember that it is best not to allow green manures to go to seed as some can actually become weeds in the garden if this is allowed to happen.

Green manures are especially useful in garden settings where the ground is traditionally dug over (and manured) in autumn, then left bare over winter. Many nutrients can be lost during this time due to the leaching action of rain (or snow). A hardy green manure sown in the autumn – while the soil still has some warmth left in it – prevents this situation and can be dug in the following spring, yielding nutrients to a newly sown or planted crop.

Role of Decaying Matter

Fresh organic matter, once added to the soil, acts as a trigger for microbe activity. Most important among these are bacteria and fungi, as well as many micro-invertebrates. Along with bacteria, fungi are the primary decomposers of dead organic matter. While the essential role in the storage, transportation and recycling of nutrients that both play has been long recognized, the importance of this is often overlooked by gardeners. Ultimately then, while Leonardo da Vinci's insightful observation that 'we know more about the celestial bodies than the soil underfoot' may no longer be strictly true, gardeners rarely appreciate the importance of decaying matter in supporting the whole garden ecosystem.

As well as breaking down dead plant material, soil fungi and other microbes play an important role in recycling a range of essential plant nutrients, especially phosphorus. Organic phosphate will slowly be released as inorganic phosphate or be incorporated into more stable organic materials and become part of the soil's organic matter.

The activity of micro-organisms is influenced by soil temperature and soil moisture, as well as the availability of organic food sources. The process is most rapid when soils are warm and moist but well drained – conditions enhanced by raised levels of humus. Phosphate can potentially be lost through soil erosion and to a lesser extent to water running over or through the soil; high levels of organic matter help mop up any excess, keeping it in the soil and preventing loss as well as potentially environmentally damaging run-off.

The organic rich layer that is usually uppermost in the soil plays a vital role in helping to recycle, and regulate the release of essential plant nutrients.

Fungi and bacteria play a vital role by holding onto a variety of nutrients, preventing them from being leached through the soil, and are in turn eaten by larger soil organisms, rendering them essential both within the soil and beyond. Far from being a problem in the garden then, decay fungi are vital components of the food chain and in supporting plant growth.

Types of Green Manure

Green manure crops suited to late summer or autumn sowing

These species will generally withstand moderate to hard frost, even for prolonged periods and can be cut down in the spring, prior to cultivation. The shorter types can also be used as cover crops on bare earth around winter vegetables or biennial crops that are to be harvested in the early spring, thereby protecting bare soil, preventing nutrient loss and creating a more stable soil environment.

	Sowing time and method	Height	Nitrogen-fixing	Term of Growth	Digging in	Notes
Alfalfa *Medicago sativa*	March to July. Broadcast at 2–3gm².	100–150cm	Yes but poor	Perennial. Grow for several months or more than one season.	Any time. Medium effort if young. Hard if left for more than one season.	Very deep rooting. Will grow on most soils. Dislikes acid or waterlogged soils but is drought-resistant.
Asilke clover *Trifolium hybridum*	Early April to late August.	30cm	Yes	Several months.	Any time. Medium effort.	Will withstand wetter soils than other clovers but more prone to drought. Shallow rooted.
Essex or red merviot clover *Trifolium pratense*	Early April to late August. Broadcast at 2–3gm².	40cm	Yes	Several months.	Easy, little effort.	Prefers good loamy soil. Can be mown or cut several times per season and used for compost.
Grazing rye *Secale cereale*	Mid-August to late November. Broadcast at 30gm².	30–60cm	No	Autumn to spring.	Before flowering. Hard work.	Grows in most soils. Keep watered during germination, or else yield is poor. Sow thickly to smother weeds.
Phacelia *Phacelia tanacetifolium*	Mid-March to Mid-September Broadcast at 2–3gm².	60–90cm	No	2 months in summer. 5–6 months over winter.	Before flowering. Easy, little effort.	Grows in most soils. Quick to grow in summer. If left, will produce mauve flowers which bees love.
Trefoil *Medicago lupulina*	Mid-March to mid-August. Broadcast at 1.5–3gm².	30–60cm	Yes	Several months to a year.	Any time. Medium effort.	Will grow in most soils but dislikes acid. Can be used for undersowing. Dense foliage.
Winter field beans *Vicia faba*	September to November 10cm deep in drills 15–20cm apart.	60–90cm	Yes	Over winter.	Before flowering. Medium effort.	Will grow on loam or heavy clay. Not drought resistant amd slow to germinate. Sow close together to prevent weeds growing between plants.
Winter tares *Vicia sativa*	Early March to mid-September, avoiding June. Broadcast at 20gm² or in rows 15cm apart and 4–5cm deep.	50–75cm	Yes	2–3 months or over winter.	Up to flowering. Easy, little effort.	Prefers heavy soils. Dislikes light or acid soil. Produces dense cover.

Green manure for spring and summer sowing

Plants for use in the spring and summer have to be quick growing to cover the ground and yield benefit within a short period. They are generally slightly tender although they can be extremely useful in the ground following the harvest of a biennial crop and prior to the establishment of another. Some lower growing species can actually be used as a catch crop around other seasonal crops.

	Sowing time and method	Height	Nitrogen-fixing	Term of Growth	Digging in	Notes
Bitter lupin *Lupinus angustifolius*	Early March to late June in rows 15cm apart, 2–3cm apart in the rows. 3–4 cm deep.	50cm	Yes	2–3 months.	Before flowering. Easy, little effort.	Prefers light slightly acidic soil. Foliage not very dense. Deep rooted.
Buckwheat *Fagopyrum esculentum*	Mid-March to late August. Broadcast at $10gm^2$ or thinly in shallow rows 20cm apart.	30cm	No	2–3 months.	Before or during flowering. Easy, no effort	Grows on poor soils. If allowed to flower, attracts hoverflies to aid pollination of crops.
Fenugreek *Trigonella foenum graecum*	Early March to late August. Broadcast at $5gm^2$ or thinly in 15cm shallow rows.	30–60cm	No	2–3 months.	Any time before flowering. Easy, little effort.	Prefers good drainage but will tolerate heavy or light soil.
Crimson clover *Trifolium incarnatum*	Early March to late August. Broadcast at $2–3gm^2$.	30–60cm	Yes	Autumn to spring.	2–3 months or over winter. Before flowering. Medium effort.	Prefers sandy loam soil but will tolerate heavy clay. Large red flowers attract bees.
Mustard *Sinapis alba*	Early March to mid-September. Broadcast at $3–5gm^2$ or thinly in rows 15cm apart.	60–90cm	No	2–3 weeks or up to 2 months.	Before flowering, toughens up after flowering. Easy before flowering.	Prefers moisture-retentive, fertile soil. A member of the brassica family, so crop rotation cycle must be considered.

PLANTING YOUR GARDEN

Selecting the plants for your garden is arguably one of the most enjoyable and exciting aspects of gardening. The plants themselves, whether they be ornamentals or edible crops, will define your garden and for many constitute the main focus of their interest. Having said this, poorly chosen plants will not perform well and do little to enhance the garden as a result. It is vital therefore that gardeners plan their choice of plants carefully according to their site and ultimately its capabilities and limitations. The worst choice is almost invariably the impulse buy; plants purchased from a nursery or garden centre on the basis of appearance alone. Choosing it just because it is pretty and planting it without considering its needs or habits can often lead to problems later.

The object of plant choice should always be to obtain, establish and maintain plants that are healthy, vigorous and (as a consequence of this) are less vulnerable to attack by pests, disease or environmental problems. Even if a plant is healthy, when too vigorous for its situation it can still prove problematic, needing constant pruning to be kept within reasonable bounds. The first step in creating and maintaining a healthy garden is to choose plants that are well suited to the conditions there. Wisely chosen plants, placed in a location that meets their requirements as fully as possible will normally thrive, require little attention and so save time and effort as a result.

OPPOSITE PAGE: **Bluebell (*Endymion non-scriptum*) and wood anemone (*Anemone nemorosa*) grow best in moist deciduous woodland.**

RIGHT: **Shade loving plants such as this hellebore often perform poorly if planted in very hot, dry conditions, although they can often tolerate sunlight.**

Right Plant, Right Place

The majority of plants, especially weeds and native species, can tell us a great deal about the environment we have in our gardens. By carefully observing which types of plants already grow well in the garden, it is possible to pick up clues not only as to which plants will thrive there, but also about ways that new planting can be improved in the garden as a whole.

All plant species have their preferred natural habitats such as wetlands, woodlands, grasslands or rocky places, and have become specially adapted to exploit these niches and out-compete other species less well adapted to them. In the case of some garden plants it is easy to match the conditions; ferns for instance will always thrive if they are planted in moist soils in a sheltered area with permanent shade, whereas Alpine species mostly need good drainage and full sun. Details such as the soil texture and pH are easily assessed but this only takes us some of the way to assessing what our gardens are like. When combined with an

Plants with woolly or grey leaves are ideal candidates for a hot dry place, as these reflect light, trap moisture, and so render them more drought-resistant.

assessment of both the climate and microclimate how-ever, this knowledge can be used to help us to select the plants best suited to the garden environment.

Many of the plants that are planted in gardens are not specifically adapted for the conditions they find, despite the best efforts to match them up. This is espe-cially true of wildflowers or wild species, which unlike more highly bred cultivars or hybrids are often very particular about their growing requirements. A weed on the other hand, while often thought of as a wild plant, is often perfectly adapted to the conditions it finds in your garden and quickly thrives. The fact that weeds thrive (at the expense of other plants that you are attempting to establish) is a lesson that gardeners need to learn to follow, as the weeds are in fact giving

vital clues to the conditions therein. Spending some time studying what naturally establishes and grows can tell a lot about the type of garden and ultimately the plants that will naturally thrive there.

Most of us have at least some ability when it comes to using plants to 'read' the environment, whether we recognize we are doing it or not. An obvious example would have to be moss growing on the north (or south in the southern hemisphere) side of a tree. It grows there because this shaded part of the trunk is cooler and moister – exactly the kind of environment needed for moss to grow and thrive. When you start trying to read the signs given by wild plants (and weeds), take note of the species that occur both within and around your garden. Get yourself a good wildflower

While often despised by gardeners as a weed that also stings, nettles (*Urtica dioica*) are nonetheless a sign of a fertile and nutrient-rich soil in a garden.

identification guide and find out what conditions these plants like to grow in. Once you have collected the details of the plants you have, you can assess the conditions of your garden.

Some species such as cuckoo flower (*Cardamine pratense*) or rushes (*Juncus spp.*) among coarse grass species are excellent indicators of soil that is wet for part or all of the year. Their presence should be a clear instruction to you that the plants you choose will need to be ones that tolerate such conditions. Dry ground on the other hand might have plants such as yarrow (*Achillea spp.*) and sheep's sorrel (*Rumex acetosella*). Fertility can also be ascertained by looking at weeds and there are few better indicators than the nettle (*Urtica spp.*) as these grow best on soils rich in nitrogen and potassium. Their presence, while sometimes a nuisance, tells you that any plants you establish there will have plenty of nutrients available for rapid growth. Indeed a former nettle patch can be an ideal site for heavy flowering and fruiting shrubs. Fertile soils that also have a high organic content will tend to support large patches of weeds such as chickweed (*Stellaria media*) and groundsel (*Senecio vulgaris*), and their presence is a sure sign that herbaceous plant species which like a rich soil will be happy there.

An area of ground inhabited by plants such as soft rush (*Juncus effusus*) and cuckoo flower (*Cardamine pratensis*) shows a site that is prone to water-logging.

Trees and Shrubs for Particular Conditions

Acidic soil types

Trees		Shrubs	
Scots pine	Pinus sylvestris (dry)	Gorse	Ulex europaeus
Corsican pine	Pinus nigra (dry)	Broom	Cytisus spp.
Lodgepole pine	Pinus contorta (peat)	Rhododendron	Rhododendron spp.
Sitka spruce	Picea sitchensis (peat)	Azalea	Camellia japonica
Norway spruce	Picea abies (peat)	Camellia	Erica and Caluna spp.
Sweet chestnut	Castanea sativa	Heathers	Gaultheria mucronata
Silver birch	Betula pendula	Prickly heather	

Calcareous soil types

Trees		Shrubs	
Beech	Fagus sylvatica	Spindle	Euonymus europaeus
Ash	Fraxinus excelsior	Hazel	Corylus avellana
Horse chestnut	Aesculushippocastanum	Lilac	Syringa vulgaris
Hawthorn	Crataegus monogyna	Snowberry	Symphoricarpus albus
Hornbeam	Carpinus betulus	Box	Buxus sempervirens
Whitebeam	Sorbus aria	Forsythia	Forsythia spp.
Tulip tree	Liriodendendron spp.	Currant	Ribes spp.

Exposed coastal sites

Trees		Shrubs	
Sycamore	Acer pseudoplatanus	Gorse	Ulex europaeus
Holm oak	Quercus ilex	Goat willow	Salix caprea
White poplar	Populus alba	Blackthorn	Prunus spinosa
Alder	Alnus glutinosa	Japanese rose	Rosa rugosa
Hawthorn	Crataegus monogyna	Elder	Sambucus nigra
Lodge pole pine	Pinus nigra	Tamarisk	Tamarix spp.

Native or Exotic Plants?

Recent years have seen calls for gardeners to grow native plants, as these (it is claimed) best support native wildlife. In certain cases this does have some merit, although in many urban garden settings, the evidence to support this is at best thin and much of our garden wildlife will take advantage of whatever it finds. The simple fact is that non-native plants frequently provide abundant food, while native wildlife will eat a huge range of species – a fact clearly attested by holes in the leaves of many non-native plants in your own garden! Be sure to avoid highly bred plants, however, as these can prove less suitable than true species, especially in respect of flowers and fruit.

Having said this, in some circumstances, native plants are better suited to the conditions in your garden than exotic imports, often requiring less fertilizer, thriving with minimal cultivation, and sometimes showing greater drought-tolerance in drier areas. Perhaps most importantly though, is the fact that native plants rarely become invasive in the way that so many imported garden plants have, and this alone may be a good enough reason in itself to plant them.

Exposed inland sites			
Trees		**Shrubs**	
Norway maple	*Acer platanoides*	Berberry (various)	*Berberis spp.*
Silver birch	*Betula pendula*	Cotoneaster	*Cotoneaster spp.*
Monterey cypress	*Cupressus macrocarpa*	Broom	*Cytisus spp. (dry sites)*
Rowan	*Sorbus aucuparia*	Gorse	*Ulex spp. (dry sites)*
White poplar	*Populus alba*	Holly	*Ilex aquifolium*
Hawthorn	*Crataegus monogyna*	Bilberry	*Vaccinium myrtillus*
Polluted atmospheric sites (urban, industrial)			
Trees		**Shrubs**	
London plane	*Platanus x acerifolia*	Berberry (various)	*Berberis spp.*
Horse chestnut	*Aesculushippocastanum*	Box	*Buxus sempervirens*
Lime (linden)	*Tilia spp.*	Snowberry	*Symphoricarpus albus*
False acacia	*Robinia pseudoacacia*	Sumac	*Rhus typhina*
Silver birch	*Betula pendula*	Holly	*Ilex spp.*
Hornbeam	*Carpinus betulus*	Cherry laurel	*Prunus laurocerasus*
Ornamental crabs	*Malus spp.*	Flowering currant	*Ribes sanguineum*
Ornamental cherries	*Prunus spp.*	Cotoneaster	*Cotoneaster spp.*
Sites with high and/or low fluctuating water tables			
Trees		**Shrubs**	
White willow	*Salix alba*	Goat willow	*Salix caprea*
Common alder	*Alnus glutinosa*	Crack willow	*Salix fragilis*
Pedunculate oak	*Quercus robur **	Purple osier	*Salix viminalis*
Hornbeam	*Carpinus betulus **	Elder	*Sambucus nigra*

* Not where water logging occurs.

Growing and Planting Trees

Trees and shrubs form the essential framework of your garden and the secret of success with these lies in careful stock selection, ground preparation and ultimately correct planting. If planted properly, they will reward you with good growth and give your garden the height that it needs.

Preparing the Ground

Despite the insistence of many books and guides, organic additives such as compost can be a mixed blessing when planting trees or shrubs, especially if they are incorporated into the planting pit. Adding compost is often said to be necessary in order to improve the soil and encourage healthy roots. In fact such a humus-enriched soil mix does improve the soil; so much so that it can actually cause the planting pit to become 'too friendly'. Quite simply, the roots like it better than the surrounding soil and rather than moving out into the surrounding soil, they circle round in it as if it were a pot of compost. This in turn produces a sort of corkscrew root arrangement known as 'girdling', which causes increasing instability of the plant as it grows.

A humus-enriched planting pit becomes 'too friendly', the roots circling round as if in a pot of compost rather than moving out into the surrounding soil.

Circling (girdling) roots are unstable, and pot-grown trees, or those planted in humus rich pits, often take on a characteristic lean and easily fall or blow over.

The best way around the problem of girdling is to actually apply organic matter across the soil surface after the tree or shrub has been planted. This is, of course, much more like the natural situation and has the dual benefit of providing a slow release of nutrient through the action of soil-dwelling micro-organisms as well as encouraging a range of soil-litter dwelling insects, including the pest-eating ground beetles. Fertilizers are also only really any use if you know that the soil is poor in particular types of nutrients. Apply fertilizers immediately after planting, but before mulching, for best effect.

Planting Trees and Shrubs

If possible, choose your own plants and seek advice from the grower if you are unsure. Always choose trees and shrubs that are vigorous, healthy and free of obvious signs of stress, damage, pests or disease. If you are buying bare-rooted stock make sure that the roots never dry out before planting and keep them covered at all times until you finally place them in the hole. Even a couple of minutes left exposed to cold or drying winds can cause a lot of damage. Remember that they are only adapted to be underground.

Plants with a defined dormant period are best planted early in that season. Therefore many deciduous species are best planted out during the early winter. Evergreens, on the other hand, tend to do well if planted either in early autumn or late spring in ground conditions where sufficient moisture is available for rapid root growth. Trees and shrubs growing in containers can be planted throughout most of the year, provided that the ground is sufficiently moist and adequate water supplies are available to water them; although they too will generally establish best in the cooler months.

It is best to have as much advance preparation as possible completed before the plants are purchased or received. At the time of planting the soil should ideally be moist and crumbly. Never plant when the soil is frozen, excessively dry or waterlogged as this may damage the roots and lower stem. Dig the pit allowing ample space to accommodate the roots, usually a quarter to half the diameter again of the

When digging on a heavy soil, dig the pit placing the spade at about 90° to the pit edge, as this will prevent the sides from becoming smeared.

Digging with the spade at about 90° to the pit edge means that the soil will be effectively 'torn' out of the ground and will enable water to escape from the pit.

Keep the roots of the bare rooted stock covered at all times prior to planting; just a few minutes of exposure can dry them and cause irreparable damage.

Use a spade handle to check that the hole is the right depth and that the tree or shrub will not sit too deeply or have exposed roots when the pit is filled.

root spread or container size. When digging on a heavy soil, dig the pit placing the spade at about 90 degrees to the pit edge as this will prevent the sides from becoming smeared. The soil will be effectively torn and water will be able to escape from the pit. This is important in ensuring the health of the roots as a pit smeared with soil on its sides will effectively fill up with water for much of the year, resulting in a wet soil environment and, as a result, extensive root die back, subsequent shoot die back and, in extreme cases, the death of the whole tree.

Place the roots into the hole when it is deep enough and check that the tree or shrub is not sitting too deeply in the hole. Equally, ensure that the roots will not be exposed when the pit is filled. As a rule of thumb, container grown trees should be planted with the compost surface about 1cm (½in) below the soil level and bare root specimens should have the topmost root at a similar depth.

Larger trees that have been 'field-grown' should ideally be positioned so the former north side faces to the north in the new situation (if possible) to ensure they

When backfilling the hole, the soil needs to be firmed in layers of no more than 15cm (6in) at a time in order to prevent large air pockets.

Once planted, the tree must be tied to the stake to properly secure them fastening the tie to the stake (not the tree itself) using a flat headed (clout) nail.

re-establish quickly. The north (or south in southern hemisphere) side is normally recognizable through deposits of algae on the shady side.

When it comes to container-grown trees, the planting pit preparation is the same as for bare rooted or rootballed trees, but the positioning of the rootball and treatment of the roots needs careful consideration. Once the pit has been dug, remove the tree from the container and lightly shake out the rootball over the excavated soil. Check the root collar area for girdling (encircling) roots and where present, sever these cleanly with a knife and remove them carefully from the rootball. Either cut through the base of the rootball using a sharp knife and spread the halves out, or alternatively tease out the lower roots using a fork before placing the rootball in the hole, so that when basal split is spread, the collar is on the same level as the ground. Add or remove soil from the pit as needed to ensure this. Tease out the circling roots at the edges of the rootball with a fork or by hand especially where plants are pot bound before filling in, firming and staking where required as for bare rooted trees.

Staking and Protection

Large shrubs and trees often require staking to prevent them from being blown over in their first season. Low stakes, that are around one third of the stem height, are now generally recommended for trees as they allow the crown and upper trunk to move in a circular motion. This encourages rapid stem thickening and the development of dense fibrous root systems that aid rapid establishment. The plants are secured to the stake by a tie that must be loosened at least once a year to prevent constriction of stems. After a year (or at most two) all stakes and ties are best removed to encourage natural development.

Where trees require staking, the stake should be positioned between the roots on the windward side of the tree (windward side refers to the direction of wind most commonly encountered on the site on a yearly average, not just on the day of planting). Rootballed or container-grown trees and shrubs can be staked using an angled stake, positioned so that it misses the rootball. Once the position of the stake has been decided, remove the tree from the hole, cover the roots (if bare rooted) and drive in the stake using a heavy hammer or drive all. Place the tree back into the hole and backfill, loosening any smeared parts of the sides using a fork in necessary. While you are filling the hole you should firm the soil as you go, in layers every 15cm (6in).

Once the tree is planted, it must be tied to the stake to properly secure it. There are of course numerous, specially designed tree ties available for sale, many of which have the advantage that they can be reused several times. Most are made of durable, long-lasting plastic or rubber, often with buckles or another adjustable fastening system to enable them to be loosened as the tree girth expands. Whatever design you use, the most important thing to remember is that the tie is secured to the stake (not the tree itself) using a flat headed (clout) nail. It is of course possible to make your own tree ties and old seatbelts, or even an old pair of tights, can be used as tree ties. If making your own try to use wide strips of material that distribute the load and prevent damage to the bark.

Ultimately, the majority of problems with staking occur when ties become too tight, or as a result of damage after storms. After bad weather check for abrasion and snapped stakes or ties and always check the ties regularly through the year for rubbing and adjust if necessary. Constriction of the stem by ties can happen surprisingly quickly, especially in the peak of the growing season during spring and early summer, meaning that fast growing trees will need frequent checking.

Deer, rabbits and other mammals may harm newly planted trees. This can be prevented by using tree protectors, the commonest of which is the spiral tree guard, used to protect the bases of newly planted trees. These are designed to expand as the stem diameter increases, thereby not constricting stem thickening. Smaller more vulnerable stock can also be protected by putting them in a tree or shrub shelter, which not only protect plants from rodents, rabbits – and sometimes deer attack – but have the additional advantage of helping stems to thicken

Deer, rabbits and other mammals may harm newly planted trees, and these are best protected either individually, or by erecting a fence around new stock.

while promoting rapid upward growth. Most are designed to last from three to five years before the material starts to degrade under the action of sunlight. Open mesh guards provide effective rabbit protection and are made with mesh rolls, supported with two or more canes or stakes. The height of mesh guards can be varied, as can the width according to the species to be protected and what it is to be protected from.

Initial Aftercare

Re-firm roots of all newly planted trees and shrubs on a regular basis, and especially after high winds or frosty weather. As soon as a heavy frost is over, check that it has not caused plants to be lifted in the soil. Frost heave, as it is called, is caused by repeated freezing and thawing of the soil that forces plants – especially smaller shrubs, or young trees – to move upwards in the soil, sometimes even pushing them out of the soil altogether. This can break the essential, fine feeder roots and if they are not quickly replanted the plant can be severely injured or even die as a result. Re-firming is readily achieved by using the heel, to exclude air pockets around the roots. Thin barked trees, such as birch and cherry, can suffer bark damage on sunny, frosty days, as the bark warms on one side (but remains frostbound on the other) and can split as a consequence. Wrapping them with fleece or hessian for the duration of a cold period can alleviate this and keeps these ornamental barked specimens healthy.

Weeds, especially grasses, can be surprisingly competitive in relation to moisture and nutrients and may even exude chemicals to inhibit the development of trees and shrubs in the first couple of years after planting, meaning that weeds must be controlled for a minimum of two years to ensure proper establishment. Mulches are one of the most useful ways of doing this and do have some ability in conserving moisture.

Watering may be needed in the first year but is only usually essential on very dry soils during the first year of establishment. In most other cases, the best strategy is to avoid watering if possible, as this will encourage the plant to root deeply and find natural sources of water. This has the long-term benefit of making the plant more drought-tolerant as well as saving water. However, if four weeks pass without appreciable rainfall, newly planted stock will generally benefit from a good watering every fortnight for the duration of the dry spell. Remember also that in their first couple of years after planting, new trees and shrubs can be susceptible to health problems meaning that you will need to check for damage to plants caused by pests and diseases on a regular basis.

Growing and Planting Herbaceous Plants and Annuals

Herbaceous Perennials

The term herbaceous perennial is a horticultural rather than scientific one and strictly means 'possessing the attributes of a herb'; that is small, perennial, non-woody, seed-bearing plants, dying down to resting buds at ground level or below. This could of course describe bulbs and other plant types and differs quite markedly from the horticultural definition. Anemones are an example where genera do not always fit comfortably into the category of herb. *Anemone blanda* for example resembles a bulb (albeit a root tuber) appearing above ground for a brief period in spring before lying dormant under the soil for much of the growing season. The related *Anemone hupehensis* on the other hand only dies down to the soil surface in winter.

To simplify things then, a herbaceous plant is normally taken to mean a non-woody plant, living for more than one year; usually growing, flowering and setting seed in the warmer months, before dying down to ground level in order to avoid adverse weather conditions. There they remain, as roots and shoot buds, until the next season when they begin the cycle again. They increase their numbers over time by forming offsets (effectively clones of the parent plant) and in time, these 'colonies' may form sizable clumps.

Planting

Herbaceous plants are generally planted in cooler periods when not fully dormant, that is either autumn or spring. The advantage of autumn planting is usually noticed on drier soils as the plants grow deeper root systems. This is because most porous (and therefore dry) soils tend to have a higher water table during winter, which enables them to establish a strong root system, before the water sinks lower during the drier months. These established roots follow the water down into the soil and the plants are potentially much more drought resistant as a result. Those planted on heavier soils however, that tend to remain moist for longer, may benefit from spring planting, as heavy soils may be wet and cold during the winter months – conditions that may cause a newly planted specimen to rot rather than root.

Herbaceous plants are generally supplied as pot-grown specimens, and these should be watered at least an hour before planting. The ground should ideally have been dug and manured at least three weeks in advance, before being levelled ready for planting. A dressing of bonemeal, or fish blood and bone, may also be applied just prior to planting. Planting should only take place when the soil is moist (but not waterlogged), ideally in weather conditions that are mild and dry. Dig a pit larger than the pot and ensure that the plant is well firmed, taking care not to compact the soil when it is returned to the pit around the rootball. While it may seem obvious, remember that pots should be removed before the plant is planted, or it will not establish.

Anemone blanda, while strictly an herbaceous plant, resembles a bulb, appearing above ground in spring but lying dormant for most of the season.

Anemone huphensis is another anemone, which has growth above the ground for almost the entire year, often barely dying down to ground level in winter.

LEFT: **Always level the whole of the site before planting so as to give a better finish; an uneven site cannot be remedied once planting has taken place.**

LEFT MIDDLE: **The whole site is then lightly trodden using the flat of the foot to remove any remaining air pockets before producing the final 'true' level with a rake.**

BOTTOM LEFT: **Remember if planting blocks of the same species that odd numbers tend to look more natural than even numbers. Give plants enough space to grow.**

Ensure that each plant has sufficient room to grow and develop – they are best planted in informal groups of three or five for the best effect. If possible, all planted areas should be designed to contain plants that have similar life spans and respond to similar maintenance and rejuvenation techniques. Some herbaceous plants are relatively short lived and will die out before others within a bed. Care should be taken immediately after to ensure that slugs and snails do not damage the crowns. Set traps and barriers around them to avoid this.

Once they are established, herbaceous perennials rarely require more than an annual application of fertilizer, provided that the initial soil preparation was thorough and included the addition of plenty of organic matter. Having said this, plants grown primarily for their ornamental foliage, such as Hosta or Rheum, may benefit from an occasional application of a liquid feed to ensure they produce plenty of lush leaves. Bulky organic material, such as leaf mould or compost, applied in spring before shoot growth is also beneficial, although care must be taken not to apply this too thickly and especially not to cover the crowns of plants resting at the soil surface as these may rot off. Specimens, such as Hosta, Anemone and other species, that die down below the soil surface, benefit particularly from this treatment, which not only helps release soil nutrient but also limits early flushes of weeds.

Deadheading of old flowerheads is not always necessary, although some, such as lupins, can effectively become weeds if allowed to set seed. In this case it

By midsummer of the first season after planting, the ground cover effect will already be well established and any gaps will quickly close in following years.

Plants such as *Rheum*, grown primarily for its ornamental foliage, may benefit from a few applications of a liquid feed to promote plenty of lush, foliar growth.

Not cutting back flowered stems of large herbaceous plants often means that the plant retains some of its interest and architectural value well into winter.

Leaving a border full of flowered stems, through the winter, adds interest over an extended time while providing valuable food for over-wintering birds.

is often best to remove all flowers as they begin to fade. However, for the majority of herbaceous plants their decorative seed heads, which persist well into the dormant season, can add interest to the garden over an extended period and may also prove a valuable food source for overwintering birds. Examples of these include teasel, Echinops and many of the larger ornamental grasses.

Cutting Back

Some shrubby perennials (often referred to as sub-shrubs), such as chrysanthemums, Phygelius and Penstemon, and many dwarf 'sub-Alpine' plants are grown alongside (and effectively treated as) herbaceous perennials. These benefit from being pruned annually. Summer and autumn flowering plants are pruned in early spring; a process where older twiggy and unproductive growth is cut hard back in order to promote the growth of new shoots which will flower in summer and autumn. Spring or winter flowering specimens are pruned as soon as flowering is over.

Herbaceous borders are traditionally cut back and 'tidied' in early winter. While this does look neat, it can encourage weeds and discourage wildlife.

This border has its left half cleared, while the right half remains in place. Notice the difference in terms of interest, wildlife shelter and ground cover on the uncut section to the right.

Renovating Herbaceous Plants

The majority of herbaceous perennial plants should be lifted, divided and replanted every three to five years, although some fast-growing and vigorous plants, such as Ajuga and Stachys, may need to be divided every year. This is done because herbaceous plants tend to become woody towards the centre over time, leading to reduced flowering and an overall loss of vigour. Lifting the plants for dividing will not only rejuvenate them but also allows for other border maintenance operations to be carried out. The site can be cleared of any weeds and organic matter such as compost or farmyard manure dug into the border. The process of division rejuvenates the whole border. In addition, it keeps the plant healthy and will prevent over-vigorous growth of fast growing species.

Lifting and dividing is normally done while the plants are dormant in late autumn or early spring. Some plants dislike cold wet conditions and these should be moved once the soil has warmed sufficiently to encourage growth. This is particularly true for any plants that are not fully hardy. While most perennials can be lifted relatively easily, some plants that are relatively long-lived, such as *Paeonia*, resent being disturbed and will take two or more years to establish again after transplanting. These are generally lifted only if absolutely necessary or if propagation material is required.

The plants are lifted, taking care not to damage the roots too much and then they are split or cut into smaller sections. Depending on the subject concerned, this may require one or a number of methods. Fibrous-rooted species such as asters can generally be teased apart by hand. Tough clumps such as Hosta may need dividing by the use of two forks placed back-to-back in the clump and forced together to prize the clump apart. Plants with thick rhizomes, such as Iris and Bergenia, often need cutting into sections with a knife. The old woody material of the centre should be discarded. Each remaining section should have a portion of root and stem or stem buds. After digging over the border and incorporating a slow-release fertilizer such as bonemeal and organic matter, the 'new' plants can be replanted. Firm them in well and keep them well watered until they are established.

Where possible, all planted areas should be designed to contain plants that have similar life spans and respond to rejuvenation techniques. Some species, Aquilegia for example, are relatively short lived, do not respond to lifting and dividing and will often die out before others within a bed. Choosing plants with similar needs will mean that it is possible to rejuvenate beds on a set cycle, say every three to four years, and avoids gaps appearing in the periods between.

Plant losses can of course occur in severe winters, when plants normally regarded as hardy are exposed to very low temperatures. Many slightly tender perennials are particularly susceptible and, if possible, these are best either lifted (or propagated) before being over-wintered under cover and replanted after the worst of the weather has passed. Any losses will almost always require replacement unless the surrounding plants can be left to fill the gap relatively quickly.

Annuals and Biennials

The term 'annual' describes a plant that germinates, flowers, and dies within a year or season. From the point of view of a garden then, this usually means a plant grown outdoors in the spring and summer which survives for just one growing season, and it includes many ornamental and food plants. However, some perennials and biennials (see below) are grown as annuals; perhaps because they are not hardy enough to survive a cold winter or in the case of edible crops like carrots and parsley (both biennials) they are grown as annual crops for their edible roots and leaves respectively, which would be reduced in quality if they were allowed to flower in the second year.

A 'biennial' plant is a flowering plant that takes two years to complete its life cycle; the first year growing leaves, stems, and roots before it enters a period of dormancy over the winter. Throughout this time, the stems of most biennials remain short and the leaves low to the ground, forming a so called 'rosette.' Biennials need a cold period (known as 'vernalization') before they will flower, although in some cases stress, including drought or nutrient imbalance, can cause premature flowering – a condition called 'bolting' in the case of edible crops.

Californian Poppy *(Eschscholzia)* is an example of an annual flowering plant, producing bloom and setting seed within the space of a single season.

The evening primrose (*Oenothera*) takes two years to complete its life cycle; growing leaves, stems, and roots in the first year, before flowering the next.

In nature there are far fewer biennials than perennials or annuals, meaning that the majority of garden biennials are actually perennials grown over a short period as, for example, winter bedding. Conversely, certain annual plants are sown in the autumn in mild areas, in order to produce early flowers the following spring, and while they are not strict biennials they are used in this way. Some short-lived perennials may appear to be biennial rather than perennial and as a last potential confusion, certain plants live as a rosette for several seasons before flowering only once and then dying – a type of life cycle known as 'monocarpic' or single flowering.

Planting

Hardy annuals are often sown in situ and thinned in a manner similar to vegetables (*see* seed, page 123). Following their introduction to a garden, many annuals freely self-seed and allowing them to do this can help add occasional colour and interest in more informal border settings. This said, be careful where you use

The seeds of some annuals such as *Eschscholzia*, germinate in autumn or mild spells during winter, enabling them to grow and flower by early summer.

The colourful nasturtium (*Tropaeolum majus*) is just one example from a range of annuals that flower more abundantly on slightly poorer soils.

them as certain species may act as alternate hosts for diseases. Plants in the cabbage family, such as sweet allysum (*Lobularia maritima*), seed very freely but act as a host for club root; meaning they should not be allowed to establish in vegetable gardens. If annuals are to be grown in pots or trays prior to planting, as is the case with tender plants or early sown vegetables raised under cover, then the planting is much the same as for herbaceous plants. Always ensure that the risk of frost has passed before planting tender specimens and that these plants are acclimatized thoroughly beforehand.

The only fertilizer treatment that may be necessary for annuals is to incorporate a base dressing of a slow release fertilizer, such as bonemeal or fish blood and bone, and the addition of organic matter at (or preferably before) planting time. Always remember that excessive fertility levels will produces lush vegetative growth at the expense of flower production – ideal for lettuces or other leafy crops but less so for ornamental displays. Indeed, if the object is to introduce a fast effective splash of colour to the garden it is worth remembering that many hardy annuals actually thrive in poorer soils, making them ideal candidates for 'low input' schemes. Dry banks are ideal for a whole range of species including field poppies (*Papaver spp.*), nasturtiums (*Tropaeolum majus*) and Californian poppy (*Eschscholzia*), all of which flower more abundantly on slightly poorer soils.

Once established, annuals are largely self sustaining, with the only regular maintenance they will need dead-heading to promote new shoot and flower development, or 'stopping' (the removal of strong central growth tips) to promote side shoot development and multiple flower production. Dead, damaged or diseased growth may also be removed as necessary.

LEFT: **Sweet alyssum (*Lobularia maritima*), seeds freely and acts as a host for club root; meaning they should not be allowed to establish in vegetable gardens.**

Bulbs such as snowdrops (*Galanthus spp.*) appear above the ground in the spring to flower, but remain dormant below ground for most of the year.

Bulbs

A bulb is an underground shoot that is surrounded by modified leaves (or thickened leaf bases) that are used as food storage organs by the dormant plant. The leaf bases do not support leaves, but contain food reserves to enable the plant to survive adverse conditions and variously resemble scales (as in lilies), or they overlap and surround the centre of the bulb (as with onions). The base of the bulb consists of a modified stem, and all growth generally occurs from this 'basal plate'; roots from the underside, new stems and leaves from the upper side. It is for this reason that they must always be planted the correct way up.

Certain bulbous plants, notably lilies and plants in the onion family (*Alliaceae*) form small bulbs, called 'bulbils'. Lilies do this mostly in their leaf axils whereas onions have a tendency to form bulbils in their flower heads. While these are mostly very small, they can be used to propagate more stock, although the catawissa or tree onion (*Allium cepa* variety *proliferum*) forms small onions in its flower head that can become large enough to harvest for pickling.

Other types of storage organs (such as corms, rhizomes, and tubers) perform a similar function and are in effect treated in a largely similar way in the garden. As a direct result, many are erroneously referred to as bulbs. Plants that form true bulbs include onion, garlic, lily, tulip, narcissus, and certain Iris species.

Planting Bulbs

While many people think of spring as the main time for bulbs, there are many species of bulbs, corms and tubers, which can be planted throughout the year. As a rule of thumb, there are three major times of the year when bulb planting takes place. Winter and spring flowering bulbs are planted from late summer to late autumn; summer flowering bulbs in spring with autumn flowering bulbs in early- to mid-summer.

This narcissus bulb shows the swollen leaf bases clustered over the base plate, essentially forming a large resting bud when the plant is dormant.

While it is always wise to check the specific requirements of any bulb you intend to plant, a useful rule of thumb is that they should be planted in a hole that is three times the depth of the bulb. If the bulb measures 5cm (2in) from top to bottom then, they should be planted 15cm (6in) deep. Of course, to every 'garden rule of thumb' there are exceptions, and shallow planting is generally best for rhizomes and squat tubers such as Cyclamen or Begonia; both of these needing to be placed with their tops almost level with the soil surface. Indeed, most tuberous roots, for example Dahlia, should be planted with stem buds near the surface. Small bulbs also generally favour shallower planting. Planting these too deeply will exhaust their energy on root and foliage growth at the expense of blossoms.

Dahlias are an example of a plant that, while essentially a slightly tender perennial, is often lifted and treated like a bulb when grown in gardens.

Deep planting can be very useful for tall-growing species or varieties. Daffodils and tulips are just two examples of types that can benefit from the additional support that an extra-deep planting will provide. Deep planting can also have the added advantage of protecting the bulb from pests such as squirrels or mice, as well as helping to prevent moisture loss during intense heat in warm or dry areas. Deep planting should be avoided in heavy or wet soils though, as the bulbs may suffer a lack of oxygen or may rot off. Conversely, tall varieties of hybrid tulip or daffodil can be over stimulated by sunlight and undergo rapid division of leaf scales if planted too shallowly in the ground. The result of this is that the bulbs rapidly divide into many smaller ones, producing smaller and fewer flowers. Whatever depth they are to be planted though, always plant them the correct way up; base plate downward in the case of true bulbs, and with the buds uppermost in the case of corms and tubers.

Bulbs, corms and tubers that are hardy enough to survive harsh conditions can be left in the ground year-round to naturalize in lawns and borders, but will need planting deeply enough to avoid damage by cultivations or other seasonal tasks. In lawns they can be planted in informal drifts to give a natural effect. Ideally, when you plant a naturalized drift, the bulbs should be closely spaced near the centre and slightly more widely spaced at the edges to give a natural effect. In borders they should be planted between the crowns of other plants to extend the season or add seasonal interest. In shrub beds they can also be used as seasonal 'accents' or as ground cover under deciduous shrubs.

Lifting and Dividing Established Bulbs

This task is frequently necessary in situations where, for example, they continue producing lots of foliage but are flowering less frequently or have ceased flowering completely. The usual reason for this is because the clump has become overcrowded. Dividing the clump is a quick and easy way to give the bulbs more space to grow and it requires no specialist tools or equipment. The best time to lift and divide bulbs is normally straight after flowering just as they are dying back. The ideal tool is a garden fork; this being used to lift clumps of bulbs, before gently separating them into smaller clumps or even individual bulbs. This also provides an opportunity to remove any unhealthy bulbs. The remaining healthy bulbs can be replanted (there or elsewhere) or stored in a cool dry place, keeping them in paper bags, nets or string sacks, ready for replanting later.

While most bulbs are best lifted and dried once they have finished flowering, some types never really become fully dormant. The latter of these must be lifted 'in the green', that is while they still have foliage on them and so in this respect they are similar to herbaceous plants. Small bulbs such as snowdrops

RIGHT: **The snakes-head fritillary (*Fritillaria meleagris*) is ideal for naturalizing in lawns, but needs planting deeply to avoid damage during maintenance.**

BELOW: **The impressive autumn flowering *Colchicum* looks great in the lawn, although the foliage that emerges in spring must also be allowed to grow and develop.**

Narcissus bulbs are an old favourite for naturalizing in lawns. Six weeks after flowering is ended, they can be cut back and regular mowing can resume.

(*Galanthus spp.*), bluebells (*Hyacinthoides spp.*) or aconites (*Eranthis spp.*) are commonly grown examples of bulbs that respond well to this treatment, establishing much more quickly with far less chance of rotting or drying out than would otherwise be achieved by planting as dry bulbs.

For the remainder, once they have bloomed, they will set seed and wither in a period of between six and twelve weeks depending upon the species. This period of dieback is necessary for the plants to build up a new energy reserve inside the bulb, which will be used to create a bloom next season. For this reason, it is best to allow them to wither completely, although it is usually possible to cut back bulb foliage or lift bulbs from the ground six to eight weeks after flowering, and when their foliage has mostly wilted or turned

yellow. If you need to lift bulbs before this, they can be lifted 'in the green' and 'heeled in;' a procedure that involves digging a shallow trench, putting the bulbs into this and covering them, leaving the leaves above the soil surface to die down naturally.

Staking Bulbs

While most species of bulbs, corms and tubers are perfectly able to support themselves, many cultivars or hybrid forms of for example lily, dahlia and gladiolus will need staking, particularly in windy or exposed settings, due to their often enlarged, showy flowers. These will need staking as soon as they reach around a third of their eventual height. Individual bulbs can be staked using thin canes or hazel rods pushed into the ground just far enough from the stem to avoid damaging the bulb or root mass. The stems can then be tied-in using twine or similar string. Larger multi-headed plants such as dahlia or closely-packed groups of plants can be supported using a single, more robust stake, tying the individual stems to this. Alternatively, a series of stakes, with an interlacing criss-cross of strings, can be used to support a whole group and is especially useful when growing flowers in rows for cutting in a bed.

Obtaining Bulbs

In the first instance most people will need to buy bulbs to plant in their garden. If doing this, it is essential to check that these come from a reputable supplier that obtains them from sustainable sources. Unfortunately, the trade in garden bulbs has often involved the collection for sale of wild-collected bulbs; an activity that destroys the beauty of natural habitats and can lead to some species becoming endangered in the wild. Not only is the loss of the plants themselves unacceptable but the process of up-rooting the bulbs can result in local soil erosion and extensive habitat disturbance. Wild collected bulbs, sold to unsuspecting gardeners, are often poor value, grow poorly and can harbour pests and diseases.

Before you obtain new supplies of bulbs then, it is important to check their origin; specifically whether they come from a cultivated source. Asking the supplier is one option, although the catalogues, seed lists and websites of responsible suppliers should include clear statements regarding their environmental policies regarding the origin of plant material.

Ground Cover and Ecological Style Plantings

The idea of carpeting the ground with densely grouped, low-growing plants is a well-established one that is often practised in municipal landscape schemes. The idea is that the dense growth will reduce the amount of weeding needed to keep plants maintained and will effectively provide 'carpets' of vegetation to add interest to the landscape. Ground cover planting can of course be used to reduce the need for maintenance in a domestic garden setting where well-chosen and carefully established plants can provide an attractive feature in their own right.

Weed suppression is of course the prime attraction of ground-cover planting; if planned and established properly, it does very well. This is because ground cover tends to form a solid mat of plants that out-compete weeds for light, nutrients and water. This is the case once established but in order to achieve this it needs time to grow and stabilize. It then requires planting at the right distance to allow plants to spread and enmesh effectively. Too close and they will compete with each other; too far apart and there are likely to be gaps that weeds will find a way though.

Heathers are very well suited to acidic soils, where they not only make excellent shrubby ground cover but also provide welcome winter colour.

Shrubby Ground Cover

Some low growing shrubs are excellent subjects for ground cover, ultimately forming a low, springy mat of vegetation. Many of these are good-looking plants themselves and among them evergreen plants tend to be the most effective in respect of their ability to suppress weeds, while offering year-round interest. Whether used to blanket a little-used corner, or to set off the rest of the garden, ground-cover plants offer a very attractive solution to low-maintenance gardening. Having said this, woody plants do tend to become larger with age, and the resulting mat of vegetation gets thicker (and deeper) over time; meaning that they are often best suited to larger gardens and more extensive landscape schemes.

When ground-cover shrubs are first planted, there will of course be more bare earth than plant cover, which obviously offers weeds an early foothold. It is

extremely important then, to prevent the bed becoming over-run before the plants properly establish. A layer of mulch approximately 5cm (2in) is a good idea; both helping to suppress weeds and retain moisture. If laid over the soil in the autumn it will also help to keep the soil warm, which should help the establishment of pot-grown shrubs and particularly evergreens planted at this time. An organic mulch layer will also help add organic matter to the soil, thereby improving its fertility, and should be topped up each year in the spring, until the plants grow into each other and form a dense covering.

Once established, ground-cover plants effectively act as a 'living mulch,' on account not only of their ability to suppress weeds but also because they reduce evaporation from the underlying soil in warm conditions; effectively lessening the effect of prolonged hot, dry spells. The choice of plants will ultimately depend of course upon the prevailing cli-

Many shrubby species are well suited to provide mixed ground cover planting, and careful selection can provide all-year-round interest in the garden.

mate, microclimate and soil conditions, as well as the general aesthetic effect you wish to promote. Free-draining sites or gardens in drought-prone areas will favour plantings of Mediterranean-type shrubs such as *Rosmarinus spp.* (rosemary), *Lavandula* (lavender) or *Cistus* (sun rose) – ideal on account of their natural drought resistance. *Thymus spp.* (thyme), spreading cultivars of *Juniperus* (juniper), *Hypericum* (St John's wort), and *Santolina* are all also worth considering for sunny sites. Conversely, shady sites will suit *Cotoneaster spp.*, cultivars of *Euonymus fortunei* (spindle), *Pachysandra terminalis* and *Vinca spp.* (periwinkle), whereas acid soils will support the many cultivars of *Erica* (bell heather) and *Calluna vulgaris* (ling), *Pieris spp.*, *Gaultheria spp.* (pernettya and rose of Sharon) or *Vaccinium* (blueberry).

Remember also that blanket coverage of a single type of plant, while it may well do the job very effectively, may also prove uninspiring and lack impact. A mixture of species and/or varieties on the other hand will inject contrast in colour, texture, and (if a variety of shapes and forms are used) architectural impact. If you do opt for a mixture of plants though, select ones that grow at roughly the same rate, and have similar site requirements.

Some climbing plants can also do a very good job of providing ground cover; offering an interesting and varied option to the art of ground cover. Climbers that are self-layering such as *Hedera* (Ivy) or attach themselves by means of twining stems or tendrils such as Clematis, Parthenocissus and Trachelospermum, offer possibilities here and often prove most useful if the need for ground cover is on a steep bank or slope.

Establishing Shrubby Groundcover

The effort needed to eradicate any existing weeds on ground intended for ground cover is well worth the time and effort that it involves. Ideally, a period of inactivity following any initial site clearance will be necessary in order to allow the re-growth of any persistent perennial weeds as well as the germination of weed seed in order to allow the removal of both of these.

The dense, self-layering growth of ivy (*Hedera spp*) offers the possibility of rapid ground cover and is especially useful on steep banks or slopes.

Sheet mulch is an effective way of suppressing weeds between shrubby specimens, but does tend to look unsightly whilst the plants are still small.

Ideally, the plants that you will need to establish ground cover most efficiently should be relatively small. The average pot size in a garden centre, for example, is typically 2-4 litre (¼–½ gallon); the ideal size for ground cover on the other hand is 0.5–1 litre. The reason for using a small plant is principally because the smaller pot size enables the planting of three to four per square metre – something that ultimately enables the establishment of more plants and full coverage in a shorter time period. The first year is the most crucial time and it is vital that new plants remain well-watered (if needed) and free from weeds to enable their rapid establishment. This can be done using sheet mulch, pegged to the ground prior to planting. Crosses are then cut through it where each plant is to go. The main disadvantage with the sheet mulching method, however, is that the sheet prevents the passage of organic matter through to the soil beneath and can interfere with natural cycles in the soil for this reason. The sheet mulch also has a tendency to show, often looking rather unsightly until the ground cover completely closes the spaces between the plants; a period that can take up to three years. Of course regular feeding throughout the growing season with liquid feeds will speed up the growth of the plants but even then it will still take up to two seasons to gain full coverage.

Establishing Herbaceous Ground Cover

Herbaceous plants can make splendid ground cover, and have an unrivalled ability to transform an otherwise dull space into a rich tapestry of leaf shapes, textures, and colours. They are often an ideal choice beneath the shade of deciduous trees or along paths and foundations, but are easily able to form impressive features in their own right. The advantage of using herbaceous ground cover rather than turf is, of course, the seasonal show of flowers, fruits, and colours. The downside is of course, that they cannot be walked on and can tend to look rather bare in the depth of winter.

A good candidate for herbaceous ground cover is of course a plant that requires minimal maintenance. Essentially there are two growth habits that may prove suitable: those that spread as 'clumps' or those that form a dense spreading carpet. Clump formers include Alchemilla, Geranium, and Hosta, which increase in size gradually but achieve most of their coverage as their foliage grows up and outward each spring. Ideally a good clump former will rarely need division in a ground-cover setting, meaning that very vigorous types, while they do achieve a rapid coverage, are usually best avoided. Carpet-forming herbaceous plants include *Lamium maculatum* and its many cultivars, Aubrieta, *Symphytum* spp. and many of the dwarf Campanula species as well as taller examples such as Bergenia and Anemone japonica. Carpeting perennials mostly spread via underground stems (rhizomes) or move across the soil surface, rooting at points where leaf nodes touch the ground and most of these will rarely need lifting or dividing if they creep outside their boundaries.

Planting herbaceous plants for ground cover is similar in many respects to planting them elsewhere, except perhaps for the closer spacing. The growth habit rates of neighbouring plants do need careful consideration, particularly if using more than one species of plant and also if your ground-cover area will be adjacent to other mixed beds or borders. The aim should be to place plants next to each other that will coexist without any undue competition between them. Clump-forming plants are of course usually less vigorous than carpet-forming species that often cover an area quite quickly, and while both forms can coexist together, you should take care not to put especially vigorous forms next to or among 'aggressive' growers. Remember also that plants must be arranged so as to be visually appealing together if a mixed planting is the intention. Using too many disparate heights and textures can look chaotic, whereas a uniform cover with only a few species can result in a rather nondescript effect.

The planting layout will of course depend upon the design, but blocks of plants should be set out in staggered rows. As with shrubby planting, a greater number of smaller plants will achieve a more rapid coverage although this will depend upon the vigour of the species. Carpet-forming plants should ideally be spaced 20 to 30cm (8 to 12in) apart whereas clump-forming species should be spaced to reflect

Herbaceous plants have an unrivalled ability to transform a space, forming an impressive seasonal show of flowers, fruits, foliar colour and contrast.

their width at maturity. If a the mature plant therefore reaches 30cm (12in) across at maturity, then the plants need to be spaced at that distance apart, as the aim is to have their foliage just overlapping. In this way, the plants will keep, reduce water loss and discourage weed growth.

Once planted, mulch the bed with a 5cm (2in) layer of mulch to suppress weeds and conserve moisture until the plants establish a good cover. The first couple of years normally proves to be a critical time, wherein weeds must be controlled. The best way to do this is by regular and thorough weeding but watering and feeding can also be extremely important to ensure steady growth. If plants do not establish well after the first year, it may of course be worth removing and replacing them with another as an area that has gaps in it will soon become infested with weeds.

Naturalistic Planting

Naturalistic planting styles are those that draw their inspiration from natural areas such as a prairie, woodland or wetland. They differ from more traditional methods of gardening in that they can appear to be less structured and more random in terms of the overall effect; mainly because the layout of the plants is inspired by the patterns and groupings of naturally occurring plant communities. Despite this, they are structured (and permanent), and the apparent lack of a designer's hand is ultimately the result of careful planning.

There are several ways that naturalistic planting arrangements can be achieved, although the two commonest methods used are block planting and drifts. Of these, block planting is the most frequently

used and involves planting similarly sized groups of the same species in irregularly repeating patterns. The groups of plants are arranged according to height and aesthetic qualities such as foliage colour and texture. Drifts on the other hand appear familiar to many people as they are more akin in style to how we imagine meadows and prairies. Instead of the regular sized blocks, the drifts are much more variable in respect of size and shape and have no obvious repetitive pattern. Small groups may repeat over and over again in the design with larger, more occasional groups providing contrast and variety.

Even though the aim is to create a random effect, plants will need dividing into general categories according to habit and form. Achieving a balance is essential and this is done by considering the ground-cover according to the relative growth habit of the plants used. Ideally, the coverage should consist of around ten per cent solitary, tall architectural specimens, forty to fifty per cent clump-forming plants and forty to fifty per cent of ground cover scattered throughout. In this way, the effect will be to give the balance of height and space that is needed. The real trick though is to avoid simply assembling a random assortment of plants. Even if these are all planted in the right conditions and grow well, without an overall structure, the feature will not look at its best. Naturalistic should never mean haphazard or formless. A good adage to help you consider this is that a collection of choice plants, arranged without thought, is no more a garden than a collection of choice words, spread randomly across a page, is a poem.

As with any type of garden feature, the choice of plants will depend upon the local conditions. Plants in a naturalistic arrangement will need to fend for themselves and must compete with the other plants around them as well as thrive in their surroundings. Ensure that species which spread very rapidly – either by seed or vegetatively – are not included as

OPPOSITE PAGE: **Even though the aim is a random effect, balance is essential; meaning a mix of solitary tall architectural, clump forming and low growing plants is needed.**

these would cause the garden to become dominated quickly by just a few species and ultimately destroy the overall effect.

Although the planting style is borrowed from nature, it is worth remembering that it is a contrivance that ultimately relies upon conventional horticultural maintenance. A well-planned naturalistic feature will however need much less maintenance once established, except for a measure of weeding mainly in the first couple of years. If woody plants are included, these will need some pruning from time to time and you may wish to lift and revitalize certain areas occasionally. On the whole, however, the best form of maintenance for these areas is a matter of a little work done often.

Ecological Planting

Ecological planting is a form of planting whereby the plants are allowed to spread and seed so as to create a changing or 'dynamic' plant community. It is most commonly seen in the form of flowering grass swards and is a form of ground cover that usually relies upon a minimal amount of intervention. It is often well suited to larger areas, but in smaller areas, such as those commonly found in domestic garden settings, it can prove rather unruly or even unsightly. However, having said that, even a small garden can have space for a little flowery mead in a turf area. Lawns converted into a wildflower habitat can be an attractive garden feature as well as proving an important refuge and habitat for many species of garden wildlife. Lawns facing the sun are especially useful, attracting bees, butterflies, and moths which in turn attract larger wildlife including birds and mammals.

In nature, grassland is moulded by the effects of geography, climate, soil and, in many cases, human intervention. Choosing the right type of grassland for your needs will depend upon all of these. Where your garden is will decide the first three by default, but the last one is mostly your choice and depends upon what you want to see in the garden.

Ecological planting enables plants to form a 'dynamic' community, such as that of a flowering grass sward and usually relies upon minimal intervention.

• 'Down-land' turf or short grass is something that occurs in many forms across the planet, particularly in temperate regions. It is usually the result of grazing by animals such as sheep and the resulting short-cropped turf contains a multitude of flower species. It is the closest model to modern garden lawns and can be maintained by regular (if infrequent) cutting by a mower on a high setting.

• 'Hay meadows' are a traditional way of managing grassland for the hay that is cut and stored for animal fodder in the summer months. The long grass frequently harboured many species of

wildflower during spring and early summer and are among the prettiest man-made habitats. The traditional forms of management often resulted in a poor soil that reduced the vigour of the grasses and favoured the growth of the wildflower species. Sadly, modern, intensive agriculture has seen a severe decline in these man-made habitats and many species of wildflowers as a consequence. Wet meadows or flood meadows are largely similar to hay meadows except that they are subjected to seasonal flooding, usually in winter, and as a consequence harbour different species. They are ideally suited for wet sites and soils. All types of meadow can be established in gardens but need to be situated carefully and cut down during the summer months, leading to a temporary unsightliness. They can be hard to establish on lawns that have been well fertilized in the past.

- 'Prairie' is a term used to describe the vast areas of flower-rich grassland that once clothed North America. It is similar to the Steppe in Europe and occurs naturally in these areas. The soils are often richer than those found in 'man-made' meadows and they are frequently very rich in wildlife and colourful flower species, many of which have become familiar plants. They are potentially much easier to establish in most gardens as the

soil fertility is less of a problem and they can be extremely decorative features, with similar mowing regimes to those of meadows.

- 'Marginal grassland' is the term often used to describe remnants of grassland plant communities that occur on field margins, roadsides or waste ground and as such have been 'marginalized.' They are often a last vital refuge for many native flower species and their dependant wildlife that were formerly common in an area. In a garden these can easily be mimicked at hedge bases or by leaving an odd corner or out of the way space. They often need little intervention except to cut them every year or two in late winter.

Grassy banks around hedgerows are often a last vital refuge for native flower species and their dependant wildlife that were formerly common in an area.

MAINTENANCE OF YOUR GARDEN

Once a garden has been planted, the regular cycle of maintenance must begin if it is to be kept healthy, functioning and consequently remaining in tip-top condition. Of course the garden is a place that should be enjoyed and there are few better ways of doing this than to get out there and look after it. There is never really an 'off season' in a garden meaning that there is always something that needs to be done. The dormant season for plants, far from being a time to stay indoors, is a busy time when pruning, cultivation, propagation and replanting are just some of the jobs for which winter is the prime season.

With spring comes the promise of warmer days and new growth, making this and the summer that follows the busiest, yet most enjoyable, time for many gardeners. However, no matter what time of the year it is there will be some interest to be found in a garden, meaning that whatever the season there is work to be done.

OPPOSITE PAGE: **Even when the desired effect is that of a naturalistic planting, regular and planned maintenance is essential if it is to remain in peak condition.**

Choosing Tools and Equipment

Choosing the right tool for the job in hand is an essential part of maintaining any garden. Whether starting from scratch or maintaining an established area, a range of tools will be necessary in order to work effectively and efficiently. However, a visit to a local supplier (or even a look at one of their catalogues) reveals a seemingly bewildering array of tools on offer, especially to those new to gardening. Some of these can be used for a variety of tasks and this versatility makes them indispensable, whereas others have quite specific purposes. Therefore the best guide when making a decision as to whether to obtain a particular item is to be frugal, and in the first instance to concentrate on essentials. In addition, remember that established designs – those that have been around for a number of years – tend to be proven in their worth. Many of the new, somewhat gimmicky items that find their way onto the shelves of stores or the pages of catalogues last only a short while and (if purchased) often prove to be far less 'indispensable' than their sales pitch claimed!

Once a list of essential purchases has been made there is still a huge range of types and brands on offer. While there are few absolutes when it comes to choosing which tools are right for an individual gardener, it is advisable to choose them carefully and ensure that they will be durable, functional and (perhaps most importantly) comfortable to use. Everyone is different in respect of their strength, build and preferences and it is a good idea to test them in the shop for weight, and length of handle so that they suit a particular build.

Having the right tool for a particular job will not only make work easier and faster but will generally yield the best results. For example, digging will always be much easier with a good quality spade and fork and these should always top any list of essential tools, on account of their versatility and frequency of use. These need to be comfortable and this is surprisingly easy to judge when buying them. The standard size for a spade or fork is a 72cm (29in) handle, and the best way to see whether this is the right size is if the top of the handle is around the hip height of the person who will be using it. Avoid any that are too short, preferably searching out a long-handled one. The importance of this is inestimable, as anyone using one that is the wrong size for their height is more likely to suffer back strain – an all too common and avoidable consequence of time spent in the garden. In addition to this, remember that 'D' handles can be uncomfortable over long periods, although they suit smaller hands better. Gardeners with larger hands will mostly do better with a 'T' handle.

Hoes are another essential item, primarily because of their value when weeding the garden. There are numerous designs and versions of these, the best of which are usually forged and have stainless steel heads.

Secateurs or other cutting tools depend upon a sharpened or 'keen' edge in order to keep them working efficiently, and should receive regular attention.

Rakes are also indispensable and the best choice here are those with good solid tines (teeth), mounted on a wooden or metal handle. Finally, a knife, a pair of secateurs, a hand trowel and a wheelbarrow (for moving things around the garden) usually complete the list of essential starter items.

Caring for Tools

In the main, the commonest and most frequent care that tools need is cleaning. The handles of tools often become dirty during use and it pays to take good care of them in order to extend their useful life. In the case of plastic or other synthetic materials this usually involves no more than washing them in a little soapy water and drying them thoroughly afterwards. However, many hand tools still use wooden handles and these are cleaned by removing as much of the soil as possible with a stiff brush. Ideally, this should be done before finishing work in the garden. If it means using water, the best way to do this is to gently moisten the implements with a damp cloth, making sure that the wood does not become 'soaked', as this may cause the grain to lift and the handle to swell. Having said this, many modern tools are varnished and so a quick scrub can be the best option for them, although even these should not be left in for a soak.

In the case of unvarnished handles, the best way to keep these in a tip-top condition is by regular applications of boiled linseed oil. This is simply done by applying the oil with a non-lint rag, allowing the wood to fully absorb the first coat before applying any more if needed. When properly and regularly applied, this prevents the wood from drying out and splintering.

Blades and other metal parts can also be kept rust free by regularly applying oil. This need only be a general-purpose household oil, although using some old engine oil is a good way of recycling. Remember that the blades of shears, forks, spades and other tools will soon rust if not regularly oiled. If any rust does accumulate on the blade, remove this with a wire brush before wiping the cleaned section with an oily rag or brush.

Sharpening Tools

Many tools depend upon a sharpened or 'keen' edge in order to keep them working efficiently. Larger blades, such as spades and hoes, may be sharpened with a fine metal file or a grindstone if one is available. Very badly damaged or worn blades may eventually need replacing if this is an option, or the whole tool may need replacing. If any doubt surrounds how repairs should be carried out it is best to consult the supplier for advice.

On the other hand, tools with fine cutting edges, especially knives, secateurs and shears, will become blunt with use and their cutting edges need regular sharpening as a consequence. A fine sharpening stone prepared with a few drops of general-purpose oil is used to sharpen blades of knives and secateurs. A straight-bladed knife can be sharpened using a pushing motion moving forward and to the side, while exerting a little downward pressure. Every four or five strokes should be punctuated by turning the knife over and, while holding the blade almost flat against the stone, brushing it across the surface to take off any rough edges. The same method can be used to sharpen secateurs, concentrating on just the outside blade of 'bypass' (parrot-beaked) secateurs. The upper surface of good quality, forged hoes can also be sharpened on an oilstone and it is worth remembering that in very stony and heavy soils, hoes may actually need sharpening several times per growing season. Once any tool has been sharpened, the job should be finished by wiping the blade with an oily rag.

Tool and Equipment Basics

Spade: a good spade is probably the most important tool there is on the allotment. Used to dig or loosen ground, or to break up clumps in the soil, a spade has a broad flat blade (called a spit) with a sharp, usually curved, lower edge. The handle should be the same height as your hip.

Fork: invaluable for cultivation, a digging fork should have roughly the same dimensions as your spade. It differs in having four strong, sharpened spikes instead of the spit. Forks are used to loosen ground, dig over a plot to lift root vegetables or dig out persistent perennial weed roots.

Swan-necked (English) hoe: the swan-necked hoe is useful for deeper hoeing and cultivating, breaking soil clods and weeding, using a chopping action. It is also used to form narrow seed drills with the blade corner, wide seed drills with the whole blade, or drawing up soil ridges around crops.

Dutch hoe: the Dutch hoe's flat, angled, sharp-edged blade destroys weeds by cutting them just under the surface. It is particularly useful between rows of young vegetables, ideal for working in fertilizer, and helps maintain a fine, dusty, weed suppressant tilth across patches of bare earth.

Rake: a typical garden rake is a toothed bar fixed transversely to a handle, that is predominantly used for light weeding, loosening, and especially levelling patches of bare soil following cultivation. It can also be used to 'comb' the surface in order to remove stones and debris.

Secateurs: secateurs or hand pruners are a scissor-like tool, strong enough to prune hard branches of trees and shrubs 25mm (1in) thick. They are available as 'bypass' (two sharp blades that cross each other like scissors), and 'anvil' (one sharp blade cutting onto a flattened base).

Knife: a folding pocket-knife is an essential piece of kit that often proves among the most versatile of tools. Essential for cutting twine or opening sacks. The ever popular multi-tool knives often have an assortment of knife blades and other tools, some of which can also be useful.

Trowel: this hand tool with a pointed, scoop-shaped metal blade is used for breaking up earth, digging small holes, and especially for planting, weeding, mixing in fertilizer or other additives, and transferring plants to pots. Stainless steel trowels are best but choose one that feels comfortable.

Hand fork: similarly sized to a trowel, a hand or weeding fork is ideal for loosening soil and (as the name suggests) dislodging weeds. Designs vary but most have three stout prongs attached to the handle. Ideal for weeding among rows of crops where a larger fork could damage the roots.

Wheelbarrow: designed for use by a single person using two handles to the rear, a wheelbarrow is an essential item for moving bulky or heavy items. One-wheel types are most manoeuvrable in small spaces, on planks or sloping ground and allow the best control when emptying.

Lawns and Grass

The perfect lawn, without a single weed or brown patch, mowed to striped perfection, has been a goal of gardeners for decades. Yet the effort and time spent to achieve this can be a real drain on resources, both financial and physical. If time needs to be spent, it is arguable that there are better uses than maintaining an area of close mown turf. That said however, a well-kept lawn does have the capability to set the rest of the garden off in a way that is almost matchless and need not be out of reach to the sustainable gardener. If rethinking your lawn strategy though, it is worth remembering that there are other alternatives to the traditional close-mown approach that can be equally attractive at a mere fraction of the effort or cost.

The main drawback of the traditional approach to lawn care lies, not in the cost in time or money, but in the effect that it has on the surrounding environment and ecology. The fertilizers, pesticides and fuel used to maintain this monoculture of close-growing grass plants, cause damage to the wildlife above and below the soil; chemical residues can leach sideways into surrounding beds or down into groundwater and the industrial processes that are used to produce the chemicals use energy and resources elsewhere. In order to change the care of a lawn to a more environmentally acceptable approach, inputs from outside the garden must be limited or removed completely.

Even in relatively small spaces, a lawn can provide an attractive groundcover option, although its maintenance can prove costly and time-consuming.

This might seem daunting but in reality it might involve little more than cutting down on the amount of mowing, and outlawing the use of fertilizers or pesticides. To remove them completely, the substitution of a mechanical 'push' mower – one that is human-motivated rather than engine-driven – will mean that your lawn is sustainable.

These simple steps will not only have an immediate improvement upon a lawn's environmental credentials but will ultimately transform what was effectively a 'green desert' into a thriving ecology. The benefits will be almost immediate, although it may take some years before the full effects are felt.

The main thing to remember is that a sustainable approach to lawn care doesn't mean that the use of the area needs to change, nor even that it will no longer be a feature in its own right. It often does mean however, that the time saved maintaining it can be spent more usefully elsewhere in the garden.

What Makes a Good Lawn?

The answer to this question alone could arguably be one of – if not the most – complex in horticulture. While a well-kept lawn can add greatly to the attractiveness of almost any garden, its use and the amount of wear it will need to withstand especially one in a small, well-used garden space, is likely to dictate its appearance and ultimately its success. Spaces that will receive frequent wear may ultimately be better suited to another

TOP RIGHT: **In a sustainable garden, a more informal lawn where the grass is allowed to grow a little longer, can provide the perfect foil for other garden plants.**

MIDDLE RIGHT: **Flower rich grassland is one way to make an area of grass not only more environmentally friendly, but also results in a feature in its own right.**

RIGHT: **Spring flowering bulbs, corms and tubers, such as these *Anemone blanda*, provide a colourful contrast when grown among other wildflowers in a lawn.**

alternative such as paving or gravel to provide the open space that is so important in providing a foil to the remaining plants in your garden. Having said this, a combination of hard surface and lawn is often the best compromise. Hard surfaces are more usable on a year-round basis but pavements often significantly reduce the amount of rainfall absorption over the garden; something that a lawn or grass area readily rectifies.

If a lawn is needed, the secret of success lies in choosing the 'right' lawn for your garden and your needs. Lawns are just communities of plants which, like any other community, can be grown quite successfully using sustainable methods. The main factor that will dictate success then, as with all other plants, lies in keeping them healthy. Lawn grasses are naturally very resilient and competitive plants, well able to stand a great deal of abuse when healthy. Provided they are given what they need, the reward will be a healthy and attractive lawn.

What is Special about Lawn Grasses?

The very familiarity of lawns means that they are all too often overlooked in the majority of garden situations. Despite the fact that it is almost ubiquitously used for ground cover, serving as a surface upon which to play games, sit, picnic and sometimes even as an ornamental area not to be walked on but simply admired, it is rare that the users take a close look at what it is made up of. A closer inspection quickly reveals that lawns are a rather variable commodity and in short, they need to be. Lawns are required to fulfil a multitude of uses, withstanding huge amounts of trampling on while enduring almost every kind of climatic extreme. It is therefore a remarkable commodity, the success of which is due in no small way to the individual plants' ability to withstand close cropping, originally by grazing animals but more lately by gardeners. The truth of the matter is that the more regularly grass is cut, the more vigorously it grows. On this basis then, establishing and maintaining a lawn should be easy.

A high quality, close-cropped lawn is however the product of time, patience and effort. While this is fine for those that have the time (and are prepared

to make the effort), to many gardeners the best lawn is essentially one that keeps a reasonable appearance without the need to spend too much time (or indeed effort) to do this. This is no impossible dream, and can be achieved with remarkable ease for those willing to make the effort at the planning stage. By selecting the best grass species for your soil, and simply working with its needs, means that the amount of work required to maintain the lawn can be reduced considerably.

Which Types of Grass Species Make the Best Lawn?

While to some, 'grass is just grass', there is a whole multitude of species available for lawn culture, and of these very many cultivars exist. While this might suddenly seem somewhat complicated, there is a simple inescapable truth at work here. Choosing the right species of grass plants for the garden situation, climate and soil, is as crucial as with any other plant. Various locations will support differing communities of grass species. Some species are hardwearing, others drought tolerant, while many need more or less mowing than others. Remember that the key to sustainable growing is working with nature, and so trying to grow the wrong grass species in a garden will only work if a gardener is prepared go to great lengths to tend it. Even then, it will probably be extremely susceptible to climatic extremes, diseases and ultimately damage. Therefore, choosing a type of lawn that has grasses suited to a particular garden environment ultimately means less time tending it and more time spent enjoying it.

Of the numerous species of turf grass available, some are more commonly grown than others. Understanding the qualities of each of these then, is an important first step in establishing a lawn.

Browntop bent *Agrostis capillaris* **and** *Agrostis castellana*: this is a fine-leaved, turf grass species that spreads with short rhizomes and occasionally by stolons. Predominantly used for fine lawns and any close mown areas.

Types of Lawn Grasses

When you are choosing a turf grass mix for a new lawn or lawn repairs, you will of course most commonly choose a selected pre-mixture. However, if you are looking for grasses for particular conditions you can always check it against the preferences of the grasses below, which if present in the seed mix, should prosper in the given conditions.

Fine-leaved species	Coarse-leaved species	Drought-tolerant species

Chewing's fescue *Festuca nigrescens*
Slender creeping red fescue
  Festuca rubra ssp. litoralis and
  fescue rubra ssp pruinosa
Hard fescue *Festuca longifolia*
Sheep's fescue *Festuca ovina*
Browntop bent *Agrostis capillaris*
  and *castellana*
Creeping bent *Agrostis stolonifera*
Velvet bent *Agrostis canina ssp.*
  canina
	Perennial ryegrass *Lolium perenne*
	Smooth stalked meadow grass
	  Poa pratensis
	Small-leaved Timothy
	  Phleum pratense ssp. bertolonii
	Tufted hair-grass
	  Deschampsia caespitosa
	Tall fescue *Festuca arundinacea*
		Smooth stalked meadow grass
		  Poa pratensis
		Chewing's fescue *Festuca nigrescens*
		Slender creeping red fescue
		  Festuca rubra ssp. litoralis and *F.*
		  rubra ssp. pruinosa
		Browntop bent
		  Agrostis capillaris and *castellana*
		Hard fescue *Festuca longifolia*
		Sheep's fescue *Festuca ovina*

Damp-tolerant species	Shade-tolerant species	Wear-tolerant species

Perennial ryegrass *Lolium perenne*
Tufted hair-grass
  Deschampsia caespitosa
Small-leaved Timothy
  Phleum pratense ssp. bertolonii
Creeping bent *Agrostis stolonifera*
Velvet bent
  Agrostis canina ssp. canina
Strong creeping red fescue
  Festuca rubra ssp. rubra
Hard fescue *Festuca longifolia*
Tall fescue *Festuca arundinacea*
	Tufted hair-grass
	  Deschampsia caespitosa
	Strong creeping red fescue
	  Festuca rubra ssp. rubra
	Hard fescue *Festuca longifolia*
	Tall fescue *Festuca arundinacea*
	Rough-stalked meadow grass *Poa*
	trivialis
	  (N.B: *P. trivialis* is best used on its
	  own due to its light leaf colour;
	  meaning that it does not blend
	  well in mixtures)
		Perennial ryegrass *Lolium perenne*
		Smooth stalked meadow grass
		  Poa pratensis
		Slender creeping red fescue
		  Festuca rubra ssp. litoralis and *F.*
		  rubra ssp. pruinosa
		Chewings fescue *Festuca nigrescens*
		Hard fescue *Festuca longifolia*
		Small-leaved Timothy
		  Phleum pratense ssp. bertolonii

Creeping bent *Agrostis stolonifera*: while this species has a similar habit to Browntop Bent, it is more tufted and has a tendency to spread more quickly with creeping stolons.

Chewings fescue *Festuca nigrescens*: densely-tufted and well-suited to a high quality lawn due to its fine leaves. It does not spread, due to its lack of rhizomes and on the whole is disease-resistant.

Hard fescue Festuca longifolia: good for close mowing and particularly good when mixed with Red Fescue. Does not produce rhizomes meaning it is not particularly suitable for areas of intense wear.

Slender creeping red fescue *Festuca rubra ssp. litoralis* **and** *Festuca rubra ssp. pruinosa*: densely-tufted,

fine-leaved and low-growing, these grasses are perfect for closely mown lawns. Once established, they spread by slender rhizomes.

Strong creeping red fescue *Festuca rubra ssp. rubra*: unlike other creeping fescues, this grass is intolerant of very close mowing but knits a lawn together with long, slender, creeping rhizomes. Best suited to chalk and limestone soils.

Sheep's fescue *Festuca ovina*: this will grow in most places including acidic, poorly drained and infertile soils. Its erratic growth habit can form swirling patterns that may not suit fine-mown lawns.

Tall fescue *Festuca arundinacea*: only really suited to areas where the lawn is to be allowed to grow taller, due to its tendency to form large dense tussocks. Unlike some other fescues, this species has coarse leaves.

Small leaved Timothy *Phleum pratense ssp. bertolonii*: blends well with both fescues and bentgrass in colour and texture and is well suited to difficult clays or in light shade.

Perennial ryegrass *Lolium perenne*: arguably the most important turf grass species for domestic lawns, chiefly due to its fast establishment rate, vigorous growth and high wear tolerance.

Smooth stalked meadow grass *Poa pratensis*: while often slow to establish, this grass is hard-wearing and persistent. It spreads using creeping rhizomes that quickly re-colonize damaged open areas. It does best on fertile chalk or limestone soils.

Tufted hair-grass *Deschampsia caespitosa*: this is a tufted grass which is suitable for heavier and moisture-retentive soils that can also tolerate shade conditions.

Seed Mixtures

In most settings, a mixture of grass species is necessary to gain the best establishment and overall quality for a lawn. Often, these seed mixtures have been specifically formulated by a supplier in order to achieve good cover of the ground and withstand wear in a range of given settings, soil types and even climates. While mixtures are common, in certain cases one species often dominates and in certain cases may even be used alone. It is perfectly feasible to select and mix a site-specific blend of species, but in practical terms (and in most situations) a pre-set mixture, purchased from a specialist supplier is normally a reliable compromise.

Establishing Lawns

Seed or Turf?

While the use of turf does have the obvious advantage of its instant effect, the cost, need for transportation and consequent fuel use means that it is not really an option for those wishing to garden in a sustainable way. Seeding is not only more economically viable but it also uses considerably fewer resources in respect of its production and transportation. In short, it is the environmentally friendly way to make a lawn. The advantage of speedy establishment, often cited in respect of turf, is also only a short term advantage – as in most situations, a lawn established from seed will be more tolerant of wear at 100 days than an equivalent area established using turf.

Establishment from Seed

Essentially, lawns are mostly raised from seed. Even turf producers begin by sowing seed, growing this on to create a product of known quality. Exactly how long establishing a decent lawn from seed takes will vary enormously, and often depends upon the grass species that is sown. Essentially, the secret of success here depends upon rapid establishment; the longer the lag-time between sowing the seed and growth commencing, the greater the chances of failure will generally be. Bentgrasses (*Agrostis spp.*) for example are ultimately strong, vigorous growing species, but have extremely small seeds; with well over a hundred thousand seeds in just one kilogramme; this means that the grass plants initially have rather weak early growth. Other species such Chewings fescue (*Festuca nigrescens*) are erect growing or tufted and so require a high number of plants to cover the ground effectively, meaning that they will need a heavier seed rate than creeping types. For this reason, most seed mixes contain a percentage (by weight) of each species used, in order that factors such as initial vigour and spread are accounted for.

The seed mixture in question will have a recommended sowing rate that should not be exceeded or skimped. Sowing the seed too densely may cause undue competition between the emerging plants, can lead to one species dominating the resulting lawn and may also encourage fungal diseases such as damping off among the seedlings. In certain situations however, higher seed rates may be used; for example in early spring when air and ground temperatures would otherwise prove less favourable for a rapid establishment. Drought, rain or waterlogging can also affect seed establishment and thus influence the seed rate, as can poorer ground conditions. For this reason, a range of sowing rates is often listed and it is important that these recommendations be followed, although as a rule of thumb, the average sowing rate is mostly around 35g per m² (1¼ oz per yd²) in favourable conditions, rising to 45g per m² (1½oz per yd²) when less so.

Before any seed can be sown, it is essential that a clean, firm seedbed of suitable tilth has been prepared. The ground should have been dug in advance and all weeds and their roots removed. However it is not advisable to add organic matter. Ideally, land not formerly used as a lawn is best dug in the autumn and left 'fallow' for the winter. This has the dual effect of allowing any existing vegetation that remains to rot down and decay in the soil while encouraging weed seeds to germinate. The latter can then be eliminated prior to sowing in order to improve the lawn's establishment. Indeed, very weedy sites often benefit from thorough weed eradication through fallowing and repeated weed control over a period of months prior to sowing if time (and patience) allows. A couple of weeks before sowing takes place, a base dressing of a phosphate and potassium-rich compound should be applied to the soil. Most general-purpose compound fertilizers are ideal for this and must be raked into the soil a short time before seeding.

The ground will need a final cultivation immediately prior to sowing the seed. This involves levelling the ground using a rake, held at a shallow angle, to break down any large clods. The art of levelling is to keep the rake angle shallow and move the high spots over into the low spots with even strokes of the rake. Hold the rake firm at the rear and let the shaft run smoothly through the front hand to do this.

All stones and large obstructions, including organic matter such as twigs or plant debris, should be removed by combing out with the teeth of the rake while holding it in a near vertical position. It is especially important to remove stones at this stage, as they tend to rise to the surface with time and can sometimes catch on mower blades as a result. For most lawns, this involves removing stones that are around 40mm

(1½in) or more, although fine turf areas will need all stones that exceed 25mm (1in) to be removed (as far as is practicable) before sowing.

The soil is then firmed with gentle treading. A light 'shuffle' across the bed applying pressure evenly with the soles of the feet is usually enough to do this. Once firmed, the soil is lightly raked one last time again at a shallow angle to produce a light, fluffy, surface that runs freely through the teeth of the rake without obstructions.

Sowing the Seed

Broadcasting is the method most commonly used to sow grass seed by hand. The method simply involves scattering the seed evenly across the area using a wide arcing throw.

The method is very straightforward and involves the following steps.

1 BELOW: Using string or garden twine and canes or pegs, divide and mark out the intended lawn area into a squared grid in multiples of 1m².

2 OVERLEAF TOP LEFT: Divide the seed into lots, each of which is enough to cover each of the marked areas for that species of mixture.

4 ABOVE: Lightly rake in the seed in order to bury it and if no rain is expected within the next twenty-four hours irrigate the whole area using a fine sprinkler.

3 BELOW: Divide each lot and sow the seed in two halves per marked area, sowing each half in opposing directions to give an even coverage.

Under ideal conditions grass seed will take approximately ten to fourteen days to germinate depending upon the temperature and moisture content of the soil. Remember that there must be an adequate supply of moisture in the soil to allow germination and growth and while the underlying soil may be moist, if the surface is allowed to dry out, the seeds or seedlings can easily dry out and die. Irrigation can help avoid this but a firm seed bed and correct sowing are the real keys to avoiding this.

Early or late sowing can avoid the problems associated with drought, particularly on dry sandy soils. However, the drawback with this is often temperature related, as most grasses do not grow actively at temperatures below 4–5°C (39–41°F) and further drops below this effectively arrest growth and development. If growth is slowed during the establishment phase, it often means that the seedlings become stressed, may be vulnerable to disease attack or from further deteriorations in the conditions.

Air and ground frosts severely check the growth of seedlings, through frost heave in loosened soil severing young roots and also by plummeting air temperatures damaging young, vulnerable leaves and stems.

On wet sites, the problems are often related more to the possibility of waterlogging than drought. A saturated seed bed lacks oxygen; a vital constituent for seed germination and healthy root growth and will result in poor germination or establishment. The depth of planting is also important as seeds which have been raked too deeply into the soil will fail as their food reserves will expire before the young seedling shoots reach the soil surface. Conversely, those left too near to the surface are prone to moisture stress. Firming the soil before sowing and restricting the raking to a shallow depth will usually avoid this. Not firming the soil before sowing can also lead to pockets of air in the soil. Such voids lack moisture, meaning that young roots growing into them quickly become drought stressed, even in relatively moist soils.

Finally, the commonest cause of poor establishment of a new lawn is competition from weeds. These compete with young seedlings for water, nutrients and light. A clean seedbed is essential and should have been obtained prior to sowing using the fallowing technique. Many annual weeds are extremely fast germinating, grow and develop rapidly, and find the conditions in a fertile seed bed much to their liking. Some, such as chickweed (*Stellaria media*), often germinate at low temperatures and have even been known to do so under snow cover, rendering them a serious competitor to early or late sown seed. The best approach therefore is to time sowings to maximize the growth of the grass, thereby giving it a fighting chance of survival.

Maintaining a Lawn

Grasses, like any other plant, need light, nutrients, moisture and space to grow. Each grass plant has just enough space and closely 'knits in' with its neighbours. The taller grass plants grow then, the less dense the number of plants in any one space becomes. This is due to the fact that as they grow taller, their needs increase and the most competitive plants win. Regular cutting, therefore, results in a dense coverage with short green leaves and a high number of plants in a given area.

Irregular cutting means fewer plants in the area, while the periodic removal of the majority of green leafy growth from the top of the plant often results in a lawn that is patchy with white or yellow leaf bases.

Mowing

Mowing is the most important, most frequently undertaken and arguably the simplest lawn maintenance task. The actual operation of mowing has a number of effects upon the sward, the most obvious of which is removing some of the top-growth. On an actively growing lawn, the more grass is removed by mowing, the more rapid its re-growth will be. This is the result of the plant's attempt to even out its root-to-shoot ratio. Essentially, if you remove top growth frequently, the grass speeds up growth to replace the deficit. Conversely, grass that is constantly mown short, has less (and shallower) root growth than that which is allowed to grow taller. Lawns that are frequently mowed also have more plants per square metre. The amount of root and shoot growth and thus sward density are then a direct consequence of mowing.

Mowing is the only maintenance task that actually improves the lawn afterwards, although a powered mower is not the most sustainable option.

Aerating a lawn can be done in two ways, either by scarifying the surface with a rake to remove the compacted mat of old vegetation (ABOVE) or by using an ordinary digging fork, pushed into the surface and rocked back and forth to relieve compaction of the soil (BELOW), allowing root penetration and improving air exchange.

The cutting height will vary according to season; cutting should be higher during the late autumn, winter and early spring when little growth is taking place. Raising the cutting height can also alleviate drought stress and help keep a lawn green through more of the summer. Remember though, that the height of cut will also be influenced by the frequency of cut. As a general rule, mowing frequency should be fixed so that you never remove more than a third of the leaf at any one mowing, thereby avoiding unnecessary stress to the plants.

Different grass species vary in their tolerance to mowing and especially in respect of the minimum cutting heights. Certain species of Fescue including strong creeping red fescue (*Festuca rubra ssp. Rubra*) and tall fescue (*Festica arundinacea*) will die out if cut at 5mm (1/5in) or below, while perennial ryegrass (*Lolium perenne*) and smooth stalked meadow grass (*Poa pratensis*) are significantly weakened if regularly cut lower than 18mm (3/4in). In this way, the cutting height and frequency will affect which species survive and grow in the lawn.

Frequent mowing also means that less material is removed at any one time and makes returning clippings a feasible option. This promotes the recycling of nutrients and feeds the lawn – grass clippings contain up to 3 per cent nitrogen, 0.7 per cent phosphorous and 2 per cent potassium by dry weight – while adding organic matter to the soil which will help retain water. Indeed, during drought conditions, clippings can act as mulch on the soil surface and so restrict water loss from the soil. On the downside, returning clippings can make turf more susceptible to disease and soil-borne pests and lead to a build up of 'thatch'.

Thatch is the general term used to describe the layers of organic fibrous material found in turf. It is a natural phenomenon of turf development and some thatch within the lawn gives resilience and some drought tolerance. Problems only usually arise when thatch layers build up to an excessive degree and cause an increase in disease, localized dry spots, leaf yellowing, proneness to scalping and a soft spongy surface. Aeration, topdressing and scarification all help here, not only by removing thatch, but also by controlling moss or creeping weeds and assisting in air and water infiltration. Scarification is normally carried out using a spring-tined rake to lightly scratch the surface and comb out the debris, and must be carried out only when the grass is growing actively.

Aeration is best carried out when the soil is just slightly moist to ensure maximum penetration into the soil without damaging its structure. This is often done manually with an ordinary digging fork and although this can seem time consuming and laborious, it is very effective for relieving localized compaction, while improving surface drainage and soil air supply. The longer term consequence of this is that it leads to increased drought resistance of the sward because of greater and deeper grass root growth, while thatch will be less prevalent because of increased microbial activity resulting from better aerated soil. The improved surface drainage encourages soil to stay warmer for longer thereby lengthening the active growing season.

Topdressing involves the application of a bulky material to the surface of the lawn. While this usually has little or only minor nutritional value, it helps restore a level surface and to control thatch build-up. Topdressing can be made up of sand and compost, or of loamy soil and compost, and is best applied when both it and the surface are dry. It must be thoroughly incorporated into the lawn surface using a brush or besom. Ideally a lawn is top dressed during the growing season so that the grass has a chance to grow through it and never so heavily that it smothers the grass. Topdressing is easier to work into the sward if the areas have been mown and scarified prior to application. The rule of thumb here is to decide upon a preferred topdressing mixture and stick with it.

Maintaining Nutrients in the Soil

Despite the claims of many organic lawn fertilizers that they are environmentally friendly, this is a dubious claim on two basic counts. Firstly, they are just as liable to over enrich the soil and result in fertilizer run-off as many other fertilizers. In addition to this, they must be manufactured, packaged and transported to

Topdressing is best done when both it and the surface are dry, during mid to late spring, and ideally on a surface that has been both scarified and mowed immediately beforehand. Spread topdressing thinly over the surface (ABOVE) before thoroughly incorporating it into the lawn surface using a brush or besom to work it in (BELOW).

TOPDRESSING MATERIALS FOR LAWNS

Sand

This has the advantage of being durable, naturally porous and resistant to compaction, meaning that it is frequently used as a major component of topdressing mixes as well as on its own.

Topsoil

The suitability of topsoil lies in no small part in its texture. Sandy soil is often ideal, whereas clay may be harder to spread. Can be used on its own, or mixed with sand and compost.

Garden compost and leaf mould

This organic matter improves the moisture-holding capacity of a rootzone, while being relatively inert and sterile. Often best used in mixtures, it needs to be well rotted. It is rich in trace elements.

---

get them to you. In short then, while they may well have organic credentials, they are not really sustainable. While it may be acceptable to use a little fertilizer while establishing the lawn, this situation should be seen as a helping hand only at the outset. The idea must ultimately be to reduce inputs and this of course includes fertilizer. The way to offset this is of course to find ways of returning nutrients from the lawn (those removed through mowing) and this is ideally done by a combination of the following.

• Mow frequently and return the clippings. This regular application of organic matter naturally recycles the nutrients therein, by encouraging the soil ecology.

• Keep the height of cut higher. This slows the speed of growth; meaning less material needs to be removed through the season and less nutrient is needed.

• Top dress with a mixture of topsoil and compost. This improves the efficiency of nutrient cycling by stimulating micro-organisms and improving air circulation.

• Include clover in the mixture. Legumes such as clover naturally capture atmospheric nitrogen and stimulate the growth of the surrounding grasses as a consequence.

• Apply a home-made liquid feed such as nettle or manure tea. This is especially useful in spring to boost grass growth and can be repeated every four to six weeks.

Watering Lawns

Grass is naturally able to deal with periods of drought by entering a period of dormancy, although this can lead to invasion by weed species. Raising the height of cut can help to reduce this problem. Another measure is to make the best use of rain that does fall. If a reservoir of captured water is available then irrigation may be possible but for most this will entail making sure that any rain that does fall can infiltrate rapidly. Well-aerated lawns allow the quickest infiltration of moisture and rain and ironically tend to lose less of this to evaporation. The last word on this though, and a serious consideration for those living in drought-prone areas, is to choose drought-resistant grass species when establishing the lawn.

Diseases of Turf Grass

In lawns fungi cause the vast majority of diseases. Having said this, not all fungi associated with turf and soils are harmful. Many are extremely beneficial as they aid the decomposition of plant materials and organic matter to release nutrients in the soil; some are also antagonistic to disease-causing organisms. The factors affecting fungal growth, development and spread are varied and diverse. Fungi do not grow well below about 5°C (41°F), but flourish around 20°C (68°C). High humidity also encourages the spread of fungi, while extreme wet or dry soil or excessive shade may weaken the grass plant, making them susceptible to disease. On the whole then, the best approach is to keep the growth of the grass as healthy as possible, thereby conferring a measure of disease resistance.

Moss

Moss will readily establish on any areas of thin turf where there is a lack of competition from grass growth. Factors that favour the growth of mosses include a moist surface, mowing too close, surface compaction, shade, low soil fertility and excessive pH. Most moss treatments – even organic or environmentally friendly versions – are purely palliative, that is they kill the moss but do not remove the problem. Dealing with the cause is normally sufficient to remove the problem and will improve the grass growth as a consequence.

Lawn Repairs

Re-seeding

Bare patches can usually be re-established quickly and easily using seed. Start by marking out the area to be repaired and break up the soil by forking it over. Rake to establish the correct level and top-up soil levels if appropriate. Consolidate the surface by treading, rake to produce the final tilth and sow grass seeds by broadcast sowing in two or more opposing directions. Rake the seed into the soil surface, ensuring the area is level with the surrounding turf.

Moss is a commonly encountered problem in lawns and it is a sign of an underlying problem such as shade, soil compaction or mowing too closely.

Overseeding

This method is used to thicken an existing lawn by thinly sowing grass seeds which will then germinate, grow and fill-in the turf surface. It is mostly done by hand broadcasting and scratching in the seed. Overseeding requires much lower seed rates than those suggested for establishing new lawns, and in some cases can be incorporated with a top-dressing mixture. Remember that sowing too thickly can lead to damage from fungal diseases. When soil conditions are dry, ensure that the seed is covered and in contact with the firmer soils underneath so that it can soak up water for germination. Lightly rolling the ground once the seed has been sown will also help.

Repairing Damaged Edges with Turf

A damaged edge can prove almost impossible to re-seed and so this handy trick combines the speed of turfing without needing to buy in turf. Start by marking out and lifting an area of turf surrounding the damaged edge. Fork over the soil to relieve surface compaction and rake it to establish the correct level, topping-up soil levels if appropriate. Re-lay the turf with the damaged edge innermost. Topdress the whole area, working it into the joints and paying particular attention to the damaged zone. The topdressing compost should ideally have a small quantity of seed mixed into it. Alternatively, the area may be overseeded once the turf is laid and topdressing applied. Ensure the area is watered when necessary.

Biennials and Perennials

In the broadest terms, garden plants can be divided up in two ways; those that have permanent woody growth above the ground, and those that do not. Annuals, biennials and perennials fall into the latter category and as such share many aspects of care and maintenance, despite differing in numerous other ways. In general terms then, their maintenance falls within three basic areas, namely: cutting plants back or providing support; weeding, pest and disease control (see Chapter 5); nutrition and environmental manipulation.

With the huge array of plants grown in gardens, there are of course many other variables that may also affect the growth of non-woody plants. Chief among these is of course the amount of time available to tend them and ultimately the effect required in respect of the overall design. In common with all types of garden maintenance, the work needed at any given time will also depend upon various factors: environmental factors (such as the weather conditions pertaining at the time); and the ground or soil conditions; as well as the plant's stage of growth or maturity.

Cutting Back Non-woody Plants

Generally, annuals and biennials need little in the way of pruning, this being largely confined to checking for and removing any dead, damaged or disease-affected material. In addition to this, a variety of other methods aimed at improving flowering or extending the flowering season are sometimes employed. On the whole then, herbaceous perennials generally differ from annuals and perennials in their need to have old, dead growth removed in the late winter, prior to the recommencement of growth in the spring.

Thinning

Most annuals, biennials and herbaceous plants produce numerous shoots, many of which tend to be thin and spindly. By removing the weaker shoots, the plant is enabled to divert its energy into the remaining shoots that will be consequentially sturdier and produce larger flowers. Generally called thinning, this technique is best carried out when the plant has reached one quarter to one third of its eventual height and is especially useful when dealing with tall perennials such as Delphinium, Phlox and Michaelmas daisy (*Aster novae-angliae* and *Aster novi-belgii*).

Stopping

This describes a technique that simply involves the removal of the growing tip of a stem in order to encourage the side shoots to develop. The tips are usually pinched out when the plant has attained a third of its ultimate height, with this encouraging otherwise dormant buds in the leaf axils to develop and grow. This in turn leads to more flowers being produced, and while these will be smaller than if the main terminal bud had been allowed to flower, the overall effect is a fuller, more striking plant. This technique is especially successful for summer and spring annual bedding plants, but is also used on a range of perennials including Helenium, Rudbeckia, Dahlia and Chrysanthemum.

Dead Heading

Unless the plant produces decorative seed heads, or if seed is to be collected for propagation purposes, it is usually preferable to remove the flowers of many annuals and some perennials as they begin to fade. This encourages further side shoots to develop and can often result in an extended flowering period. This is especially important in the case of freely seeding plants if you do not wish them to self-sow and come up in following seasons. As the season draws to a close though, the need to cut back diminishes, with seed heads and old growth from late flowering perennials usually being best left until early in the following season, as this may provide additional winter food for resident birds and mammals.

Cutting Back

Some shrubby perennials such as Phygelius, Penstemon and Chrysanthemum spp. do not always die back to ground level but usually benefit from being pruned back almost to ground level in early spring. In this way, they are treated like true herbaceous specimens, and encouraged to produce new basal shoots that will flower in summer and autumn.

Providing Support

Taller-growing herbaceous and annual plants usually require some form of support in order to display them effectively and protect them from damage. This is especially true of tall-growing herbaceous plants that can be extremely prone to wind damage, especially when varieties have been planted that have large showy flowers, for example some Delphinium cultivars and many Dahlia species. Indeed a variety of plants will benefit from a stake, including tall annuals such as sunflowers and many annual edible crops such as outdoor bush tomato and sweetcorn which should be staked in a windy or exposed setting.

Staking plants is important not only for appearances. Allowing them to grow, bloom and (if appropriate) fruit, without toppling over, breaking, or smothering smaller plants nearby, will benefit the garden as a whole. What is more, a firmly staked plant often has the benefit of improved air circulation, meaning that it will also be less likely to be affected by fungal diseases. Staking must be done early though, preferably when the plant is young, if the full benefit is to be gained from it.

If staking edible crops, aside from the benefits of cleaner produce that is less susceptible to damage or disease, supports also make cultivation and harvesting easier and result in a more efficient use of space, ultimately equating to higher yields from the available space. Having said this, staking is a form of 'intensification'; in other words it will inevitably lead to more time spent preparing the plot, and tying in the growing plants. If this sounds like too much effort, the best idea would be to select and grow specimens that do not need support.

When staking taller specimens, the ultimate size of the plant should be considered. Remember that the stake has to prevent the weight of the plant from toppling and may therefore need to be suitably sized as a consequence. In the majority of cases, supports should never exceed one third of the stem height. This is partly to hide them from view, but also to encourage more robust growth. This will of course depend upon the method of support used and the situation.

Staking Methods

Stakes are an ideal way of supporting individual plants, particularly those with one central stem such as sunflowers (*Helianthus annuus*), although they can also be used as a central anchor point for multi-stemmed specimens.

Cages and frames are particularly good for bushier specimens that need all-round support, and have the added bonus of cutting out the need for tying. Having said this, the design of some types can make pruning or pinching out side-shoots difficult, resulting in crowded growth inside the cage itself.

One of the simplest and most attractive home-made plant supports is to construct a pyramid or cone made with straight cut branches of hazel.

Trellises are essentially a lattice work frame, traditionally made of timber, although synthetic substitutes are increasingly common. There are many designs available, some of which can be fixed onto a wall to provide support for climbers while others can be used as 'free-standing' supports in their own right.

Smaller 'twiggy' material can be used to make 'pea-sticks'; an ideal way to support lower growing annuals and of course (as the name suggests) peas.

Although hazel is the material traditionally used to make temporary plant supports, any straight growing branch-wood can be used for the purpose.

Wires may be attached to a wall or fence to provide support for climbing plants in a similar way to a trellis. Wires can also be stretched horizontally between posts or stakes to provide support for plants grown as a row crop, or as a crisscross framework for climbers.

Sticks and twigs are used either as protection for seedlings or support for low-growing plants. Twiggy sticks are often called 'pea sticks' by gardeners, due to their long established use in supporting shorter varieties of peas and beans.

Staking Materials

There is a whole range of materials that can be used to support plants and each of these has their relative merits and drawbacks. Ideally, the best materials are those available to hand but if materials need to be obtained, then careful thought should be given to exactly what they will be required to do.

Natural materials, such as timber, bamboo, branchwood or twigs are freely obtainable and provided care is taken over their origin, tend to be a renewable resource. Ideally, these materials should be locally produced and if space permits they should be produced within your own garden. The fact that they are natural in origin does mean that they tend to rot and need replacing, sometimes on a yearly basis.

Synthetic materials include a range of materials, including plastics, UPVC, carbon fibre poles, galvanized or plastic-coated metal. There is a huge number of brands and designs available, almost all of which have two things in common; they are durable and (as a consequence of their manufacture) quite costly. Arguably though, their longevity offsets these initial costs.

Tying Materials

The way that you attach the plant to a support is arguably just as important as the support itself. Ideally ties must be flexible and slightly loose to allow the plant room to grow without tearing, ripping or scarring the plant stem. Natural materials such as raffia or twine do of course have the advantage of being biodegradable;

RIGHT: **With a little imagination, it is possible to make quite complex and even architectural structures using materials grown sustainably on-site.**

BOTTOM RIGHT: **Larger stakes can be used to make more substantial structures such as this, where they provide posts to support wires for tying-in fruit canes.**

they can be composted and if combined with natural supports mean that the whole system is derived from renewable sources.

Synthetic materials are mostly made of coated wire, Velcro, plastic or rubber and there are a numerous 'systems' available. While some of these can be reused, the majority cannot, and they must be disposed of and not composted. This, combined with the manufacturing processes involved, usually bring them into the class of non-sustainable resources. Having said all of this, it is possible to recycle and reuse a whole variety of synthetic materials. Polythene can be cut into strips to make durable and flexible ties, as could old cloth strips, the latter of which can even be composted provided it is from natural fibres.

Ultimately then, the most important aspect when selecting staking and tying materials is to consider their origins, whether they are renewable, whether they can be used again and if not, whether they will biodegrade safely (that is, can they be composted).

Nutrition

Annuals, biennials and perennials have something of an unfair reputation as being hungry, heavy-feeding crops. This is mostly due to unreasonable expectations regarding their rate of growth and capacity to yield fruit and flowers. However, if the initial soil preparation has been thorough and included the addition of bulky organic matter such as well-rotted manure or compost, the need for a fertilizer is instantly lessened due to the activities of soil organisms. Of course some plants, especially annual bedding and vegetable crops, do need an added boost through the season, and these often benefit from regular applications of

a liquid feed such as compost or manure 'tea.' For established beds of perennial plants though, the nutrient cycling – and ultimately the growth of the plants – can be enhanced and maintained by regular additions of bulky organic materials such as well-rotted farmyard manure or compost, applied in spring.

Mulching

Mulching an established herbaceous bed with an organic material has many potential benefits aside from that of simply adding organic matter to the soil. It has a considerable effect upon the overall soil environment and will (to a certain extent) help to keep the plant's roots warm in winter and cool in summer. This often proves useful as it assists the new growth in the spring, as ordinarily plants only commence active growth once the soil starts to warm up. A layer of mulch does however encourage surface rooting, meaning that in drought-prone areas, it is likely to need topping up periodically through the season to prevent these roots

Mulch, placed around the base of plants in the early spring has the dual benefit of suppressing weeds, while providing much needed organic matter.

becoming damaged. On the other hand, a mulch layer can help to reduce soil water loss through evaporation. It does this in two main ways: partly by shading the soil surface and also by directly slowing down the direct loss of water vapour from the soil to the atmosphere. Evaporation from the soil surface draws more water from further down, by a process known as capillary action. The drying action of this has obvious detrimental effects upon the soil's water reserve that may in turn lead to stress within the plants. A surface layer of mulch essentially breaks this 'wicking' action, thereby limiting water loss through evaporation.

Mulch is also a useful way of reducing the numbers of weeds growing in a planted bed, particularly in the earliest part of a growing season when its ability to inhibit germinating weed seedlings can be a bonus in the shorter days when time in the garden can often be limited by the short days. This said, mulch will not inhibit established, vigorous perennial weeds, such as couch grass (*Elymus spp.*) and bindweed (*Convolvulus spp.*).

Special Considerations when Mulching Herbaceous Plants

Most herbaceous plants have a tendency to die down to ground level and form winter resting buds at the surface. These buds are very vulnerable to rot if covered by mulch, particularly one that tends to become wet and sticky due to the effects of winter weather. This condition – known commonly as crown rot – can seriously affect herbaceous plants in the spring, causing gaps in planted areas later in the year. A few such as Hosta or Dicentera on the other hand, actually die down to resting buds that are below the surface and are more like bulbs as a consequence. Mulches cause less of a problem for these plants as they quickly emerge through the mulch once growth commences in spring.

A general rule is to mulch lightly in between the plants, avoiding the crowns and using a light open substance such as spent mushroom compost or well-rotted garden compost. In addition, timing the application of mulch so that it is only applied at the point when growth commences in the spring can avoid the worst of the problems and often enables a more generous application to be made.

Maintaining Woody Plants

Essentially, woody plant care is similar to any other form of plant care. They need water, light, the correct soil type, pH, and enough nutrients, as well as a suitable climate, if they are to survive and thrive. Despite this, they differ greatly in the fact that they have permanent woody growth, both above and below ground. Add to this the fact that many of them – especially trees – live for a very long time and it quickly becomes apparent that they are basically very different from any other garden plants.

Therefore, the main aspects of their care and maintenance lie in the control of their growth and in ensuring that the parts below the ground are not forgotten but receive the attention and care they deserve.

Caring for the Parts above Ground

Pruning Basics

There has been so much written about pruning that it may seem that nothing that could said here could possibly add to it. Indeed, there is so much varied opinion, not only in print but also between gardeners, that it can seem a confusing, even daunting subject for both the novice and more experienced gardeners. The simple, inescapable truth though is that there is no great mystery surrounding pruning and, like most jobs in the garden, it merely involves the application of simple and straightforward principles. There are arguably two things that are essentially the hallmark of competent pruning:

- A planned, careful and methodical approach to the work undertaken.

- A good working knowledge of the requirements of those plant species that are to be pruned.

Before starting to prune then, it is important to know why the work is being done. Surprisingly often, people actually begin pruning a shrub with no real long-term objective. Pruning is something for which the real results may not always be apparent for months

QUESTIONS TO ASK BEFORE STARTING TO PRUNE

In order to formulate a plan, it can be useful to find out as much about the subject to be pruned as possible. The following questions are not necessarily an exhaustive list, nor will all of the questions be applicable in every situation. The essential point here is to ensure that you have found out as much as possible in order to ensure that the job is done efficiently and most important, correctly.

- Where if the shrub located?

- What species is it?

- How large is it?

- Can you estimate the age of the shrub?

- Are there any specific climatic or microclimatic factors, likely to affect its growth?

- What are the specific pruning requirements of this species? Where can you find this out?

- What is the overall condition of the specimen?

- Does it require any form of remedial pruning work?

- Are branches causing an obstruction or nuisance?

- When was the last time the specimen was pruned?

- What is the aesthetic character of the shrub?

- How much waste will pruning operations generate? How will you dispose of/utilize this?

- What tools are needed for the job?

and in the case of trees, years. Before starting to prune then, it is essential to ask 'why am I doing this'?

Remember also that every pruning situation is different and, although experience can equip a gardener well to tackle even the most challenging 'Thicket from Hell', prior thought and a plan of action will enable work to progress more efficiently and help avoid mistakes. Correct identification of the species in question is always preferable, at least as far as the genus. Remember though, that even species within a genus can have a variety of different pruning requirements. Few genera have uniform requirements across all of the species contained therein.

Arguably then, the most important skills to develop are plant identification skills! Once the plant that is the intended subject has been correctly identified, the answer is only a textbook away. Essentially then the order is to find out what the plant needs and then to make a plan.

Why is it Necessary to Prune Plants?

Pruning is almost always done to control the growth of woody plants. A variety of reasons may make this necessary, but perhaps the commonest in gardens is because they have outgrown their situations, or because they are kept in a particular shape (such as a fan shape) against a wall or a hedge. Other specimens are pruned because of the effect it has on their appearance; pruning often has the effect of improving the flower or fruit size of some shrubs and climbers and yet other shrubs may have young growth that has brightly coloured stems or leaves.

Choosing the Right Tools

In the first instance it is essential to take a good look at the plant(s) that are to be pruned and assess what equipment will be needed to do the job. The commonest (and arguably most indispensable) of these is undoubtedly a pair of secateurs, which are used to snip through thinner growth up to around 15mm (½in) in diameter. For thicker growth a pair of loppers that are used on branches up to 25mm (1in) thick will be needed. These are useful in situations where secateurs may not easily reach, for example in dense or tangled shrubs. Normally, loppers should not be used for very thick branches or they may easily be damaged although several designs now exist for ratchet-operated loppers that can cut through growth of up to 50mm (2in).

Above these thicknesses a pruning saw becomes essential. Again many designs exist but the most useful are the curved or Grecian type and a bow saw for

Pruning Equipment

Secateurs
When small branches are to be removed it is often easiest to use secateurs and remove the branch in one go. Secateurs are the commonest type of pruning tool and are best used on twiggy material about the width of a pencil.

Loppers
Used on branches up to 25mm (1in) thick, loppers are useful in situations where secateurs may not easily reach, such as in dense tangled shrubs. They should not be used for very thick branches or they may easily be damaged.

Grecian saw
Use on branches up to 50mm (2in) diameter where the branches are very crowded. It cuts on a pulling cut making its use above shoulder height very easy.

Bow saw
Used for cutting larger branches. Available in various sizes. They cut with a pushing cut, making their prolonged use above shoulder height rather tiring.

really thick wood. Always ensure that the right tools are available for the job, as not doing so will make the job harder and may actually end up causing more harm than good.

Deciding What Needs to be Done

Correctly identifying the plant and checking what sort of pruning it needs is vital. Pruning is something for which the real results may not always be apparent for months and, in the case of trees, years. A few general points are common to most species however and, if unsure, provide an excellent starting point.

The first and simplest thing that can be done is to remove the 'D's; in other words all of the dead, dying, damaged or diseased wood. Remember though, that deadwood is very important to the ecology of a garden, especially what is called 'standing deadwood' in trees. This is often removed to ensure that dead branches do not fall suddenly; injuring plants or people that are unfortunate enough to be below, or perhaps buildings or other structures. If it does prove necessary to remove deadwood it should be left for wildlife and not removed and burned as is often recommended. On the other hand, diseased material should be removed

and burned, especially if there is a chance that it will spread and affect other plants.

The 'C's can also be considered now; the removal of criss-crossing branches and crowded growth allowing new, rejuvenating growth in many species. Once all of the above items have been addressed, the next step would normally be the removal of any unwanted growth which is growing across paths or crowding out other surrounding specimens. Always take care (arguably the most important 'C'!) when doing this though, as simply removing large amounts of plant material, because it is deemed to be in the way, may cause the plant to assume an unbalanced form that is difficult (if not impossible) to counter with further pruning.

Once this material is cleared, it is possible to see what further work needs to be done. Creating balance, form and a pleasing shape in the pruned specimen requires a keen eye, as well as knowledge of what type of pruning benefits that particular plant. It is always worth taking a little time over this, as acting too hastily at this stage can easily spoil the job. Pruning is one of a few jobs in the garden that is best viewed intermittently from a distance, in order to judge the next step.

Heading cuts involve shortening a branch, making the cut immediately above healthy buds, and tend to stimulate vigorous re-growth in that area.

Thinning is a pruning technique that involves removing a whole branch, and tends to limit shock responses and dense re-growth in the growing season.

Always remember though that some species react well to pruning while others do not. Therefore, reading up on the specific requirements of the bush or tree in hand is essential if you are going to get the best results, and well worth the time that it takes.

Pruning Cuts

When removing branches, there are two basic types of pruning cuts. These are 'heading' – the removal of a part of a shoot or limb – and 'thinning' – the removal of the entire shoot or limb.

Heading stimulates re-growth near the cut and is the most invigorating type of pruning cut, resulting in thick compact growth and a loss of natural form – such as might be found in a formally pruned hedge.

Thinning on the other hand leaves some shoots undistributed, and so tip (or apical) dominance is maintained and new growth occurs only at the undisturbed shoot tips. Thinning generally provides a more natural growth form, as only around one third of the growth would be thinned at one time, thereby permitting the natural flowering and fruiting cycle to continue.

Pruning cuts should always be cleanly done, using sharp-bladed cutters or a saw, thereby avoiding tearing. When removing a whole limb, always try leave as short a stub as possible. If you are heading back (shortening) a branch, it is important that the cut is 1–3mm (1/8in) above a bud and that the cut itself does not damage the bud. Remember that a branch can only be cut once; if you cut the wrong branch, you cannot rejoin it effectively to the plant from whence it came. Always check that you know the full extent of a branch and what effect its removal will have prior to making the cut.

Be careful, when using a saw close to a trunk or stem, to remove heavier thicker branches. The weight of the branch can sometimes cause splitting and tearing to the main stem wood or bark. Injuries such as these often increase the likelihood of disease affecting the plant.

LEFT: **When thinning the growth of a shrub, use a saw to remove thicker growth as near to the base as possible to prevent a crowded collection of old stumps.**

Pruning out Infected Wood

Where infection is to be pruned out, the plant should be assessed to ascertain how much infected wood needs to be removed and whether this will ultimately damage the overall shape. Severely affected plants may be best removed and destroyed to prevent further spread of the disease. Make cuts well below the infection into clean unaffected wood. Also, clean pruning tools after each cut using a household disinfectant. (N.B: this must be done especially thoroughly when moving between plants in order to minimize cross-infection and spread of disease). Dispose of all infected prunings carefully, preferably by burning them.

Pruning Cuts and Healing

Any wounds or cuts (such as those made by pruning) made to a woody stem brings about a healing response from the plant. The tissue, that is located just below the bark (*cambium*), grows rapidly and forms a 'callus' over the bare face of the wound. This healing is a gradual process that is directly related to the general health and vigour of the shrub or tree in question.

When removing dead wood, ensure that cuts are made back to living tissue as healing via callus formation is only possible from this living tissue. Cuts should always be made to a point as close to a branch or bud as is practically possible. Careless pruning often results in 'snags' left projecting beyond this point. These will eventually die back to tissue in the region of the nearest bud or branch. When removing diseased wood, extra care is often needed. Infection may have spread well beyond the dead or the visibly infected portion. Fire Blight (*Erwinia amylovora*) for instance, often extends backwards beyond the first visible signs into the branch.

Making a Clean Cut

It is vital to avoid tearing of the stem or branch during pruning as this can cause two major problems. Firstly, it leaves a much larger area exposed to possible infection, from pests and/or diseases, entering the wound. Secondly, the healing process may well be impaired and slowed down in the region of the tear. Where a

Cuts should always be made to a point as close to a branch or bud as is practically possible, so as to avoid 'snags' left projecting beyond this point.

severe tear occurs while removing a side branch, it is possible that it may have removed some heartwood and left an area where water may collect. This will eventually result in decay and allow cavities to form.

Angle of Cut

The general aim of all pruning cuts should be to make the cut as close as possible to the stem and to keep the wound as small as possible. Opinions do of course vary but many so called authorities still recommend that the cut be angled so as to shed water away from the stem and the wound. The angle of the cut will be dictated to a large extent by the nature, thickness and mechanics of the main stem. It is worth pointing out here that a 'square-on cut' will leave the smallest wound area and therefore lessen the general chances of disease entry.

SQUARE CUTS VERSUS SLOPING CUTS

Despite much debate as to the merits of both these techniques, the question of correctness of either sloping or straight cuts appears to be rooted in the tradition of practitioners and not on the basis of scientific evidence. Most scientific literature on the subject of pruning ignores the issue, meaning that the traditionally cited wisdom (water will not sit on the wound) is not a scientific fact. While it may initially seem to be a sensible view, it could only be rigidly applied to stems that were growing at or near to 90° perpendicular. Stems held laterally or emanating from the ground at an angle would (by this reckoning) not need sloping cuts as their very growth habit would negate the chances of water sitting atop the stem. In addition, even the sloping angle of a cut (whether by design or branch orientation) would naturally absorb water alighting upon the surface through capillary action. This, and the natural tendency of water to form condensation droplets across an uneven surface (even if vertical), would ensure that some water remained.

The main disadvantages of water entering a wound arise from the freeze/thaw action causing damage to the structure of the old stem, and moist surfaces being more vulnerable to inoculation by bacteria or fungi. However, research carried out in the United Kingdom suggests that the most important factors affecting the incidence of disease entry through wounds hinge around the amount of disease spores present (that is whether the disease was there or not); cultivar (of the plant); wound age (old cuts proving less susceptible); and the climatic conditions (most are prevalent in warm, wet times). From this, it could be concluded that correct hygiene of pruning tools, and the pruning of subjects during cold winter periods or drier summer weather, would allow cuts to age prior to the onset of favourable conditions for spore dispersal in the autumn period.

One inescapable fact is however, that the larger each individual cut (especially when multiplied by the total number of cuts on each plant) the greater the statistical likelihood of disease occurrence will be. This is because there will be more fresh, open wound areas upon which airborne disease spores may alight.

Interestingly, the likelihood of a wound to bleed will also affect the possibility of infection. Pathogens need favourable conditions in which to grow once inoculated. The sap exuded from a wound is characteristically nutrient rich (especially in spring) and provides a rich nutrient solution for bacterial or fungal spores. In addition to this, some of the sap that bleeds to the surface often retreats within a few minutes into the wood, carrying any alighting spores with it. In this way they can find a favourable and sheltered growth site and do not need continued moisture on the wound surface.

The advantages of square cuts

- Small wound area.
- Reduced chances of 'ribboning'.
- Reduced chances of bud damage in case of opposite buds.

The advantage of sloping cuts

- Reduced chances of bud damage in case of alternate buds.

Timing of Pruning

Timing is crucial when pruning woody plants, as many woody ornamentals are pruned according to their date of flowering. Spring-flowering plants, such as Forsythia, are normally pruned only after they bloom as pruning them during the dormant season will remove flower buds formed the previous autumn. On the other hand, summer-flowering plants are generally pruned during the dormant winter season. The growth and flowering habit of the shrub must therefore be considered in deciding when to prune, although timing will also vary according to position and locality, together with environmental factors such as soil type, rainfall, or exposure to wind and sunshine. Therefore, shrubs are often grouped in respect of their pruning needs according to their flowering or growth habits:

Shrubs that Flower on the Current Season's Wood or Growth

These subjects usually flower in the middle of, or towards the end of, a growing season. The earlier part of the season is spent in producing growth from buds that have rested during the dormant season. These shrubs are pruned by removing all shoots during the spring of each year. Timing is important – if the operation is left too late then growth will have already commenced meaning that its removal will weaken the plant. By removing the previous year's growth, the plant concentrates more vigour into fewer growths and produces a reduced number of flowers although these will be of a greater size. Examples include *Buddleja davidii*, *Caryopteris*, *Perovskia* and *Spiraea japonica*.

Shrubs that Flower from the Previous Year's Wood

Many hardy deciduous shrubs fall within this group and they can be divided into the following categories:

Deciduous Shrubs that Flower on Strong Young Growth

Flowering either very early, often before leaf or shoot growth with flower buds opening directly upon the older wood (for example *Ribes* and *Forsythia*) or on short laterals in early summer (for example *Philadelphus* or *Weigela*). These are pruned immediately after flowering, by cutting back flowered growth to strong young shoots lower down. This allows for new younger growth to develop fully in the extra light and air before flowering next year. In addition to this, up to a fifth of the oldest stems are cut to near their base each year.

Deciduous Shrubs that Flower from New Growth from or near Ground Level

These characteristically complete their flowering by late spring, meaning that the flowers appear around the same time as the foliage, for example: *Kerria*, *Neillia* and *Prunus triloba*. They are pruned immediately after flowering, by removing previously flowering shoots back to vigorous side-shoots and removing a third of stems by cutting them back to ground level each year.

Deciduous (mostly medium to large) Shrubs that Form a Well-branched Framework

These are all generally shrubs that need little in the way of regular pruning, as their whole attraction lies

in their natural growth habit, while some react poorly when pruned. Examples include snowy mespilus (*Amelanchier*), *Coryopsis*, witch hazel (*Hamamelis*) and lilac (*Syringa*). Most are pruned in late winter after flowering (when still dormant) usually limiting pruning to the removal of crossing or badly-positioned shoots. Deciduous magnolias also fall into this category and are pruned in the same way, although they are not worked on until late summer.

Deciduous Shrubs with Flowers Born Terminally on Previous Year's Growth during mid- to Late-Summer

These are often shrubs that require only a very light level of pruning such as lacecap and mophead hydrangeas. In early spring, the dead flower heads are cut back to the first (or at least a pair of) strong buds, while one in four of the oldest stems are cut out to near ground level in order to encourage new ones from the base.

Deciduous Shrubs that Produce Flowering Spurs on the Older Wood

These are shrubs with branches upon which spurs develop from year to year and occur even on really old wood. This habit is most common in members of the rose family, for example *Malus*, *Pyrus* and *Prunus*. They normally need very little in the form of pruning except occasional stopping during the growing season to encourage more spur formation.

Hard Pruning

Many shrubs benefit from being cut back hard annually. This can be done for a variety of reasons but is commonly seen on semi-hardy subjects such as Fuchsia to promote new young shoots, flowers, foliage or stems, for example *Cornus* (for coloured stems), *Eucalyptus* (to retain young shoots with juvenile foliage) and *Cotinus coggyia* (to promote young shoots of coloured foliage). Hard pruning is almost always carried out in early- to mid-spring and involves cutting the stems back to a stool (essentially a stump of a pre-determined size) or in a few cases, such as *Rubus cockburniana*, to ground level.

Evergreen Shrubs

Provided there is sufficient room for their develop-ment, most evergreen subjects require little by way of pruning. Pruning is often limited to the removal of dead flowers (dead heading), or removing wayward shoots or branches affecting the overall symmetry of the shrub. Dead, diseased and dying shoots may be removed at any time of year while winter-damaged growth is removed between April and May.

Some evergreen shrubs flowering on current or the previous year's wood, are actually grown principally for their foliage and as such, this is the main focus of the effects of pruning. Examples of this include *Elaeagnus*, *Fatsia*, *Hebe*, Portugal laurel (*Prunus lusitanica*) and *Rosmarinus*. Most need no regular pruning, but will benefit if any vigorous or badly posi-tioned growths are removed in the spring.

Many evergreen shrubs or sub-shrubs benefit from harder pruning to maintain a compact habit or increase their flowering potential, for example *Santolina*, *Hypericum* and *Mahonia aquifolium*.

Others such as lavender and the heathers *Calluna* or *Erica vagans*, benefit from regular annual trimming to promote young foliage and/or flower development and also to prevent them from becoming leggy. This is usually done in spring by cutting back the flowered shoots to 1.5 to 2.5cm (½ to 1in) from older wood.

Climbers and Wall Shrubs

Many shrubs and climbers are grown against or within the shelter of walls. Among these there are those plants that can be considered true climbers, with the remain-der being more correctly known as wall shrubs, need-ing to be pruned, trained and supported in order to maintain this habit. South- or west-facing walls often provide more sheltered conditions, thereby increasing the range that can be grown in what may otherwise be inhospitable conditions within a garden. The grouping includes a wide range of species that have consider-able variation in form and habit that can be grouped according to their growth habits and requirements.

Pruning evergreens is often limited to the removal of dead flowers, and removing wayward shoots or branches affecting the shrub's overall symmetry.

Ivy *Hedera helix* (RIGHT) and *Hydrangea petiolaris* (BOTTOM RIGHT) produce adventitious roots from their stems that cling tightly to the wall or support on which they are grown.

True Climbers

These are subjects that cling hard against the wall or support and include familiar examples such as the common Ivy *Hedera helix* and *Hydrangea petiolaris*. These plants produce adventitious roots from their stems that cling tightly to the wall or support on which it is grown. Pruning options usually involve clipping the whole surface area once or twice a year in the case of ivy, usually before and during the growing season to retain a good cover without allowing stems to grow out from the wall, although most self-clinging climbers need little or no pruning or clipping other than perhaps cutting back the mature branches when and if required.

Shrubs Trained Hard against a Wall

These are natural climbers which are frequently also grown by tying them to some form of support system. They are grouped into four main categories for pruning purposes:

- Those that are pruned back to a permanent framework and spur system, for example *Wisteria*, where a few permanent branches are trained to provide a framework and the remaining growths pruned back in summer and again hard in winter to promote spur formation for fruit and flower production.

- Subjects that are pruned annually after flowering by removing old wood. This is done to encourage young wood that then produces flowers the next year. This can result in much of the older wood being removed although the oldest wood is usually left. Care must be taken with many climbers of this type as the old growths tend to twine around each other, for example honeysuckle *Lonicera*.

- Climbers that are pruned back hard each year, often to near ground level. These grow rapidly, flowering on growth produced the same season.

Old growth is removed in spring of each year. Many Clematis plants in the *jackmanii* and *viticella* groups are pruned in this way.

- Shrubs that gain height by means of their scandent growth habit, for example *Forsythia suspensa*. These types tend to produce large growths, which clamber and may need pruning to restrict their growth.

Non-Climbing Shrubs Planted Against a Wall

Shrubs that are non-climbing may still be trained to provide coverage of a wall or fence. For instance a system of branches may be trained into a fan design and laterals may be pruned to promote flowers and fruit; a system that is well suited to *Chaenomeles speciosa* and *Prunus triloba* 'Multiplex'. However, less formal arrangements may also be used and these often suit slightly tender shrubs such as *Abutilon megapotamicum*, *Ceanothus* and *Fremontodendron*. In general the pruning of these takes place in early spring, where flowered shoots are cut back to two or four buds from the main framework branches. Early flowering specimens such as *Pyracantha* on the other hand, are pruned in late summer.

Finally, shrubs are grown against a wall for additional support or shelter. Most of these are somewhat tender and pruning is usually only necessary to keep the shrub within bounds, mostly involving the removal of older wood in order to restrict the plant's size.

Renovating Shrubs through Pruning

Old shrubs, or those that have become neglected, often become overgrown, full of crowded stems and dead wood. As a consequence of this, any new growth is weak, and flower production often decreases. If this happens, it may well be possible to prune them in order to rejuvenate their growth.

Complete renovation is the most drastic way to prune a neglected or outgrown shrub, and is a method that can be attempted on almost all deciduous shrubs. It simply involves removing all stems to 10–20cm (4–8in) from the ground or to a low framework of branches around 20-45cm (8-18in) high. This often results in dense re-growth, which may need subsequent thinning out as the season progresses, to select the strongest, best placed shoots.

A staggered renovation is a more gradual affair, usually taking place over two or three years. This allows a measure of judgement, both in gauging its response to the treatment as well as maintaining the natural shape and can prove an ideal approach for shrubs where the response is uncertain. The first year involves the removal of dead, damaged, diseased, crossing and rubbing shoots down to ground level, to a maximum of half the growth while cutting back the remaining older stems by half, to a vigorous side shoot or healthy outward-facing bud. In the second year, new shoots are thinned out (if excessive), while the remaining older branches are shortened or cut back. In the third year (if the process is extended this far) any remaining older stems are removed before returning to the normal pruning regime in subsequent years.

Hedges

There are many deciduous and evergreen shrubs that respond to clipping or trimming by producing dense or compact growth, and therefore they make ideal hedges. It should be remembered that 'clipping' and 'trimming' a hedge is really only a form of pruning and that the same basic principles of pruning apply. Depending upon their habit of growth and subsequent clipping or trimming, hedges are categorized into two main types.

Formal hedges are usually grown to provide a barrier, screen or windbreak or as a 'backdrop' to an ornamental planting scheme. The aim is to produce a hedge of the required height and width but one that is also sufficiently dense in its growth. Formal hedges should always be slightly wider at the base than at the top; if it were the other way around the top growth might shade out the lower and restrict its growth as well as making it vulnerable to damage from snow or wind. When clipping a formal hedge, start at the bottom and establish the width required before working upwards.

The frequency of clipping for a formal hedge will depend upon the particular plant species used together with the amount of growth and also, perhaps, the standard of maintenance required. Typically, a formal hedge will be trimmed as often as every four to six weeks from mid-spring until early autumn, or as little as twice per year in the case of less formal hedges.

On the other hand, informal hedges, while they may serve the same purpose as a formal hedge, often have the added attraction of floral display and/or fruits. This can make them an attractive feature in their own right, and one that is lower in maintenance as they generally require less pruning or trimming. Many flowering shrubs can be grown as an informal hedge with good examples including *Berberis stenophylla*, Deutzia, and shrub roses. They are pruned in exactly the same way as if they were a specimen shrub.

Caring for the Roots

The roots of woody plants, like those of any other plants, perform certain basic functions which are vital to the health and wellbeing of the plant. Essentially, they take up water and nutrients, provide physical support, grow, move towards water and over time thicken and develop; in order to enable this; the soil must be the right kind of environment. Roots are alive and must therefore breathe. Soil then, must contain sufficient air (oxygen) or the roots will die; it must be moist, cohesive (and thereby supportive), as well as rich in nutrient. Essentially, it must not be toxic to life processes.

Even soils that would otherwise be suitable for a given tree or shrub species may prove inhospitable if the optimum structure is not maintained. This is rarely a problem in cultivated ground but if it becomes

Ground that is compacted, covered with paving or buildings, can ultimately cause roots a problem due to shortage of oxygen and organic matter.

compacted, waterlogged or is covered with paving or buildings, the conditions rapidly deteriorate; mainly due to a lack of oxygen and a shortage of organic matter. This leads to a depletion of the micro-organisms in the soil environment, which in turn limits nutrient cycling and ultimately the nutrient flow to plants. In short the roots, even if they can survive the asphyxiating conditions, find themselves in a soil that is essentially sterile. Not only this, many roots depend upon symbiotic relationships with nitrogen-fixing bacteria (in the case of the pea family) and *Mycorrhiza*, which form intimate associations with roots and assist greatly with the uptake of nutrient.

Put simply then, without an air supply, the soil becomes a toxic wasteland that roots will struggle in and if the roots struggle, so does the whole plant. Ironically, for even the largest tree, it is the top 30cm (1ft) of the root system that is the most important region. This is because the majority of soil organisms need oxygen in order to survive, and this quickly becomes depleted deeper into the soil. As tree and shrub roots often depend intimately upon their activities, the result is that rooting is usually limited to a fairly narrow band of the soil. The shallow rooting tendency of most trees and shrubs often renders them extremely vulnerable to damage, even in a garden setting. In such a location frequent cultivations in their root-zones can prove damaging, despite otherwise being favourable to the soil.

While young trees and shrubs are dominated by tap roots that anchor the trees directly into the ground, as they grow, anchorage is increasingly provided by lateral roots which radiate from the top of the tap root. These act like 'guy ropes' and prevent root rotation gradually coming to dominate the root system getting longer and thicker and branching as they grow. As the root system develops and becomes more extensive, the roots of larger shrubs and especially trees form a rigid mass – like wheel spokes – that fuse over time to form what is known as a root plate, which is often solid and similar to the crown's dimensions. Ironically, these are simply the culmination of a much larger, more important root network, involved in the harvesting of water and nutrient, vital for the health and wellbeing of the plant.

The spread of the root-zone for most woody plants is at least twice the spread of the above ground parts (that is, trunk and branches) and it is extremely important that roots are kept in a state of good health. Essentially, this simply means avoiding compaction, and whenever possible forgoing cultivation. The easiest solution here is actually remarkably similar and involves spreading a layer of springy, open mulch around their bases. If the ground has already become compacted, it can be aerated quite simply using a

Providing a deep, springy layer of mulch around the base of trees or shrubs helps prevent compaction and maintains a healthy environment for their roots.

digging fork. This is best done when the soil is slightly moist to ensure maximum penetration into the soil, without damaging its structure, and should only be done from the edge of the crown or top-growth outward. Done manually, this can seem time-consuming and laborious, but it is very effective for relieving localized compaction while improving surface drainage and soil air supply. An ideal mixture for the mulch would consist of leaf-mould or other compost, mixed with partially rotted woodchip, spread across the root-zone to a depth of around 5 to 8cm (2 to 3in). The resulting cover remains open, allows easy penetration of water, and prevents compaction at or near the surface while gradually breaking down into a food source for soil organisms. It should need topping up every couple of years.

Many garden plants such as this spider flower (*Cleome*) produce abundant seed that can be collected and used to grow plants in the following season.

Propagation Basics

Despite a seemingly huge variety of methods employed in the propagation of plants, there are two basic types of plant propagation: vegetative – taking cuttings, for example – and sowing seed. The ability to successfully raise plants from either existing stock or seed that is either collected or purchased is often seen as the 'true mark of a gardener' and can prove not only economically desirable but also the most sustainable option in most situations.

Successful propagation of most plants generally requires only a few items of simple equipment including trays, pots, and compost. A propagator or greenhouse is not a requirement but can greatly aid the success rate and early growth. Perhaps more importantly, though, is the consideration of space. Even a modest-sized nursery will need space to be allocated, where there will be enough space not only for raising the seeds or cuttings but also for putting out the pots for growing the new plants on. Remember also that seedlings and young plants require frequent care during the growing season, although this care and patience will be well worth it in the end as the plants grow large enough to plant out and take their place in the garden.

Propagation from Seed

Seed can essentially be classed in three ways. The commonest and easiest type is that which can be collected, dried and stored prior to sowing – the so called 'orthodox' seed. Nuts and many larger seeds are difficult to store as they will only germinate when fresh and as such are usually referred to as 'recalcitrant' seed. The remaining type are the berries and softer fruits that not only need the soft fruit removing before they can be sown, but the resultant seed is often short lived (recalcitrant) and must be sown at once to retain its viability (ability to germinate and grow).

What do Seeds Need to Start Germination?

Germination, put simply, is the resumption of growth of the embryonic plant inside the seed. This embryo lies in a dormant state, only barely alive until conditions are correct for growth to resume; with some seeds – such as poppies – being able to survive successfully in this dormant state for fifty years or more.

Most however, are capable of lasting for only a few years before the embryo dies and the seed becomes 'unviable'. The term viable seed is the term used to describe seed that is alive and in a healthy state, thereby allowing germination; as time passes, the amount of viable seed usually decreases under normal storage conditions.

In order to germinate, seeds require moisture, warmth and oxygen, with most seeds germinating best between 18.5° to 24°C (65° to 75°F) and although the majority of seeds will happily germinate in light some, such as periwinkle *Vinca*, *Viola* and *Verbena*, germinate best in the dark. While the majority of seeds are easy to grow, a few species have specific germination requirements that require knowledge of the particular species. Bought seed of course have specific instructions on their packaging, while self-collected seed on the other hand may require a bit of guesswork. As a general rule, small dust-like seeds such as thyme, basil or Begonia, probably need light to germinate. If you suspect this to be the case, make sure that the seed is well pressed into the moist mixture, but do not cover it. Conversely, larger seed is most commonly covered to twice its thickness, preferably using a light substance such as finely sieved compost to do this.

Some seed can be a little trickier to get started than others and the commonest problem is caused by cold temperature dormancy. This is mostly found in plant

species that have their origins in cooler climates. However, the way around this is relatively straightforward and simply involves a treatment called 'stratification'. This involves covering them in some damp material, such as compost, leaf mould or sand depending upon their size. Large seed can be kept in organic matter but smaller seed is best mixed with sand to make sowing easier later on. Keeping seeds in a refrigerator at about 4.5°C (40°F) for up to three months, removing them after this time when they should be ready to germinate. There are many examples of seeds that germinate better after stratification, some common ones being oaks and hellebores.

Sowing Seed in the Open

Most garden soils are well suited for raising seed and only slight modifications are usually necessary to do so successfully. The real secret of success lies in preparing the ground in a way that will enable the seed to germinate evenly and grow in a uniform environment; it involves the preparation of a seedbed capable of providing the seed with the environment that it needs.

Preparing a seedbed is quite simple. Following cultivation, the ground is levelled using a rake held at a shallow angle, to break down any large clods. The art of levelling is to keep the rake angle shallow and move the high spots over into the low spots with even strokes of the rake. To do this, hold the rake firm at the rear and let the shaft run smoothly through the front hand. All stones and large obstructions, including organic matter such as twigs or other plant debris, should be removed by combing it out with the teeth of the rake while holding the rake in a near vertical position. The soil is then firmed with light treading, using the flat of the foot, before lightly raking one last time, again at a shallow angle, to produce a light, fluffy surface that runs freely through the teeth of the rake without obstructions; the perfect environment for sowing and growing seeds.

The seed of most hardy plants will germinate quite successfully once the temperature gets above 7°C (45°F). While the seeds carry their own food supply that provides them with everything they need for those

To form a seed bed, the soil is first raked thoroughly to produce a light, 'fluffy' surface that runs freely through the teeth of the rake without obstructions.

Scattering it over the surface of the compost sows small seed; it is important that this is done sparingly so as to avoid overcrowding of seedlings.

first crucial days following germination, once the plant begins to establish and grow it needs soil-borne nutrients; meaning that the soil it is growing in needs to be of the right fertility for the plant. Poorer soils can benefit from the addition of a base dressing of fish blood and bone, for example, prior to sowing in order to give the boost that the developing plant needs. Richer, loamy soils on the other hand, need only be properly dug and prepared to support seed germination.

The method used to sow seed will of course depend upon its intended purpose. 'Broadcasting', for example, is an ancient form of seed sowing that is normally used to sow seed in the position in which it will finally grow, often well suited to large areas like lawns or green manure crops. As the name suggests, it involves a 'broad, casting action' that separates the seed to an even spacing. It is simple,

TOP RIGHT: **In order to ensure that the seed is sown in a straight row, it is a good idea to set a tight string line along the entire length of the intended row.**

MIDDLE RIGHT: **Using the string line as a guide, draw the corner of a 'swan necked' hoe to create a drill of about 1–2 cm depth, depending upon the seed's requirements.**

RIGHT: **Sow seed thinly along the row, station sowing any that are large enough to handle by placing two or three at intervals that will form the final plant spacing.**

yet remarkably easy to do badly. The easiest way to do this on a smaller scale is to split the seed into two halves, mixing small seed with fine sand. Scatter the seed carefully through, from a closed hand, between the thumb and crooked forefinger, letting it run out in even arcs as you move your arm from side to side. Sow each half of the seed at a 90° angle to the other, thereby assuring an even distribution of the seed. Gently rake the seed in once sown and lightly water if needed.

In gardens though, the most commonly practised method of sowing seed outdoors involves sowing it in rows. The row is a straight line, set with the object of using the space and ultimately the seed itself economically. The row is set with a taut string line, against which the corner of a swan necked hoe is drawn, thereby creating a shallow drill of about 1 to 2 cm (½ to ¾in) in depth, depending upon the seed's individual requirements. Dry ground can be watered after the drill is made before sowing the seed thinly, and fine seed can

be mixed with silver sand to make it easier to distribute evenly. Seeds of larger growing plants, particularly those with seed that is large enough to handle, can easily be 'station-sown', placing two or three seeds at intervals that will be the eventual plant spacing. If all three germinate, then the two weaker ones are removed or transplanted to gaps where none germinated.

Seeds such as peas and beans benefit from being sown in a wide row; a practice whereby two rows are effectively station sown at once, on each side of a wide drill that is 15cm (6in) across. The drill is made with the flat of the hoe and following sowing, the soil is carefully raked back, ensuring that the seeds are not disturbed from their stations.

When you sow a row or area of seeds, you should get into the habit of labelling it straight away. Try to avoid using the packet to do this as they are easily blown away, eaten by insects or just tend to deteriorate. Re-usable plastic or home-made wooden labels are probably the best option. Each label should have the name and variety of the plant sown. In addition to this you may wish to put down the date that you sowed it and if, for example, it was pre-treated by soaking. This can help you to build up your own knowledge of what works for you (and indeed what doesn't) in your own garden.

Protecting Young Seedlings

Seed beds, with their fine, fluffed earth, often act as magnets to birds and animals. Some may wish to take the seed from the ground but in truth, most will find it more attractive as a dust bath or litter tray! Once the seedlings emerge though, birds often find them irresistible and they can cause considerable damage, so the latter must be kept out using some form of barrier. This is easily achieved, as any structures do not need to be large, permanent or even particularly sturdy. The simplest method can be to form a low tunnel of chicken wire, supporting this on hoops, 'cloche style'. For larger areas, a series of stakes hammered into the ground can be covered with netting to keep the birds at bay. Small twiggy sticks, or sticks with cotton stretched between, are also effective but less easily removed to allow you to tend and weed the seedbed.

Where necessary, seedlings can be encouraged to germinate more quickly by providing a protective cover from the elements such as a cloche, or fleece.

Thinning and Transplanting Seedlings Raised Outdoors

As they grow, plants need space to develop. Those that are growing too closely compete not only for space but also for light, water and nutrient and, in addition to this competitive stress, also become prone to a variety of fungal diseases as the air cannot move around them. Thinning them out helps avoid the majority of these problems and will result in larger, stronger and healthier plants in the long run.

In essence, thinning is two processes rolled into one. Firstly, it is the removal of all the plants that are excess to requirements. Secondly, it is the selection of the strongest plants that will be retained for use. Before starting to thin, dry ground must be watered, preferably the evening before. If a row is being thinned, a measuring stick marked with the appropriate plant spacing can be used to show the approximate position of the individual plants. Remove all the plants in between each of the markers, selecting the healthiest plant at or near the mark on the stick to remain. If there are no plants, then one can be transplanted there. When pulling the plants out, it is a good idea to put a finger either side of the one that is being kept, to ensure that its roots are not disturbed. Once finished, the row should be watered with a fine rose on a watering can to re-firm the soil around the remaining plants. The seedlings that have been removed can be put on the compost heap. Avoid thinning with this method on hot, dry days or in windy conditions, as the remaining seedlings may become water stressed if their roots are disturbed. The alternative in this case is to snip the seedlings off at ground level with a pair of sharp scissors, thereby avoiding root disturbance.

Transplanting Seedlings

Seedlings raised in open ground can be transplanted as soon as they are large enough to handle; usually once the first true leaves (that is not the initial seed leaves) have appeared. The conditions for transplanting outdoor seedlings are ideally during damp overcast weather, as this will aid in helping to avoid the seedlings' roots drying out. As with thinning the plants,

When watering seed sown indoors use a fine upturned rose on a watering can to ensure as little disturbance as possible to the compost and seedlings.

they will need watering the evening before. It is best to dig up only a few plants at a time, discarding any that are weak, damaged or appear to be sick. Seedlings can be placed in a plastic bag to maintain humidity around them while they are out of the ground.

If seedlings are to be replanted in rows then a line can be set, in a similar manner to the way that it is set for preparing a seed drill, with the plant positions determined by their eventual size. The seedlings are planted using a dibber or a thin trowel, firming lightly around the base before moving on to the next. Once the row is completed, water them in.

Sowing Seed Under Cover

Sowing seed under glass is a good way of both extending the growing season and raising those tender plants that can only survive outside in the warmer months of the year. Plants raised under glass can be grown on until they reach a size where they are better able to resist pest attack and can also be planted out at their final spacing, thereby avoiding the need for thinning or gapping up in rows. In short it offers a greater variety and choice in the garden.

Tender specimens, or those intended for early harvest, can be sown under cover, using trays or pots for small seed, and individual pots for larger types.

A variety of containers may be used to raise seed under cover, the commonest form being the plastic seed tray that has now largely replaced wooden seed trays. Wooden seed trays, of course, have a lovely rustic and organic appeal but are in fact difficult to keep clean and may well harbour plant diseases. The best 'plastic' trays are actually made of durable polyurethane, meaning they can be re-used, and are much better than the flimsy, thin moulded plastic that is really only intended for single use. However, for those wishing to raise only a few plants, small, 9cm (3½in) pots provide a smaller, space-saving alternative.

Small pots and modular trays offer the advantage of not subjecting the developing plant to any root disturbance from sowing to being planted out in their eventual position. The same is true of some of the biodegradable pots that are sold on the market. Indeed, home-made paper pots using newspaper are better (environmentally speaking) than any bought product, although any bought items made from recycled material should ideally be favoured over 'new' items.

Finally, it is perfectly feasible to use (or, more properly, re-use) plastic cups, vegetable packing trays and any other throw-away items in the interest of helping

to avoid them going on a one-way trip to the landfill site. Old plastic bottles make good individual propagation cowls for small pots and 'milky' plastic bags can also be used to cover the tops of pots and trays to maintain humidity. Recycling is, when all is said and done, something that can save you money as well as save the environment.

The Need for Heat

Most seeds have a preferred temperature within which they will grow. A warm greenhouse, conservatory or living room will often provide this, although seeds needing constant high temperatures may need a propagator. These are, in effect, mini hothouses that help to keep the seed in a warm moist environment both above and below the soil line. Many gardeners think that they need one of these but cheaper alternatives are often possible using recycled materials. Expensive propagators can involve the use of electric soil warming cables, the real luxury ones possessing thermostats to control the soil temperature. Most are designed for greenhouse use, but some models exist that are narrow enough for use on a windowsill. They are, without doubt, a luxury though, and it is possible to grow seeds quite successfully without one.

Once seeds begin to germinate they can be moved gradually into a less humid environment. The trays or pots can be freed of plastic covers and bags, or the propagator lid can be vented and, after a few days, removed. As soon as the seedlings reach a size where they can be handled – usually once the second set of leaves appear – they should be carefully pricked out into individual pots or larger boxes and trays. Always handle them by the leaves, gently lifting each seedling from beneath, using a dibber. Never hold them by the stems as this can cause a great deal of damage to the developing plant. They should be spaced at least 5cm (2in) apart to allow subsequent development. Keep them warm and sheltered, watering them with a fine, upturned rose in a watering can. They must be gradually hardened off (acclimatized to outdoor conditions) in a frame or similar before planting out.

Hardening-off Plants
Raised Under Cover

Plants that have been grown in a glasshouse cannot be put outdoors straight away as their growth is too soft to withstand the cold. This is overcome by gradually hardening them off; in other words a gradual acclimatization to outdoor conditions. This is done in stages, initially by removing covers from the seedlings and, once they are growing well, by moving young plants from the glasshouse into a cold frame. If the plants were raised in a cold frame, from there they can be planted out under cloches, low polythene tunnels or horticultural fleece. Cloches and cold frames should then have their covers removed or the fleece rolled back during the day, replacing this at night for

a week or two, before planting out and removing the cloches or fleece completely after a couple of weeks, according to the weather conditions

Even if young plants have been hardened off prior to planting out, they will still suffer a certain amount of stress as a result of their move. The degree to which this affects their growth in the long term will of course vary, and depends upon the steps taken to avoid the problem.

It is worth remembering that no matter how carefully they are handled while planting some, albeit slight, damage is still likely to occur. Roots, stems and leaves can all be affected, and the plant will need to recover from this while dealing with the challenge of establishing itself in its new home. As a rule of thumb, the younger the plant, the more quickly it will re-acclimatize. Having said

Seeds sown under cover germinate rapidly and are usually ready to be transplanted or potted on once they have formed their first set of 'true' leaves.

this though, very young plants are naturally more susceptible to other stresses, meaning that it may well be better to grow them on a little first.

The fact that the plant experiences a change of location can also cause problems at first, although typically young plants recover from this quite quickly. Plants that have been grown in a sheltered location, for example, initially struggle if they are planted in an open situation, even if the site is not particularly windy. Equally, plants grown in an open sunny situation would not benefit from being transplanted to a cool shady place.

The real trick then is to ensure that they are gradually acclimatized to their new setting. Plants not used to an open setting may need a little shelter, or light shade for a few days as they get used to their new home. Remember also, that even if they come from a similar location to that which they are planted into, they may well have been growing in close proximity to one another; gaining benefit from the humidity this promotes. However, once planted or transplanted they will be at their final spacing and this sudden isolation, while beneficial in the longer term, can cause a measure of water stress in those first few days. Be prepared to cover them with some fleece if a sudden cold snap threatens and make sure they get enough water while their roots are establishing.

Protecting Vulnerable Stock

Some newly-planted specimens attract the unwanted attention of pests such as birds or rabbits and, in these cases, it is important to keep the pests out. Fortunately, they can easily be deterred by covering the specimens temporarily with netting. If birds and rabbits prove to be a major problem it may be worth making more permanent fences or cages to grow crops inside.

Frames or hoops, fixed over vegetable beds can be used to support various protection according to the season; fleece or polythene in early spring and autumn, netting to keep pests out and shade in the height of summer. If opting for a more permanent protective structure though, it is a good idea to make sure that it can be moved off, as this will allow access to maintain the plants and ultimately to cultivate the ground in the following spring.

Even though you will need to water new plants regularly, be careful not to overdo it. Many plants, including most root crops and members of the onion family, need only be watered during their establishment and even then do not like to be too wet. Feeding is also not necessary in the early stages, and in many cases it can prove detrimental to young sensitive roots. As a rule of thumb, if you applied a fertilizer before planting, you won't need to apply any more for two to three weeks after putting plants in when they show visible signs of growth.

Collecting Seed from the Garden

To many gardeners the idea of collecting seed seems a rather complicated, fiddly and time-consuming pastime, best avoided and left to the 'experts.' After all, seeds are available to buy from a huge number of outlets, are usually relatively cheap, and come with a ready set of instructions on handy packaging. Having said this, those with a sizable garden could save money by collecting seed and, perhaps more importantly, it is a sustainable option that involves no external inputs. Commercial supplies of seed usually originate from seed or plant material from a different area – or in some cases even another country – and may not always be best suited for the conditions in your local area. By gathering and propagating locally produced seed, you are helping to maintain what is essentially referred to as a 'landrace'; essentially a strain of that species or variety that is ideally suited for the area within which it is grown. Lastly, collecting and saving seed also removes the possibility that the seeds of prized plants become virtually lost to gardeners if they are no longer offered for sale or if they become difficult to find – as often happens to traditional or 'heirloom' varieties. Even without all of these obvious advantages, the inescapable truth is that collecting and saving seed often proves both enjoyable and satisfying.

Seeds can be collected from any garden plant that produces viable seeds, but hybrids should normally be avoided. Hybrids are produced from very specific crosses made by plant breeders, which often yield seeds that are either sterile or produce plants that are not true to type; that is they will not resemble their parent. This latter problem of variation can also occur with seeds taken from plants that have been naturally cross-pollinated by the wind or insects; a frequent result when different species or cultivars of a plant are grown together in a garden. Ideally, seed should only be collected from self-pollinated, non-hybrid and pure-bred species or varieties. Many annuals, particularly non-hybrid vegetables, yield seeds that can be saved. Some gardeners become so enthusiastic about seed saving that they join seed-saver groups that specialize in keeping heirloom varieties, many of which are essentially the ancestral forms of modern cultivars.

In order to collect the seed, the plant must of course be allowed to produce them in the first place. Once the flowers fade, the plants should be checked weekly for seed formation and ripeness. Of course, plants vary in respect of their seed-head type, meaning that there are several methods that can be used to collect and separate the seeds from the plant.

Seeds that form within pods, such as poppies, peas, and beans, often remain on the plant for a long time after maturity but can also start to disperse as soon as they ripen. The pods are gathered at the point when they are just ripening (that is starting to dry on the plant) before bringing them indoors to air-dry. The whole pod is collected and once fully dry it is broken open to remove the seed.

Seeds of many ornamental annuals, herbaceous perennials, and herbs disperse very quickly as soon as they are ripe by scattering. As a consequence of this, the seed-heads must be regularly inspected to assess their maturity. Remember that picking unripe seed-heads will result in a harvest of immature and therefore unviable seed. Once at the point of ripening, gather them, ideally on a dry day, placing the seed heads in paper bag. In the case of plants such as Impatiens or Geranium, which have exploding seed pods capable of ejecting their seeds over long distances, the trick is to tie a paper bag or lightweight fabric bag around the flower heads before the seeds ripen in order to catch them as they scatter.

Plants with seeds encased in a fleshy fruit, such as tomatoes, squashes, melons or berries, need to have their seed separated from the pulp and be cleaned

A QUICK GUIDE TO COLLECTING SEED

- Seed is best collected on a dry, windless day.
- Only select healthy, pest- and disease-free plants, with seedpods that look ready to 'split'.
- Carefully cut off the entire seed-head, and put it into a paper (not plastic) bag.
- Make sure that the seed-head is upside-down in the paper bag, and close it, taking care not to crush the pods.
- Label the bag before putting it into a dry place for the seeds to ripen; the seeds will fall into the bag when they are completely dry.
- Check on the drying seeds regularly and when most of the pods have opened, tip out the contents onto a dry surface and separate seeds from any bits of seed-head or pod still attached.
- Store the cleaned seed in a small dry envelope, sealing and labelling this carefully.
- Store the packaged seed in a cool, dry place until ready to be used.

Storing Seed

- Packets of saved seed can be kept for longer periods if maintained in constant cool, dry conditions. The best way of doing this is to place them in airtight storage containers which are then stored at 4°C (39°F). A household refrigerator will easily do this, while the airtight container maintains dry conditions.
- Seeds of many plants can remain viable for up to five years if properly stored although most are best sown in the following season. Some plants such as Delphinium, Helleborus, onion and parsley produce short-lived seeds (that is ones that must ideally be sown immediately after they ripen) and they often lose viability if stored.
- Before planting, it is a good idea to check seed stored for more than a year to test its germination rate, as the effort to sow them directly in the garden may turn out to be a waste of time and effort if viability (and therefore the germination rate) is low. To check this, place a few of the seeds between paper towels that are kept constantly moist and between 18–21°C (65–70°F), checking them daily for germination. If the germination rate is seventy per cent or less, it may be worth obtaining new seed.

before they can be stored. This is simply done by letting the fruit become slightly overripe before squashing or extracting the pulp and seeds together. Dispose of the skin and non-seeded flesh and put the remaining pulp into some water for a day or two. After this time, put the mix in a strainer and run water through it until the seeds are clean. Spread the seeds out on a glass or metal dish (not paper or the seeds will stick to it) and put them in a well-aired place to dry. Large seeds may take a week to dry whereas smaller seeds should be ready after around four days.

In order to make sure that the collected seeds are viable next season, they must be stored in airtight containers in a cool, dry location. Ideally the containers should include a sachet of silica gel (a moisture-absorbing substance sold at photographic or craft shops) in each container before sealing it.

Lastly, remember that the seed of some plants is best sown immediately after harvesting; and it is worth finding out what the germination requirements are of all of the seeds you collect. An ideal and cheap way to do this is by consulting a seed catalogue. Remember that these are not only helpful in purchasing seed, but provide an excellent repository of information outlining how to raise them, normal flowering time, cultural requirements and disease resistance.

A Note of Caution

While it may prove tempting to collect and bring home seeds or plants seen while on holiday, particularly in foreign countries, this is often the way that serious insect pests and diseases are introduced. Not only that, but an introduced, (non-native) plant may become a noxious weed, not only in the garden to which it is imported but also to the wider environment if (and ultimately when) it escapes. Many countries operate strict import policies as a result and impose heavy fines on anyone found transgressing these.

Remember that the global cost of damage caused by introduced weeds has been estimated to be close to five per cent of global GDP (gross domestic product). Add to this the fact that virtually all ecosystem types on the planet are affected by invasive species and it quickly becomes clear that they pose a major threat. If you want to raise the seed of a new species, it is better to buy some from a reputable seed supplier in your own country, even if from that point forward you collect and save the seed yourself.

Famous Garden Escapees

• Water hyacinth (*Eichhornia Crassipes)* is a water weed native to the Amazon, once used as an ornamental, which clogs lakes or waterways in Africa and Southeast Asia. In Spain, its removal from 75km of the Guadiana river has cost nearly 15 million Euros.

• Japanese knotweed (*Fallopia japonica*) is an herbaceous plant introduced to Europe in the mid-nineteenth century as an ornamental garden plant. It rapidly became very invasive and is now one of the few plants to be legislated for in UK law.

Vegetative Propagation

In nature, most new plants are the result of seeds or spores. In certain circumstances however, plants produce offspring in other ways; a tendency that gardeners have long taken advantage of in order to raise plants quickly and easily from existing stock. The vegetative parts of the plant are simply the stems, roots and leaves and in certain circumstances, all of these parts can be used to produce a new plant; although the ease of this varies considerably between species. Most fruit trees, for instance, are propagated asexually, using a bud or a twig from a tree that produces exceptionally good fruit. When this bud or twig becomes an adult tree, it has the same qualities as the 'mother' tree and is essentially an identical clone of the mother plant. Other plants may be propagated more simply, as they have specialized roots, stems and leaves that have a tendency to form new plants; a natural inclination that renders vegetative propagation easy.

Plant Parts that can be used for Propagation

'Rhizomes', usually grow underground and although they appear root-like, are actually horizontal stems that often send out roots and shoots. 'Stolons' are similar to rhizomes, but these usually exist above ground level and sprout from an existing stem. Many of these are easily propagated, with iris and bamboo being common examples of plants propagated from rhizomes. 'Runners' are similar to stolons but arise from a crown bud and creep over the ground. Examples of plants propagated from runners are strawberries and spider plants.

Bulbs, such as tulips, onions and lilies consist of swollen leaves on a short stem. They are easily propagated from natural offsets that form next to the parent bulb or from sections of the bulb itself. In some species such as lilies, individual scales can be separated and propagated. Lilies also produce small bulbils in their leaf axils that will also produce bulbs if grown on for two to four years in a rich light soil. This same procedure applies for plants that form from offset corms, such as gladiolus

'Corms' are similar to bulbs and often confused with them. Structurally, however, a corm is different, consisting of a stem that is swollen as a food store. It is shorter and broader than a bulb. The leaves of the stem are modified as thin, dry membranes that enclose the corm and protect it against injury and drying. Examples of corms are Crocus and Gladiolus. True corms are usually propagated from offsets or from seed.

'Tubers' are underground swollen stems or roots that store food. An example of a stem tuber plant is a potato. These are used individually to produce new offspring, and are generally sold as seed potatoes. Root tubers such as Dahlia, Cyclamen and Anemone can be divided while dormant, provided that each divided segment has a bud attached that will form new shoots.

Before cuttings can be taken it is important that any tools to be used are sharpened, so as to ensure that they cut cleanly and precisely.

Methods Commonly Used in Vegetative Propagation

Root cuttings

Some plants can be propagated from roots. To produce a new plant from a root cutting, there must be a shoot bud present or it must be possible for the cutting to form one. The ability of root cuttings to form these buds depends on the time of year. The dormant (resting) season is usually best with Phlox and Euphorbia being examples of plants that may readily be propagated from root cuttings. They should be taken from newer root growth, making cuttings 3–10cm (1¼–4in) long from roots that are 1 to 1½cm (³⁄₈–½in) in diameter. A useful tip here is to cut straight through the end of the root closest to the stem but cut the other end on a slant. This allows you to remember which end is the top (the straight cut) and which is the bottom (the diagonal cut). Cuttings taken from

The stem of most plants needs to be cut just below a node (the point where leaves are attached to the stem) as it is here that roots are most likely to form.

Remove any leaves or side-growths on the lower stem before inserting it into compost, making sure that no leaves are touching each other or the compost.

dormant roots are placed in a moist rooting medium at 5°C (41°F) for around three weeks before they are planted upright in the pots. Thereafter, they are kept moist and warm in a bright location until growth is ready to plant out.

Stem Propagation

Many trees, shrubs and herbaceous plants are propagated from stem parts. A root system must be formed on a stem either before or after that stem has been removed from the parent plant. The two commonest methods used are layering and by stem cuttings.

The main difficulty involved in producing new plants from stem cuttings is keeping the stems alive while they form new roots. Some plant stems root better when the wood is soft and actively growing; others root best from mature wood. Cuttings taken from plants that are actively growing are called 'softwood cuttings'. These cuttings are taken from first-year branches that have not yet become woody. Many flowering shrubs are often propagated by softwood cuttings with late spring and early summer being the best times

When cutting the stems for hardwood cuttings, the uppermost edge is cut with a slanted cut, meaning that it is always easy to recognize which is the top.

Hardwood cuttings need healthy wood from the previous summer that is about 'pencil thickness' cut into sections approximately 15–20cm (6–8in) in length.

for success with this method. Take cuttings 5–10cm (2–4in) long. Larger cuttings produce larger plants sooner, but they are prone to more rapid water loss. Make cuts slightly below a leaf node (the point where the leaf meets the stem) and remove any leaves on the lower section. Insert them into compost, making sure that no leaves are touching each other or the compost. Remove any cuttings immediately from the tray or pot if they die and pot healthy cuttings up promptly once they recommence growth following rooting.

Cuttings taken after the wood is mature are known as 'hardwood cuttings' and these are taken while the plant is dormant. Cuttings can be taken two weeks after leaf fall and before bud burst. Healthy wood that was produced the previous summer and is about pencil thickness is selected and cut into sections of approximately 15–20cm (6–8in). Several cuttings can be made from the same branch of some shrubs. The basal cuts are made just below a node, and upper cuts slightly above a bud. The upper cut should be

The cuttings are then inserted vertically in moist sandy topsoil or sand leaving about $1/3$ of their length above ground, and placed in a cool shady place.

slanted so that a cutting is less likely to be inserted into the compost upside down. Bury cuttings vertically in moist sandy topsoil or sand leaving 2½ – 5cm (1–2in) of cutting above ground, and put them in a cool shady place, taking care not to let them freeze. In spring, remove the cuttings from storage and plant them at the same depth in pots or open ground in a sheltered position and in dappled shade. Keep them moist until a root system forms and transplant them the following spring while they are still dormant.

TOP LEFT: **Lift a whole clump of a well established herbaceous crown and begin by pushing a digging fork into the middle of the crown.**

BOTTOM LEFT: **Using another fork of a similar size, push this into the crown next to the first fork so that the tines are parallel with each other.**

BELOW: **Pull the fork handles together then push them apart, to break the crown into two. Repeat if necessary and replant the sections.**

Layering

Layering is a simple job where a young branch is bent down to the soil and pegged down. The tip is then bent back upward forming a 'leg' and the bend is covered with soil. At the point of the bend roots will form, as the bend interferes with the flow of sap thereby encouraging root formation. Sap flow can be further reduced by twisting the stem, or cutting a 'tongue' in the lower side of the bark with a sharp knife. The stem will need earthing up throughout the summer to encourage stem rooting. Species suited to this method include Magnolia and Corylus (hazel).

Division

Division is a method usually practised only on herbaceous plants and it involves cutting or breaking up a crown or clump of suckers into segments. Each segment must have a bud and some roots and these are replanted. The clump is carefully dug up and split apart with two spades or forks, or 'chopped' with a shovel or large knife if the clump is firmly massed. Autumn-flowering perennials are commonly divided in spring, while those flowering in spring and summer are best done in the autumn.

Propagating Bulbs, Corms and Tubers

Bulbs, corm-forming and (most) tuberous species, if propagated from seed, can take from three to five years to reach mature flower size. Add to this the fact that many modern cultivars are extremely highly bred and therefore hybrids of uncertain origin; traits such as flower colour, size, habit or disease resistance cannot be guaranteed and the offspring may be highly variable as a result. For these reasons, the plants are normally propagated from small, embryonic plants that naturally form on the parent. There are a number of these including 'offsets' in the case of Allium, Crocus, Iris and Lilium; 'cormels' in the case of Gladiolus; or bulbils or 'bulblets' in the case of Allium, Narcissus and

Lilium. These are all naturally produced and easy to separate from the parent. In essence it is similar to dividing an herbaceous plant.

In the strictest terms, the miniature bulbs, known as bulblets, are only formed on 'true bulbs', for example Allium, Amaryllis, Crinum and Narcissus. They often naturally form around the base plate of the parent bulb and when these grow to full size, they are known as offsets. Offsets can be separated from the mother bulb and replanted into beds. The number of growing seasons required for the offsets to reach flowering size will depend upon the kind of bulb and size of the offset.

In certain bulb species though, the bulb can be divided into sections in order to force them into making new plants; techniques known as 'chipping' (in the case of, for example Allium, Narcissus and Hyacinth), 'scaling' (in the case of, for example Narcissus and Lilium), or 'scooping' (in the case of, for example Hyacinthus).

Chipping involves cutting the dormant bulb into several vertical sections (halves, quarters or eighths for instance) ensuring that each has a section of the base plate. These sections can then be planted upright in a mixture of equal volumes of leaf mould and sand. Over a few weeks, bulblets will develop from the basal plate between the bulb scales. These can then be transplanted into beds or pots to continue development.

Corms such as Gladiolus and Watsonia produce new corms on top of the old withered corm. Miniature corms called 'cormels' are often produced between the old and new corms though, and these can be separated from the mother corms and stored over winter for planting in the spring. These cormels usually require two or three years of growth to reach flowering size meaning that they may well be best grown in pots for the first year or so.

Tubers such as Cyclamen, tuberous roots such as Dahlia or Ranunculus and rhizomes such as bearded iris and Hemerocallis are propagated by cutting them into sections, each containing at least one bud. Special care should be taken when dividing the tuberous roots of Dahlia to ensure that each tuberous root has a piece of crown bearing a healthy bud.

GARDENING WITHOUT HARMFUL CHEMICALS

Conventional approaches to dealing with the yearly onslaught of garden pests and diseases was to carefully observe the plants and 'hit' the offending creatures with a spray thereby removing the problem in one fell swoop. The spray approach left a bitter legacy over the years however, with many chemicals proving steadily less effective and pests and diseases acquiring immunity to their effects. This in turn led to more spraying, a rise in the amounts of toxic residues in the environment and untold damage as a result. Ultimately, the sad irony is that often the only insects remaining in gardens are the very pests that the sprays were intended to control.

Controlling many of these problems is easier than might be supposed however, and frequently it simply involves working with nature to create a more natural environment. The insects and other creatures living in a garden are all part of a complex natural ecosystem, with probably less than one per cent of species encountered ever becoming garden pests. The other ninety-nine per cent are then merely 'innocent' garden residents, some of whom even prove to be 'beneficials' – a term that is used to denote one creature that eats or kills pests – while the remainder have no real effect on your garden plants whatsoever; except perhaps by contributing towards the normal healthy environment needed for growth.

It is worth remembering that pests and diseases are a fact of life and indeed nature itself. In every garden, each year sees the loss of some plants and even

experienced gardeners have to accept some of these losses. If these remain at just a few, or if those lost are small and easily replaced, then it is not really a problem. However, if plant losses rise, the effect can be more severe, meaning that it pays to be vigilant. Early losses can also be a warning of a greater problem in the making and if a plant is looking sickly, finding out what has caused the problem should be a priority. Once the cause is known, action can be taken in order to stop the problem from worsening.

Keeping your plants healthy is, of course, one of the keys to gardening success and while an outbreak of pests or disease can be very damaging, they are often rarer than is supposed. The occasional pest or limited disease occurrence may well be tolerable, provided that it is controlled and prevented from spreading. Often the real secret lies in maintaining plants in a healthy condition, thereby rendering them hardier and more resilient to the onslaught of pests and diseases. In a few cases though, some pests and diseases present a serious threat to garden plants, particularly if their effects are sudden and extreme. The sight of plants suffering under the onslaught of some sudden unexpected ailment can be extremely disheartening, particularly if you don't know what is causing it. Fortunately, the vast majority of conditions that afflict garden plants are relatively uncommon, and for those commoner remaining ills, the vast majority produce characteristic symptoms that make it possible to diagnose, and hopefully, treat the problem.

However, despite their relative rarity, the range of garden plants and abundance of potential problems means that even the few conditions that are likely to be encountered in a garden can add up to what seems an extensive list. The solution then is to become familiar with the basics of diagnosis. If you can get

OPPOSITE PAGE: **Bees, such as this mining bee pictured here on a cuckoo flower (*Cardamine pratensis*), are an essential part of both garden and wider ecology, but are extremely sensitive to pesticides and rapidly decline when and where these are used.**

Pests often only become apparent once they reach epidemic proportions such as here with this glasshouse mealy bug on a Cruel plant (*Araujia sericifera*).

Hares and deer are often the source of damage to newly planted tree stock during the winter, where the thin bark is stripped to get at the tissue below.

the problem down to a general cause, for example a pest, disease, or an environmentally related ailment (known as a disorder), diagnosing the specific cause and of course choosing the most appropriate treatment becomes more likely. This is vital, as the wrong diagnosis and wrong treatment can waste time and money, while of course ultimately failing to help the plants in question.

Recognizing the Cause of Problems

This can be a complex area, even for experienced gardeners, and ultimately a great deal can be learned from experience. It is important to understand the life cycles and (in the case of pests) the behaviour of the organisms responsible for ill health in the plants growing in the garden. The tendency of some gardeners to obliterate anything seen crawling on plants is a common overreaction and often serves merely to exterminate an innocent and often useful garden resident. It should always be remembered that only a fraction of the creatures seen in a garden are actually harmful; meaning that learning which are pests – and of course which are not – is essential.

Vigilance is extremely important then, and involves taking a regular 'close-up' look at plants to check for early symptoms of attack. This enables a swift diagnosis and can help show which plants are susceptible to particular pests or diseases.

What is a Pest?

Essentially a pest is an animal. This definition ranges from almost microscopic invertebrates such as the red spider mite; through visible pests such as aphids, beetles and molluscs (slugs and snails); to larger more visible creatures such as rabbits, birds and deer. What they all have in common is that they cause harm by directly eating the plant. Some chew, a great many suck juices from the stems and leaves while others steal

Even though not generally known as plant pests, wasps and ants often attack and damage ripe fruit in autumn, lured by the sugar.

fruit or blossom. One of the most disturbing aspects of pest infestations is that they have a tendency to arrive (seemingly quite suddenly) in large numbers and are often specific to one or a few related plant types. While most pests are visible, some are very small and may need a magnifying glass to see them. Others hide away out of sight and, in such cases, the only evidence of their presence is the damage caused by their feeding. In essence, there is nothing to beat regularly inspecting plants that are known to be susceptible and acting quickly at the first signs of their arrival.

What is a Disease?

Plant diseases are caused by microscopic parasites, which attack plants at the cellular level. As a consequence they cannot be seen with the naked eye, or with a hand lens, meaning they are only usually noticed once harm has occurred. By this point, however, obvious and sometimes extensive symptoms appear, often with an alarming suddenness and plant losses can be severe as a result. Despite this, diseases frequently start

Often, the only evidence of pests are signs of their activities, with rabbits for example often most apparent through droppings (TOP), burrows (MIDDLE) or damage to plants (BELOW).

The horse chestnut leaf-miner (*Cameraria ohridella*) while damaging to the tree's appearance, has little effect on its long term survival or overall health.

as a localized infection on the plant, meaning that prompt action can help save the rest of the plant or those around it. Plant diseases and their control are a complex area, although in essence they boil down to three major causes: fungi, bacteria and viruses.

Fungi are small, either unicellular or colonial, masses of cells, the vast majority of which are beneficial or benign to plants. Many of these have complex life cycles and are only visible at the reproductive phase or after damage occurs.

Bacteria are primitive, single-celled organisms which enter and infect individual plant cells. Once inside the plant they can reproduce rapidly, mostly causing harm due to toxins released inside the plant.

Viruses are small life forms that are incapable of independent life outside a particular host plant's cells. Essentially they hijack the cell and cause it to make copies of the virus, often killing the cell and sometimes debilitating or even killing the whole plant as a result of this.

Disease Symptoms

Disease symptoms can be tricky to diagnose but a few of the commoner ones are outlined here. Blights are usually noticed as a softening and death of tissue in patches, whereas damping off is a localized blight of the stem near the soil. Wilts, as the name suggests, are sudden wilting, usually of the stem tips, whereas foot rot (lower stem) and root rots are often less visible until close examination. The term 'anthracnose' usually refers to any skin tissue where black lesions appear, with leaf spots specifically affecting that area. Scab also affects the skin, being a hard corky layer on the stem's leaves and fruits of the plant. Cankers are areas of flaking or bleeding bark tissue, whereas yellowing and 'mosaics' are often disease related.

A few other disease-like conditions can be less threatening and are actually an interesting addition to the diversity in your garden. Galls for instance – and there are many of these – are what is called a 'hyperplasic deformation' of the plant tissue and are often caused by tiny mites, midges or wasps. They are mostly harmless and can occasionally be extremely curious shapes. Other deformations also occur such

CLOCKWISE FROM ABOVE: The fungal disease brown rot (*Monilinia fructicola*) affects ripe fruit, in warm, moist, humid conditions and can destroy an entire crop in just a few days.

Powdery mildew is a fungal disease which flourishes on many cucurbits (gourd family) in warm, dry weather and can reduce the crop and eventually kill the plants.

Rose black spot (*Diplocarpon rosae*) is a specific fungal disease of roses that causes dark blotches on the leaves, which drop prematurely and weaken the plant.

On a living tree, the chicken of the woods fungus (*Laetiporus sulphurous*) cause heart-rot of wood and can destabilize a tree by hollowing out its centre.

Fire blight is a bacterial disease affecting the rose family where new shoots wilt, turn brown or black, curve back, and give a shepherd's crook appearance.

as 'Witches Broom', and these can have a variety of causes such as bacteria, fungi, mites, aphids, and even mistletoe plants. Lastly, the plant may simply be showing a genetic abnormality such as 'fasciation', where normally round stems are flattened, suggesting many stems have fused together, although in truth only one stem gives rise to the condition.

Although this *Rhododendron* looks diseased, the yellowing and poor condition is the result of the plant being grown in a soil containing too much lime.

While resembling a disease, this *Camellia* flower has actually been damaged by early morning sun on a frosty morning, causing the petals to turn brown.

How do Pests and Diseases Spread?

Diseases are almost always either already present in the garden, or transported to the plant by a 'vector' such as the wind, water, an insect or other animal. Gardeners also unwittingly spread them on soil, organic or other plant matter brought to the site. Even soil clinging to boots – if it comes from elsewhere – can spread diseases and some pests. Good cultural practices and paying heed to hygiene will often eliminate much of this human element, but the natural methods of their spread are less easy to prevent.

On the other hand, the relatively large size of most pests means that they usually migrate to suitable 'host' plants by themselves, often in a predictable seasonal pattern or 'outbreak.' Having said this, the wind frequently blows small pests over great distances, and these outbreaks tend to be less predictable as a result. Many pests are only active at certain times of the year meaning that, in most cases, knowing when they are likely to appear should engender gardeners with an added sense of vigilance. Not all plant pests or diseases are able to attack healthy plants however, tending to concentrate their efforts upon weakened, dying or dead material. Coral spot (a disease of woody plants), botrytis (grey mould) and the majority of slug species are common examples of this. Nevertheless, if they are allowed to multiply by, for instance, poor hygiene they occasionally become 'aggressive' and start damaging otherwise healthy plants.

What is a Plant Disorder?

A disorder describes the situation when a plant experiences a physical change to its normal functions; this usually being brought about by adverse environmental stresses. Disorders differ from temporary stress responses – such as wilting – in that they are irreversible, being the product of a fundamental change in the plant's growth pattern. Ironically, many disorders resemble damage caused by diseases or pests, with physically stressed plants sometimes becoming far sicker than if they actually had been invaded by a pest or disease-causing organism in the first place. Disorders differ from pests and diseases in that they are, on the whole, an avoidable problem. If plants begin to show signs of physical stress and damage it often reveals that there is a problem; the majority of which can be rectified if action is taken promptly.

Prevention is Better than Cure

The best way to control problems is to ensure that plants remain healthy by giving them the conditions that favour plant growth, but not pests or diseases. Healthy plants are often more resistant to diseases and stresses that might otherwise cause ill health. In addition, a healthy balanced garden, full of the appropriate types of plant, is also the ideal environment for beneficial organisms. Traps, barriers, 'scarers' and repellents can also be effective methods of dissuading pests as long as they do not prove too tempting or disruptive to the other, more desirable inhabitants of the garden.

Beneficial Organisms

Encouraging beneficial organisms into the garden is an important first step toward balancing its ecology and removing the greatest part of the threat posed by pests. All pests are species that naturally tend to become numerous and as such they are almost always a food source for a whole array of 'predators' (animals that eat them); 'parasitoids' (animals that lay eggs that hatch and eat them); and 'parasites' (true diseases of the pest itself). These can be bought for use in the greenhouse but they are often less effective outdoors and in these cases it is often better to enlist the help of a 'local volunteer force'. A garden can easily become a haven for beneficial insects, attracted there by the plants it contains or the suitability of the habitat, which will in turn provide a relentless service eating as many pests as possible. With an army of natural pest killers at work, the numbers of pests drop rapidly and the normal balance of predator and prey ensures the nuisance does not become too problematic.

Water related stresses are as debilitating as any disease; in this case a fern, planted in a sunny situation has become dehydrated and died back as a result.

Physical stresses can be the result of human activities. This tree has gradually grown around this barbed wire, causing constriction of the bark.

Planting for Pest Control

Many nurseries, websites and garden magazine adverts offer 'beneficial' species for sale as 'biological control'. While these do of course work, they can be expensive and it is possible to save some money, while still protecting plants, simply by planting the right plants to attract native beneficial insects into your garden. Once in there, this hoard of helpers will begin to control many garden pests naturally and without the environmental consequences of pesticides or the need for expenditure.

The most bewildering aspect for many gardeners new to the idea of natural pest control can be the sheer array of beneficial insects offered for sale as biological control. To make it worse, in nature there are very many more, most of which are barely visible to the human eye. The best idea then is to start by learning to recognize the more familiar types that are easily seen and build up a working knowledge from there.

Commonly encountered garden beneficials include the familiar garden ladybird; hoverflies (the stripy flies that land on flowers); and lacewings (green lacy-winged night flyers); all of which have less familiar larvae that are voracious predators of aphids. Even the much-maligned wasp (otherwise known as a 'jasper' or 'yellow jacket') can be a friend in the early summer, gathering up many a garden pest – especially caterpillars – to feed its young. Closer to the soil, the aptly named ground beetles (the ferocious looking, fast running, black ones) count slugs among their prey while many other beetles also eat their fill of pest species.

Often smaller (and consequentially inconspicuous) are the many 'parasitoids' that are the unsung heroes of the garden. The majority of these are tiny wasps, a few fly and mite species, as well as a host of micro-organisms. Some of them are so effective that they have been harnessed for their commercial value as pest controls. Parasitoids live within a host (the pest insect) for just part of their life cycle; the adult laying her eggs on the pest insect, with the resultant larvae feeding upon and killing it.

Without these natural predators, pest populations would explode later in the year, due to their prodigious reproductive abilities. A single black bean aphid (*Aphis fabae*), landing on a broad bean at the start of the summer could (theoretically) give rise to 2,000,000,000,000,000 offspring by the start of the autumn; a staggering amount equivalent to a million tons of aphids! This, of course, never happens as most of them are eaten by something or other but it does give cause to reflect that it is just as well that so many creatures eat aphids. By encouraging beneficial species into gardens this doomsday scenario is avoided, although in order to be successful they must be provided with the essentials of life: food (the pests themselves), shelter, hibernation sites, and a safe habitat to conduct their lives.

Best Plants

All that is needed in most gardens is a small area, or a series of small patches, interspersed with crops or dividing borders, which are given over to flowering plants chosen so as to attract and harbour beneficial insects. The ideal balance in a garden would be to dedicate five to ten per cent of the growing space to flowers that will attract beneficial insects, and these can be tucked away in odd corners, or where a space becomes vacant. Remember that diversity in respect of any planting is vital in terms of success using this method. Quite simply, the more diverse you make a garden, the more habitats, shelter, and alternative food sources are likely to be provided for predators.

Ironically, to be really effective, a mixture of plants must be chosen that will attract not only beneficial insects but also the pests themselves. Whilst this might seem an insane idea, it is actually the best way to ensure success. In short, if predators are attracted, but there is no food for them, they will not linger there. If on the other hand, the plants first attract pests, then their presence provides an ideal breeding ground for their predators and parasites.

Many beneficial insect species have periods in their life cycles when they survive only on nectar and pollen, hence the need to provide attractant food plants for them and ensure an adequate supply of food. Hoverflies are a prime example of this, where the larvae feed on aphids, while the adults consume only pollen and nectar. Always choose plants that have different heights and flowering seasons, especially those that flower early and late in the season to keep beneficial species going for as long as possible. Remember that even a gap of a few weeks without suitable flowers will disrupt the colonization process, as the adults will have no food source and may well migrate onward in search of new feeding grounds.

As a rule of thumb, small flowers produced in large quantities are much more valuable than a single, large bloom and many members of the mint, carrot and daisy families are excellent insect-attracting plants for just this reason. On a vegetable patch, letting some of the salad and cabbage crops bloom is useful, not only for the purposes of seed collection, but also because they are excellent attractors of beneficial species. If using annuals, remember also that many have short flowering seasons, meaning that it is a good idea to plant small batches every three or four weeks over a month or so to extend their season. Dead heading flowers will also extend the flowering period of individual plants.

Shelter for breeding adults is also important and a good way to help beneficial insects to over winter in the garden is by making shelters for them. These might be for individual species, such as ladybird shelters or lacewing hotels that can even be impregnated with a chemical that attracts the over-wintering adults in the autumn. Alternatively, a more general habitat stack could be constructed that will provide for the needs of a whole host of creatures including the beneficial ones.

Finally, remember that insect-attracting borders or patches need to be thought of as a long-term or even permanent component of a garden. Don't be too over eager for excellent results in the first season as the benefits tend to be cumulative, and as the border matures, resident populations of beneficial insects will become established and thrive; meaning that the garden will become a more natural and balanced environment for the healthy production of both vegetables and flowers.

TOP RIGHT: **Globe artichoke (*Cynara cardunculus*) attracts predatory wasps, hoverflies, and if the seed heads are left, birds, all of which can help to control pests.**

RIGHT: **Yarrow (*Achillea millefolium*) is ideal for attracting hoverflies, the larvae of which are voracious predators of aphids. Old seed heads also attract birds.**

Beneficial Insects and Attractant Plants

While some beneficial insects enter gardens as hungry vagrants that are in search of prey, others have a varied life cycle in which the adults specialize in different foods from the juvenile phases. Flowers are often an excellent way to attract many of the latter type of insect to a garden, by providing a steady food source and consequently encouraging them to search for pest insects for their young. The right choice of garden flowers will ultimately increase the numbers of beneficial insects and improve the health and wellbeing of the plants as a consequence.

Beneficial Insect	Pest Usually Controlled	What to Plant to Attract Them
Hoverflies, robber flies, lacewings, parasitic wasps, ladybirds	Aphid, mealy bug and others	*Achillea filipendulina*, *Lobularia maritima* (alyssum), cosmos, *Tanacetum vulgare* (tansy), shasta daisy (or other daisy flowers), *Angelica gigas*, *Daucus carota* (carrot flowers only), *Foeniculum vulgare* (fennel), *Iberis* (candytuft), *Limonium latifolium* (statice), lupin, *Petroselinum crispum* (parsley), *Anethum graveolens* (dill), *Melissa officinalis* (lemon balm), *Petroselinum crispum* (parsley), *Mentha spp.* (mint), *Nepeta* (catnip)
Ground beetles	Slugs, small caterpillars and grubs	Amaranthus, *Thymus* (thyme), *Rosmarinus* (rosemary)
Damsel bugs and other carnivorous bugs	Many insect eggs, thrips, aphids, mites, scales, whiteflies	*Petroselinum crispum* (parsley), *Digitalis* (foxglove)
Ichneumon wasp	Caterpillars	*Anethum graveolens* (dill)
Beneficial mites	Thrips, fungus gnats, other mites	*Helianthus annulus*, shasta daisy
Tachinid flies	Caterpillars, beetle and fly larvae	*Melissa officinalis* (lemon balm), *Petroselinum crispum* (parsley)

Traps and Barriers

Coloured, sticky traps, pheromone traps and pitfall traps (like beer traps for slugs) can all be used to control pests, although they are most commonly served as a monitoring system, warning of the presence or increase in undesirable pest numbers. On this basis, traps can be useful in timing control measures; yellow, sticky traps used to detect rising numbers of whiteflies, aphids, thrips, leafhoppers and other small flying insects; while traps that use pheromones or attractive scents to tantalize adult insects are usually used to monitor pest species of moths and butterflies. Pitfall traps are easily made by sinking cups or jars into the ground and filling them with yeast and water or stale beer in order to trap slugs.

Any material that is fine enough to keep pests out can be used as a barrier. Screens can keep out large insects, birds and rabbits, but can also prevent pollinating insects from reaching a plant, resulting in lack of seed or fruit. Cardboard and metal collars will prevent cutworms from reaching young transplants; whereas sticky bands placed on tree trunks trap beetles and soil-hibernating pests. Copper strips are available for slug control, and supposedly react with the slugs' slime to shock them. Sharp particles, such as crushed eggshells, are also used as a barrier against slugs.

Successional Planting for Beneficial Insects

Successional flowering will help to support beneficial insects through the whole season. Of course, the choice of plants depends greatly upon the type of garden or allotment you have and there are many species to choose from. Remember that they can be planted in various parts of the garden and can often make good permanent features either between beds or as a border to the whole plot.

Season	Plants
Late winter to spring	*Viburnum tinus*, *Euphorbia characias*, tulips (especially botanical species), *Bellis perennis* (wild type not doubles), *Aubrieta deltoidea* (attracts early aphids for emerging predators)
Late spring to early summer	*Viburnum lantana*, *Viburnum opulus*, *Crataegus monogyna* (hawthorn), coriander, dill, fennel, yarrow (including cultivated forms)
Mid-summer	Alyssum (annual type), coriander, fennel, dill, caraway, *Verbena bonariense*, *Limnanthes douglasi* (poached egg plant), *Escholzia californica* (Californian poppy), *Eupatorium cannabinum*, Gypsophila, yarrow, dwarf sunflowers, ox-eye daisies
Late summer	Coriander, dill, *Argyranthemum*, dwarf sunflowers, *Lobularia maritima* (white alyssum), *Echinacea purpurea*, honeysuckle, asters
Autumn	*Lobularia maritima* (white allysum), ivy (flowers), dwarf sunflowers, single Chrysanthemums, Michaelmas daisies

Insecticidal Soaps

These are made from the salts of fatty acids and should not be confused with ordinary cleaning soaps. Insecticidal soaps kill only what they touch and are effective against soft-bodied pests such as aphids, thrips, crawler stage scales, whiteflies, leafhoppers and mites. Insecticidal soaps may cause burning on some plants, particularly those with hairy leaves and it is best to test insecticidal soap on a single leaf if you are unsure, as burning will usually occur within twenty four hours.

Young transplants, cuttings, and plants with soft young growth are more susceptible to damage. Soap mixed with hard water may also be less effective and more toxic to the treated plants.

Scarecrows are a 'fun' way of deterring crop damage from birds, but in reality have a limited lifespan before the birds learn that they are not a real threat.

Traps, Barriers and Deterrents

Beer traps and slug deterrents (granules and copper strips, greasebands)	Traps are an effective way of both controlling pests and finding out which ones you actually have. Deterrents are physical barriers over which the pest cannot or will not pass. There are many types and their effectiveness can vary.
Bug nets in glasshouse	Greenhouse vents are problematic in terms of pest control in that they allow both pests in and purchased biological control out. Bug nets are put in place to avoid this happening.
Fleece on frames	Frames covered in horticultural fleece can be used over outdoor crops to help keep pests out and control the temperature.
Fleece stretched over a crop	Fleece can be used to create a favourable microclimate around young plants. It also acts as a barrier to airborne pests. On the downside though, it can keep out airborne predators from pests that overwinter in the soil.
Fruit nets (over fruit)	Fruit nets are especially useful for summer soft fruit crops that can quickly be devastated by birds.
Individual cloches	Cloches can act as barriers to a wide variety of airborne pests. Any pests that are sealed into this environment may however find the perfect environment within which to thrive.
Mesh cages for trees	Mesh cages are usually used to keep rabbits and hares at bay. They are usually simple constructions that use three or more stakes driven into the ground with chicken wire (or similar) attached to them.
Rabbit fencing	A continuous barrier to prevent rabbits entering areas where plants are growing. The base of the wire should be buried below ground level to prevent the rabbits burrowing a passage beneath it.

Botanicals

Derived from plants, botanical insecticides include pyrethrum, garlic extract, citrus oil extracts and neem oil. While some of these are poisons, most are deterrants, acting rapidly to stop feeding by insects, although they may not kill the pest for hours or days. Their major disadvantages are that they must be applied frequently, may be difficult to obtain, and although generally less toxic than conventional pesticides, many are still toxic and may harm other beneficial garden residents.

Easy to make Home Made 'Natural' Pesticides

Many natural plant products, while effective, yield rather nasty toxic compounds. The following are just a few examples of mixtures that can be made using safe ingredients.

Chive Extract

Put some fresh leaves in water for two to three days before straining. Add one part soft soap to every 100 parts of the liquid and thin the resulting mixture one

Scarecrow, noisy scarers, and bird scarer	Bird scarers have the drawback of a limited lifespan before the birds learn that they are not a real threat. They can of course be changed and most bird scarers are only needed on a seasonal basis.
String stretched over seedlings e.g. grass, wire netting over peas	Aerial barriers can protect against bird attack. They may only be needed for the duration of the crop's life or even less.
Traps – sticky, coloured in glasshouse	Sticky traps can cause a certain degree of control for flying adults of insect pests. They are not as effective as they are sometimes thought to be and are in fact more use to show whether a particular pest is present or not, thereby allowing appropriate control measures to be put in place.
Traps – pheromone	Pheromone traps are used to detect the presence of insects. The pheromones attract members of the opposite sex and the appearance of the target species allows you to begin looking for and controlling the damaging young.
Tree guards – rabbit (spiral)	Spiral guards are useful for protecting the bark of newly planted trees from rabbits and hares in winter and early spring. These guards expand as the tree develops but they are best removed completely after about a year.
Tree shelter	These protect newly planted trees from vertebrate pests and from the worst rigours of the environment by providing a favourable microclimate around them. They naturally degrade under the action of sunlight but are best removed after two to three years.
Twiggy branches over plants	Arched over young plants, these can be an effective deterrent to predators such as birds and cats. They do not prevent the migration of beneficial predators to the plants.

part in four parts water before spraying. This is primarily effective against insects.

Stinging Nettle Extract

This is made by boiling a bucket of stinging nettles for twenty to thirty minutes in water, before straining it and leaving it to stand for a day. Add one part soft soap to every 100 parts of the liquid and thin the resulting mixture one part in four parts water before spraying. This is primarily effective against aphids and caterpillars, but may protect against other pests.

Garlic Extract

This is made by soaking mashed garlic in water for a couple of days before straining. Add one part soft soap to every 100 parts of the liquid and thin the resulting mixture one part in four parts water before spraying. This is primarily effective against insects.

Onion Extract

This is made by leaving the leaves for a few days in water, then straining it. Add one part soft soap to every 100 parts of the liquid before spraying. This is primarily effective against aphids and caterpillars.

Organic Pesticides	
Bacillus thuringiensis	These are bacterial spores that produce a toxic protein that is useful against caterpillars but will not cause any harm to beneficial species. It works quickly, paralysing the caterpillar and preventing further damage, although it quickly degrades in sunlight and needs frequent re-application throughout the growing season.
Bordeaux mixture	A compound containing copper and sulphur used to control various fungal diseases including apple scab and potato blight. It is harmful to fish or livestock and frequent use can lead to a build up of copper in the soil that can be harmful to worms.
Derris	A chemical extracted from the roots of Derris and *Longocarpus spp.*, the insecticidal ingredient is a naturally occurring substance called 'rotenone', which is useful against a variety of insects including aphids, caterpillars, sawflies and plant-eating beetles. It can prove harmful to some beneficial species, but is harmless to bees.
Insecticidal soap	This is not soap in the sense of a washing soap but is made from the salts of fatty acids, extracted from plant material. They work only on direct contact but can be effective against a wide variety of insect pests, especially aphids, mealybugs, spider mites, thrips and whiteflies. It can also be used for caterpillars and leafhoppers, though larger bodied insects can be more difficult to control with soaps alone. It can damage sensitive plant species, including many brassicas, and especially plants under drought stress. If unsure, treat a portion of the plant, and wait at least 24 hours to see if any damage occurs before treating an entire group of plants.
Pyrethrum	This is extracted from the flower-heads of *Chrysanthemum cinerariaefolium* and *Chrysanthemum coccineum (syn. Chrysanthemum roseum)* and is occasionally called Dalmatian or Persian insect powder. The insecticidal agents are naturally occurring 'pyrethrins' which are especially effective against aphids. It does not persist for long but can cause harm to beneficial species.
Plant oils	Their effectiveness varies but most depend upon coming into contact with the pest itself and suffocating it although some, like neem tree oil, do appear to have insecticidal properties.
Sulphur	An effective fungicide against a variety of plant fungus including powdery mildew, greymould and blackspot. It can prove harmful to predatory mites and can cause damage to certain sensitive species.

Stale Beer

Put this outside in a shallow container, sunk into the ground so that the edge is at soil level. Cover the top with a slate or tile, held up on small stones to ensure that it does not fill up with rain. It should then attract slugs or snails, which crawl into the container and quickly drown. The success of this method is often quite remarkable, meaning that you will need to empty the container and refill it regularly to maintain its efficiency.

Companion Planting

Recent years have seen an increased interest among gardeners in potential natural affinities and aversions shown by many commonly cultivated garden plants for other plant species. The practice, by which these tendencies are exploited to the full, is commonly known as 'companion planting' and has its devotees, although it is not universally accepted and is dismissed by some as being unscientific or without proof. As a result, despite numerous books and

articles extolling its virtues, many gardeners still cling to the ideal of traditional, tidy, neat rows of crops, in immaculately weeded plots.

While companion planting is often viewed (or arguably sold) as something new, this idea is a long way off the mark. Indeed, the practice has its origins in antiquity, with the Roman agriculturist Varro, noting that 'walnut trees close by, make the border of the farm sterile'. This is arguably the first written reference to companion planting and ironically, modern science has shown that Varro was actually right in his assertion. Walnut trees do in fact release a chemical called 'juglone', which inhibits the growth of nearby plants. It is a form of natural weed control commonly called 'allelopathy', and is something that gardeners have observed for centuries between cultivated plants without ever knowing exactly why it happened. Therefore, all that is truly 'new' is the sheer wealth of amassed knowledge on the subject, which is now recorded and readily available to modern day gardeners.

Companion planting could best be described as the establishment of two or more plant species in close proximity, so that some cultural benefit (pest control, higher yield, and so on) is derived for one or more of the species involved. The most frequently cited reasons for this are that either the smell of the volatile oils in the companion plant discourages certain pests, or that plants have shapes which confuse the pest recognition ability. The truth of the matter is often more complex however, and the real secret of the practice lies in its tendency to mirror the complexity of nature itself.

RIGHT: **Mexican Marigold (*Tagetes patula*) has root secretions that allegedly kill nematodes, and a fragrance thought to repel harmful insects from crops.**

BOTTOM RIGHT: **The alleged ability of Mexican marigold to repel whitefly, have made it a common sight planted among both indoor and outdoor tomatoes.**

Companion planting mimics natural settings where numerous species grow together and as a consequence, makes it difficult for pests to locate host plants.

How Does it Work?

While companion planting has a long history, the mechanisms of beneficial plant interaction have not always been particularly well understood. Traditional recommendations used by many practitioners seem to have evolved from an interesting combination of historical observation, horticultural science, and a few, sometimes unconventional sources. Several processes may actually be responsible for the efficacy of plant combinations and it is rare for truly good companions to work simply at one level. Certain companion species are selected for their attractiveness to pests, which in turn serves to distract them from the main crop. Legumes – such as peas or beans – have the ability to fix atmospheric nitrogen for their own use and, in doing so, benefit neighbouring plants with an enhanced supply of this essential nutrient during and even after their growth. More interestingly perhaps is the ability of some plants to exude chemicals from roots or aerial parts that suppress or repel pests; protecting neighbouring plants as an added bonus. The African marigold is a fine example of such a plant, releasing a chemical called 'thiopene' (a nematode repellent) thereby rendering it a good companion for a number of garden crops. While useful in the right circumstances however, a negative counterbalance to the practice is that of 'plant antagonism' (inappropriate companions that have a detrimental effect upon each others growth) meaning that care must be taken to avoid 'clashing species'.

The most noticeable benefit to companion planting could be simply said to be a more general mixing of plants and (in some cases such as vegetable gardens) a more efficient use of available land. Plants may help each other directly by providing shelter from wind or bright sunlight or acting as ground cover to prevent weeds. In addition to this, if pests or adverse conditions reduce or destroy a single species or cultivar, then others in the garden remain, meaning that all is not lost. The theory works on many different levels, and is about choosing plants that have additional properties and functions, beyond simply being ornamental or food items, and using them in combination with one another.

Is there any Scientific Evidence that it Really Works?

When compared to the wealth of 'garden lore' on the subject, there is surprisingly little scientific evidence of the effectiveness of companion planting combinations. Even the briefest of chats with a confirmed organic gardener will doubtless provide plenty of anecdotal evidence but little in respect of hard evidence. While 'conventional' gardeners might still dispute the validity of anecdotal evidence, there seems to be a general consensus that there really are benefits to be had from diverse planting arrangements. Numerous studies have been, and continue to be, carried out although not all of these provide something useful for the home gardener or allotment grower. One interesting Estonian study added evidence to the steadily swelling body of evidence underpinning the practice of companion planting and it is something that anyone can do at home. The researchers showed that French marigold (*Tagetes patula*) was extremely good in preventing cabbage white butterflies (*Pieris brassicae*) from laying eggs. Amazingly, the butterflies were attracted to and nectared (fed) from the flowers but did not feel inclined to lay eggs upon the adjacent cabbage. Yellow flowered varieties were deemed the best. Later in the same year Salvia viridis (*syn Salvia horminium*) – the annual or painted sage – provided a similar effect when flowering reached its peak. Onions and pot marigold (*Calendula officinalis*) on the other hand were not very good at preventing this particular pest despite their traditionally being used as companions for cabbages.

Does it Work for all Plants?

While the general principle of diverse planting arrangements is generally a sound one, it would be a mistake to think that it is a hard and fast rule for all plants. Insects repelled by one plant may well just wander across the garden and find another to harm. Some plants can also prove to be a mixed blessing, and have good points outweighed by negative ones. Wild brambles growing in orchards are an example where the benefit of harbouring useful predators in the early growing season can be offset by their habit of acting as a host and possible transmission source for diseases later in the summer. A few plants (such as the walnut mentioned above) are antagonistic to a wide range of plants making them difficult to grow alongside any other crops, and even the more tolerant ones still tend to have a few companions that they just can't get along with. Knowing which ones make good partners is certainly the key to success.

Bear in mind that the lack of 'scientific certainty' means that it is sometimes necessary to experiment before committing to a companion species. Nasturtiums, for example, are often cited as an effective aphid control, although many a gardener will wonder if they do this by attracting all the aphids to themselves! What works in one locality may not always work elsewhere; meaning that personal experimentation may yet be the key to success in this interesting yet uncertain area.

Companion planting generally works best when it mimics nature. Almost invariably, the longer the practice is maintained, the greater the benefits generally are as, like any natural habitat, the stability of the system increases with age. Wild communities, in the early stages of development, are prone to fluctuations; often resulting in populations that suffer higher incidence of disease outbreaks or are prone to crashes in population numbers. The same is true of plants (and animals) in recently established gardens, where outbreaks of weeds or pests are often most severe in the period immediately after its establishment. The more complex and diverse communities become, the fewer the fluctuations are in respect of numbers of a given species, and the more stable the communities tend to become. As the number of species increases, so does the web of interdependencies. Pest outbreaks become infrequent as predator numbers become more constant and when combined with other good horticultural practices such as hygiene or crop rotation, the incidence of diseases is much reduced.

However, the lack of hard science means that rules of thumb are (in many cases) still the basis of companion planting, and arguably, gardening in general. Science rarely has all the answers, meaning that garden lore, while inexact, is a rich and diverse source of wisdom passed down through countless generations, which can still enliven the practice of gardening into the present day.

Crops and their Companion Plants at a Glance

Crop	Companion plants	Crop	Companion plants
Apples	Chives, Foxgloves, Wallflowers, Nasturtiums, Garlic, Onions, Leeks, Carrots, Celery.	Cabbages	Beans, Beetroot, Celery, Mint, Thyme, Sage, Onions, Rosemary, Dill, Potatoes, Chamomile, Oregano, Hyssop, Wormwood (Southernwood), Nasturtiums, Tansy, Coriander, Radishes, Lettuces, Peas, Chervil, Cucumber, Nasturtium.
Apricots	Basil, Tansy, Worm wood Southernwood) Lettuce, Carrots, Cucumber, Onions, Strawberries, Beetroot, Cabbages, Radishes, Tagetes.	Carrots	Peas, Radishes, Lettuce, Chives, Sage, Onions, Leeks, Tomato, Raspberries, Tansy.
Asparagus	Tomatoes, Parsley, Basil, Onions, Carrots, Cabbage, Beetroot, Lettuce, Chamomile, Kohlrabi, Courgettes (Zucchini), Summer Savoury.	Cauliflowers	Cauliflowers, Celery, Tansy, Nasturtium, Spinach, Strawberries.
Aubergine	Beans, Marigolds, Parsley, Tomato, Asparagus.	Celery	Parsley, Apples, Carrots, Tomatoes, Strawberries, Borage, Lettuce, Spinach, Sage, Pyrethrum.
Beans	Carrots, Cucumbers, Cabbages, Celery, Lettuce, Peas, Parsley, Cauliflower, Spinach, Summer Savoury, Strawberries, Sweet corn, Potato, Parsnips, Peas, Potatoes, Peppers, Beans, Radishes, Garlic.	Courgette (Zucchini)	Nasturtiums, Sunflowers, Squash, Cucumber.
Broad Beans	Potatoes, Sweet corn, Peaches, Tansy, Garlic, Basil, Wormwood (Southernwood).	Cucumbers	Cucumbers, Potatoes (early crop only), Beans, Celery, Lettuce, Sweet corn, Savoy Cabbages, Sunflowers, Nasturtiums, Broad Beans, Potatoes, Melons, Tomatoes, Cucumber, Squash, Tansy.
Dwarf Beans	Beetroot, Potatoes. Peas, Beans, Potatoes, Radishes, Carrots, Cucumber, Sweet Corn, Turnips.	Kohlrabi	Beetroot, Onions, Tomatoes, Asparagus, Celery, Parsley, Basil, Carrots, Chives, Marigolds, Foxgloves, Garlic, Sweet Corn, Nasturtium, Cucumber.
Beetroot	Beetroot, Onions, Kohlrabi, Lettuce, Cabbage, Dwarf Beans, Potatoes, Peas, Beans, Cabbage, Sweet Corn, Broad Beans, Green Beans, Nasturtium, Marigolds, Foxgloves, Horse Radish, Egg Plant.	Garlic	Roses, Apples, Peaches, Turnips, Peas, Nasturtiums.
Brussels Sprouts	Nasturtiums, Pumpkin, Sweet Corn, Marigold.	Grapevines	Grapevines, Geraniums, Mulberries, Hyssop, Basil, Tansy.

Crop Antagonists

Some plants are actually highly antagonistic to one another and will cause detriment if grown together. You are always best avoiding planting the following combinations.

Crop	Antagonist	Crop	Antagonist
Asparagus, Beans, Peas.	Onion and its relatives.	Carrots	Dill
Cabbage family	Strawberries	Fennel, Cabbage family, Sweet corn, Potato	Tomato
Cucumber, Asparagus, Pumpkin and Summer Squash	Potato	Beans, Potato	Sunflower
Beans	Beets	Cucumber	Aromatic Herbs
Beans	Kohlrabi	Radish	Hyssop
Peas	Gladiolus	Lettuce	Parsley

Companion Nutrition

Plants may help each other indirectly by improving the soil or by acting as 'mineral accumulators'. These plants use leaves they are about to shed as dumping grounds for unwanted minerals and by-products, which will then feed the soil organisms and ultimately future crops. Many minerals are essential to the health of plants, although some may be needed in only minute amounts (so known as trace elements).

Element	Benefit(s)	Supplied by
Boron	Apples and brassicas	Euphorbia
Calcium	Binds plant cells together	Beech and broom
Copper	Leaf growth	Yarrow
Cobalt	Leaf growth	Vetch
Iron	Leaf growth	Beans and foxgloves
Magnesium	Leaf and root growth	Oaks and potatoes
Manganese	Beet	Comfrey
Nitrogen	Vegetative growth	Any legume
Phosphorus	Root growth	Oak leaf
Potassium	Fruiting and disease resistance	Apple leaves and sunflowers
Silica	Toughens plants, disease resistance	Onions and stinging nettles
Sulphur	Disease resistance	Brassicas and horseradish

Natural Weed Control

No matter what steps are taken to minimize the maintenance in a garden there will always be some weeds to contend with; indeed, the constant battle against these unwanted plants is one of the great certainties of any garden. If left unchecked, even for just a couple of weeks, they can begin to assert themselves among garden plants, from which they 'steal' vital nutrients, compete for light and water and, if not rapidly controlled, will overrun, spoil or even kill all but the most vigorous specimens. As if this wasn't enough, weeds can survive being cut down or pulled up and their seed often lasts for years in the soil; while others are capable of harbouring pests or diseases. Despite all of this, the problem is not unsolvable and, if dealt with early, just a short time spent each week is enough to control them.

What is a Weed?

A plant that is described as a weed is one that, without help or encouragement, establishes itself in a garden and competes with cultivated specimens; that is, ones that have been deliberately planted. They do this by robbing cultivated garden plants of nutrients, light and arguably most important of all, water; being able to do this because they are species that have evolved to colonize, compete and become dominant. Most are specialists in establishing on disturbed ground – such as is often found on a cultivated plot – and frequently have rapid growth rates when compared to cultivated specimens. In natural habitats this competitive capability is held in check by established neighbouring plants, but natural stability is rare in many gardens, where vegetation is constantly cleared and soil disturbed by a regular cycle of cultivation. In most cases though, it is their unwantedness that proves their major crime in the garden as they tend to look unsightly and, if unchecked, rapidly take control of an area.

While many common weeds are native plants and owe their competitive edge to this alone, others are introduced plants that have become weeds because they do not have the constraints of the habitats from whence they came. These are often the most serious weeds in a garden and can sometimes become so troublesome as to assume a national importance. Invasive species do differ though, according to region

Most weeds establish quickly on disturbed ground, can grow in cool conditions and have rapid growth rates compared to cultivated specimens.

or country and it is best therefore to read up on, and be aware of, the invasive species known to be problematic in a particular region. This ensures that their purchase can be avoided; as despite the environmental risk they carry, some nurseries still sell some, even though they are known to be invasive.

The term weed is a relative one however, and any plant that is able to propagate itself and spread freely can become a weed in a garden setting if not properly controlled. Even if gardeners are prepared to tolerate this up to a point, there may come a time when they become too prolific. Don't make the mistake of thinking that a pretty plant can't become a weed then, and choose plants carefully from the outset to avoid introducing problems.

Another source of cultivated weeds can be seen in a vegetable garden and are the 'remnants' of a previous crop. These plants, called 'volunteer' weeds, are usually easily dealt with, although some can interfere with the crop rotation by acting as a host for diseases in the intervening time between cropping cycles. Equally, some 'wild' weeds also host plant diseases that can subsequently spread to cultivated crops. Charlock (*Sinapis arvensis*) and shepherd's purse (*Capsella bursa-patoris*) for example, can host clubroot, while eelworm may be harboured by chickweed (*Stellaria media*), fat hen (*Chenopodium album*) and shepherd's purse. Cucumber 'mosaic' virus, a potentially devastating disease affecting not only cucumbers, but also melons, courgettes, marrows and so on, is carried by a range of weeds including chickweed and groundsel (*Senecio vulgaris*).

Most weeds are easily dealt with, although there are always a few that seem to resist all efforts to eradicate them. No weed is completely invincible however and the only really successful strategy for weed control is persistence.

What are the Problems with Using Herbicides?

The majority of herbicides (weed-killers) are toxic compounds that can harm other crops or persist in the environment. There could always be the odd exception of course; such as might be found where highly persistent invasive alien weeds, such as Japanese knotweed (*Fal-*

lopia japonica), cannot be effectively controlled by hand weeding or mulches alone, and present not only a threat within the garden, but also to the wider environment.

Weed Types

The weeds that plague your garden often share some attributes with the crops they compete with and as such, they can be divided into three groups.

Annual weeds germinate, grow, flower and set seed within one growing season. Some species, known as ephemerals, are extremely fast growing and complete their lifecycle well within a growing season, allowing them to produce successive generations over a year; a strategy that enables them to exploit brief windows of opportunity in order to grow and set seed. Many of these are known then as winter annuals, due to their habit of germinating in late summer or autumn, overwintering and setting seed the following summer. A few hardier examples such as chickweed (*Stellaria media*), can actually germinate under snow cover, meaning they can commence their growth at the first sign of spring, often before the surrounding crops do.

Biennial weeds are actually short lived perennials that grow from seed during one growing season, overwintering as a rosette of leaves close to the soil surface before flowering, setting seed and dying the following growing season. Biennial weeds such as spear thistle (*Cirsium vulgare*) are relatively common in garden settings with the exception of vegetable patches and annual flower beds, where the regular cropping cycle often keeps them at bay.

Perennial weeds live for more than two years and can become established either by seed or by vegetative parts, such as roots or rhizomes that are frequently moved around during cultivation, or contained in imported topsoil or compost. Seedling perennials are usually no more difficult to control than any other weed seedlings, although once established, they can be very difficult to control and often prove very competitive among vegetable crops. Examples of perennial weeds include blackberry (*Rubus fruticosus*), nettle (*Urtica dioica*), dandelion (*Taraxacum officinalis*) and dock (*Rumex obtusifolius*).

Ways to Control Weeds

Physical control of weeds usually involves hand weeding, hoeing and forking over, and despite the effort they involve, in most cases they are perfectly viable provided they are done regularly. It also represents the least environmentally detrimental method of weed control. The real trick is to be able to recognize weeds when they are very young; even when they are just seedlings, as it is then that they are most vulnerable and your efforts at weeding can be most effective. In the case of shallow rooted plants such as Anemone, Rhododendron and Magnolia, or crops such as Brassicas and onions, any cultivation needs to be limited to shallow hoeing however, as digging can cause severe root disturbance. Perennial weeds, especially those with extensive root systems or which spread by rhizomes in the soil, such as couch grass (*Elymus repens*), bindweed (*Convolvulus arvensis*)

Hand weeding is a perfectly viable solution, which if done regularly, also represents the most environmentally friendly method of weed control.

and horsetail (*Equisetum arvense*) may be difficult to control by hand weeding alone, especially if they become established among perennial plants.

Mulch is a layer of material that is laid over the surface of a soil or other growing medium, often to suppress growth or prevent germination of weed seed. While often cited as a means of weed control, mulch can have other important benefits for the ecology of the garden although not all types of mulch have equal benefit. Mulching an established border will have the dual benefits of helping to keep the plant's roots warm in winter but cool in summer. A mulch layer will also reduce soil water loss through evaporation, partly by shading the soil surface and also by directly slowing down the loss of water vapour from the soil to the atmosphere. Mulch also aids plant development by gradually raising soil fertility and encouraging nutrient cycling. If they are applied and their levels maintained, natural, organic mulches will actually harbour many beneficial insects such as carnivorous beetles that will help keep the plants healthy by eating pests.

To be effective, mulches must be laid on a bare surface as they will not inhibit established weeds, especially the vigorous perennial weeds such as couch grass or bindweed. They should also be laid on soil that is warm and moist, either in autumn or spring. The weed control benefits are mostly due to the mulch preventing the germinating weed seedling from reaching the sunlight or by 'drawing' the weed up so that it is spindly and can be easily removed or pulled. They will not however inhibit established weeds – especially vigorous perennial ones – and these must be removed by hand as they appear. If mulch is laid to a sufficient, even, depth – say 5cm (2in) or more – it will develop a dry dusty surface that will deter the germination of weed seeds that land on it. While this is only a temporary measure it can help reduce the need for weeding at the busiest times of the year.

Synthetic materials, especially if they are impermeable such as black polythene, will inhibit oxygen and water infiltration into the soil and even some organic materials, such as grass clippings, can pack down on the surface and form a water-resistant layer. Finally as mulches do encourage surface rooting it is a practice that must be continued if started, if the plants are not to suffer detrimental effects later.

MULCH MATERIALS

The materials that can be used for mulching are very varied in their composition and the effects that they have. They are generally classified into organic and inorganic types. Organic mulches are mainly bulky materials of living origin. Inorganic mulches, on the other hand, may include some naturally occurring but non-living materials such as synthetic materials of artificial origin. In the inorganic category; the materials may be subdivided further into loose fill materials and sheet materials.

Bark/Composted Woodchip

This is an excellent material from the point of view that it is recycled but also because it will gradually break down and yield organic matter to the soil below. It lowers the chance of germinating weeds and is possibly the best material for encouraging beetles.

Woodchip mulch.

Garden Compost

This often makes excellent mulch from the point of view of soil fertility and the boost it gives to beneficial insects but it can be an excellent place for germinating weeds to become established and also large quantities can be difficult to produce.

Straw

Straw is a moderately good material to use around the bases of plants in the summer, most famously under fruiting strawberries. While it is surprisingly durable, it eventually rots down, although it should be chopped into short lengths prior to use.

Black Polythene

This is quick and easy to lay and is a common material that can readily be obtained from many suppliers. It does not allow for water penetration into the soil, however, and is generally best restricted to use under paths or for temporary coverage.

Woven Plastic Sheet

This is an improvement on black polythene due to its porous nature, although it has the similar disadvantage of gradually denuding the humus content from the soil below by preventing organic matter from reaching there. Use in similar places to polythene as a water permeable substitute.

Woven plastic sheet.

Grit, Pebbles Gravel or Sand

These inorganic materials are very durable although they often become incorporated into the topsoil layer because of the actions of worms and other organisms. They are an ideal substrate on dry gardens, around alpine plants and in pots or troughs. If laid on top of sheet mulch, they tend to stay cleaner.

GETTING THE BEST FROM YOUR GARDEN

The real key to success with sustainable gardening begins with a good design. Planning the garden also provides a chance for everyone that uses it to have a real say in what they want to do there and can actually mean that the final product is all the better for it; in essence the function of the space depends upon those most likely to use it. Once the function has been established then, the process of designing it can begin in earnest. A thorough appraisal and survey of the site is the best way to start and can be done quite simply using a few simple techniques.

Why Survey a Garden?

Surveying a garden before any form of planning, design or re-design is attempted will not only help prevent rushed or ill-considered decisions, but often proves to be time saving in the long run. As well as allowing time to prepare, it can also help determine which plants might be successfully grown, as a thorough survey involves recording not just the measurements of your garden but also its characteristics such as microclimate, soil type, existing features and views. Ultimately the plan produced will help to plan any changes needed. A survey should, therefore, cover the following points.

The prevailing climate will greatly influence the success of a plan. Check the direction of the prevailing winds, the annual rainfall, time of the year rain falls, annual temperatures, and whether frosts are experienced. All of

these things can easily be checked by talking with neighbours or contacting a local meteorological station.

Sun and shade are extremely important factors in the choice of plants that will thrive there. Try and assess how much sun and shade the garden receives and where it falls at different times during the day; always bearing in mind that even the sunniest garden may have shady pockets created by shadows from nearby houses, fences, hedges or trees.

Identify the soil type and note down the existing vegetation, as this often gives a multitude of clues as to what will grow there. Look up the requirements of these plants in a textbook, and talk to neighbouring gardeners about their experiences to build a picture of the plants that should thrive there. Take note of any drainage problems you encounter.

Note the position of all the existing features both on and nearby the site including trees, garden beds, driveways, garden sheds, and so on. Decide on any that are to be retained or removed in the 'new' garden. Always note down the position of services, including water mains, gas mains, sewers, meters, taps, power lines (underground and overhead), and so on.

As well as the site's physical dimensions, look for views, both on and off the site and those from indoors as these are also important. Ask yourself if there are views that you wish to retain – possibly using a feature within or outside the garden as a focal point – or whether privacy is a priority, thereby necessitating screening or barrier planting.

Finally, check with the local planning department or similar authority that no legal restrictions exist. Gardens are often in areas subject to planning restriction or control, which may affect their use or development. Typically this relates to structures over a certain height or the planting and removal of trees.

OPPOSITE PAGE: **King cup (Caltha palustris) thrives only in wet, ideally waterlogged, ground; knowing what a plant needs is essential if it is to survive.**

ESSENTIAL TIPS FOR MEASURING YOUR GARDEN

Two's company

Always work with a friend. It makes life easier especially when trying to keep a tape straight to take measurements. One person should normally be in charge of measuring and the other in charge of recording the information. It also helps to have someone to discuss things with and of course it is always nice to have a bit of company.

Divide the area into triangles

Since the time of the Ancient Greeks, the value of the triangle as a shape for surveying land has been recognized. The most obvious way to do this on a rectangular garden is to measure the outside and then to measure from corner to corner as a cross check.

Use two tapes to mark the position of a fixed site feature

You will need to plot the position of features such as trees or flower beds and this is best measured at right angles from a nearby straight edge such as a boundary line. Stretch a tape along this edge. Place the start (the '0' end) of a second tape nearest the object you are measuring toward and move the other end in an arc across the tape along the edge. The shortest distance you measure across this arc is the distance at a right angle from the first tape line. Note this measurement and how far along the first tape it occurs. This makes it easy to plot where things are.

Take photos as you go

Photos are always ideal to have as a reminder and to have to hand when drawing up your ground plan sketch, or particularly when you start to draw up the final design for the garden. A good tip is to blow up a few of the photos and cover them with tracing paper for you to sketch your ideas on and get an idea what a finished garden would look like.

Make a sun chart

Find out which are the sunniest and which the darkest parts of the site are. Every few hours, record where the sun is shining on a plan. Keep in mind that the site's exposure to sunlight will also vary at different times of the year. Ensure that you note the direction where prevailing winds tend to come from.

Taking Stock and Inventory

Once you have an existing ground plan, this can be appraised to see what may be done with it. Remember that a garden is fundamentally the same as any other living space, in that its design should always reflect exactly what it is needed for. If the garden is a space predominantly for outdoor living and entertaining, then the design should reflect that. Of course, children or pets have different needs that will need consideration, always bearing in mind that these can and do change over time. Having said this, a garden does not have to be based purely around one need, and the real trick of making a garden inventory is to make two lists. The first list should contain all the things that are considered essential needs – cooking, relaxing, a safe play area and so on. If this list is not too long already, then a second list should be made that includes all of the things that are preferred (but not essential) activities. These two lists then set out the functions and potential functions of the garden. The second list should contain all the features that might be included and although it will of course be heavily influenced by the first list, it should be aimed at the aesthetics of the garden as much as at its actual functions.

Once the list has been made, consider what space is needed for all the functions and make a rough sketch of where they may take place. If space is limited, then a compromise will decide what the garden will be for. Make sure that careful thought is given at this stage to the whole year. An outdoor dining and sun lounging area may be great in midsummer but if the garden is in a cooler area, will it really offer the best use of the space all year round? Equally, if home produce is your goal, consider how many vegetables are ever likely to eaten and whether there will be time to tend them. A small plot may give an ample supply while not taking too much time.

Remember that certain features are not ideal where young children will be spending time. Ponds, thorny or poisonous plants can all prove troublesome. On the other hand, children love water and seeing the life it contains, meaning a pond may follow as children grow. This is in line with the thinking that making and maintaining a garden is a continual process, which is always evolving according to your needs. If your needs change, then so can the garden. It is all part of the fun of it.

Once this is done, it is time to look at whether any sort of theme is applicable and how this may affect the approach. A dry sunny space may suit a Mediterranean or 'xeriscape' theme (see below); while a permanently wet site may be better as a bog garden. If space permits, and the microclimate is varied, several elements can be carefully combined, although it pays to be realistic about what can be achieved, to what extent these various elements will combine and ultimately how much work they will require to maintain.

BASIC DESIGN PRINCIPLES

Unity. This is the quality that ties a design together. Avoid clashes and things that appear out of place by using similar materials, patterns, shapes and colours throughout the design and tying these in to the house and surroundings.

Rhythm and **line** Is the use of a logical order and flow in the design. Remember that strong lines are important with flowing shapes befitting larger naturalistic gardens and geometric shapes often more befitting smaller courtyard settings.

Scale simply refers to the relative size of each element or part of the garden in relation to the space in which it is placed. Any feature included should be neither too small and insignificant or large and overpowering for the whole scheme.

Balance refers to the use of space in relation to other features in the garden. It is a matter of taste but too many features in too small a space can feel cluttered whereas too much open space can leave the occupants feeling exposed.

Variety and **contrast** should not conflict with the need for unity. A certain amount of variety promotes the potential interest, and is all the easier in large gardens but this needs to be artfully juxtaposed in order to achieve a balance.

Functionality is always vital in any personal living space. For example, leaving areas for refuse or household recycling near to the house, or allowing space for a washing line, can all too easily be overlooked. It is mostly a simple matter of applying common sense and avoiding problems and conflict by design.

Dry Gardens

Water conservation in gardens has become an increasingly important issue in recent years, often prompted by local or regional water shortages. Dry gardening (often referred to as 'Xeriscaping' and 'xerogardening') refers to a method of gardening that reduces or eliminates the need for additional watering and proves especially useful in areas that do not have easily accessible supplies of fresh water. Even in areas where water is less scarce, the environmental cost of storing, filtering and pumping water to houses is one that really should be avoided for uses other than those essential to daily living. The

In very hot dry places, xeriscaping means gardening at the extreme, where every last drop of water is precious and the plants are highly adapted to cope.

potential of any dry garden site can of course be maximized if this is considered in the initial planning phase and, if the design is carefully considered, it becomes perfectly feasible to garden in dry conditions.

However, water-efficient gardens need not be entirely drought tolerant, and are frequently divided into zones with different water requirements. If the intention is to have some shorter-term planting – a vegetable garden for example – then this will need more water than the rest, typically called an 'oasis'. Moving away from these well-watered oases are 'transition zones' of moderate water use, containing plants that require less frequent irrigation (ideally no supplemental water or very infrequent irrigation during prolonged dry periods) and less maintenance. The remaining areas then are essentially no-watering or 'arid zones' that rely totally upon that which falls as rain. A landscape divided in this way is said to have been 'hydro-zoned'.

When choosing where to site these zones, consider the surroundings first. An oasis for example is best placed nearby to a large structure such as a house or shed; where it can benefit from rain runoff (or is close to the site of any stored rainwater) and shade (which reduces evaporation, keeping more water in the soil). No water zones on the other hand might well be the furthest away from the house or other structures with the transition zones forming a buffer between the two.

Good soil preparation is of course very important and soil testing can help determine not only the best plants to use, but also highlight any amendments needed to improve the soil for them. In oases and moderate water-use zones for example, adding compost will increase the soil's water-holding capacity, whereas the low water-use zone may only need the soil to be loosened in order to improve root development and allow rapid, deep infiltration of water and air that will be needed by plant roots.

TOP LEFT: **Even in relatively cool temperate climates, slight localized variations in temperature and rainfall can result in a warm, dry microclimate prevailing.**

LEFT: **The plants used in xeriscaping are often quite architectural and well suited to an urban setting where they contrast well with the formal surroundings.**

In dry places, succulents can be used to good effect, especially when planted in drifts to 'soften' edges that would otherwise be harsh, lifeless edges.

Even in relatively cool locations, some rather exotic looking specimens, such as this *Opuntia*, can be grown, provided that the soil drainage is very good.

Planting a Dry Garden

The plants that can be used in any particular dry garden will of course depend upon the prevailing climate and indeed the garden's own unique microclimate. Start by finding out what the rainfall patterns for the garden are; ideally establishing not only how much rain falls per year, but also whether it is spread throughout the year, or concentrated in short bursts. Plants whose natural requirements are appropriate to the local climate should always be emphasized, as they must be able to withstand the full range of climatic variables. Ideally, a water-efficient garden has plants arranged in receding layers, with oases acting as focal points, in which bright, eye-catching or verdant plant growth accentuates the steady transition to more subtle (and more drought-tolerant) planting.

Closely cropped, densely planted green expanses of lawn are essentially thirsty, high-maintenance features that are not especially drought tolerant. Having said this, the lawn can still be maintained in most settings by raising the height of cut and ensuring that it is well aerated. This in itself will improve the drought tolerance and make it remain greener for longer. In addition, adding clover to the mixture will help retain a green element even in more severe drought and can be cut in the same way as the grass itself.

Not only is yucca hardy and drought tolerant, it also rewards the gardener from time to time with a magnificent flower spike, laden with cream blooms.

Really water-needy plants can be grouped together near to structures, perhaps planting them in containers so the roots will get more water rather than them seeping into the surrounding soil, where it can encourage the growth of weeds. An alternative to using containers is to create a retaining wall (essentially a very large container), which has the added benefit of making your oasis plants stand out more.

Plants should also be arranged, based on the amount of sunlight they need (and of course how much is available). The sunny side of a wall, trellis or even a hedge will get a lot more sunlight than the opposing side, making these the ideal place for 'sun-worshipping' species.

Even where plants are to be watered, there needs to be a water-thrifty way to do this. Drip irrigation is an ideal way and while it is possible to do this with timers and seep hoses, these can prove expensive.

LEFT: **The bright yellow blooms of this *Helichrysum*, are freely produced above a mat of foliage in summer and autumn on a free draining soil in full sun.**

BELOW: **Plants with hairy or 'silver' leaves are well suited for use in a dry garden, as this is an adaptation to avoid water loss and overheating by the plant.**

RIGHT: *Pachysandra* is an example of a plant well suited for dry shade, where its thick, leathery leaves provide an effective weed-suppressing ground cover.

A simpler method is to use old plastic bottles, with pinpricked sides, sunk into the ground and filled with water. These will gradually release water to the plants and minimize water evaporation, while removing the chance of runoff or seepage away from the plants. If watering plants, try to do this in the late evening or early morning, to minimize water loss through evaporation. Mulching planted beds will also help to reduce erosion and suppress weeds. Organic (especially wood-based) mulch will retain moisture, and as it decomposes, will steadily improve the soil. Provided it is topped up each year, it will also greatly increase the soil's water-holding capacity over time.

Water that is harvested from roofs and paving during storms can be used to reduce the need for supplemental irrigation. Roof runoff for example can be used to create a so-called 'rain garden', by excavating a depression or creating a ditch to capture the runoff and planting the area with water-loving species. Directing water in this way drastically reduces the need for supplemental irrigation in oases, as well as moderate or even low-watering zones. However, a rain garden does need careful grading to channel and capture the runoff, meaning that it will need careful planning at the design stage. Impermeable plastic mulch can play a key role in helping channel harvested water from one area to another, and can be 'artfully disguised' using pebbles and stones as for example a dry 'river-bed', thereby making it into a functional and decorative feature in its own right.

Collecting rainfall that falls on roofs of houses or garden buildings means that there is a reserve of water for those plants that need it in the drier months.

In some gardens, water has a tendency to collect in low lying areas, making these places ideal for growing moisture-dependent plant species.

Certain plant species are specifically adapted to grow in moist or wet ground with willow (*Salix spp*) even thriving in permanently waterlogged soils.

Wet Gardens

Wet sites can seem the bane of the gardener, as they seemingly consist of sticky, difficult to work soil for much of the year. On the whole though, a wet site tends to be less problematic where the plants themselves are concerned and there is a whole range of species and possibilities that can be chosen to make the best of the conditions. As a general rule however, most plants do not thrive if their roots remain permanently wet for extended periods of time. Most of the moisture-loving species prefer seasonal wetness and are more specifically adapted to fluctuations in soil moisture. In areas with very poor drainage then, particularly if the ground is distinctly marshy, it is only those plants that can persist under almost permanently wet conditions that will really thrive. Before getting to work on a wet site then, it is extremely important to establish whether the soil is permanently wet, marginally wet, or wet for only a few days at a time. Consider also the soil type: plants growing in sandy or light soils that are wet but drain quickly are less likely to be damaged than those growing in heavy clay soils that drain slowly and mostly stay wet. The season is also important, with plants often withstanding flooding much more ably in spring and summer than in the autumn or winter.

Therefore, when planning a garden on a wet site it is important to look at and assess the various levels across the site. Water of course, always flows down a slope, meaning that moisture will tend to accumulate in low-lying areas, particularly if something is preventing its drainage. Soil that becomes compacted, particularly if this occurs at the surface, will only add to the problem, trapping water at the surface and effectively preventing gaseous exchange – that is entry of oxygen and the prevention of carbon dioxide and other poisonous gases from escaping. The net result of this (for most plants) is that it renders their roots unable to process nutrients with the net result being weak and spindly growth.

If a garden is prone to surface water (puddles) in spring or following heavy rain, this is a fair indication that the soil is either compacted near the surface or that it suffers from poor drainage. The first of these can be overcome by breaking up the surface with a

Thriving in moist or even permanently wet ground, the kingcup or marsh marigold (*Caltha palustris*) is most at home in a slightly shaded spot.

fork when dry but poor drainage can be more problematic and the best option here is often to choose plants that perform well in moist conditions. While this solves the immediate problem, water-loving plants can quickly become stressed if conditions become drier during the summer months, wilting quickly when deprived of water. Plants that like consistent moisture all season may (ironically) need frequent watering on seasonally waterlogged sites as its effect renders them less drought resistant, meaning that they do not always represent the best option in a sustainable garden.

Growing Plants in Raised Beds

A raised bed is a worthy compromise for those gardening on land that is seasonally or permanently wet, as it provides even drainage throughout the growing season. In addition, it also means that plants have their feeding roots near the surface where they can breathe, while allowing deeper, 'water harvesting' roots to follow the water level down into the underlying soil as it naturally fluctuates through the year. As a result, water

is conserved; there being less need for much of the year and when it is applied, it can be done more sparingly with little or no waste through runoff.

A raised bed is of course, ideally suited to the no-dig approach of managing the soil and means that the bed will need to be reached on all sides from a permanent path. This effectively limits the useful size of a bed to around a maximum of 1.2m (4ft) wide, thereby enabling weeding, planting, maintenance or harvesting of crops to take place without ever needing to walk on the soil. After all, if the object is to maintain good structure and avoid compaction, the best way of doing this is to avoid standing on the bed. If constructing a series of beds, particularly if the object is the production of vegetables or other edible produce, the beds will need setting out with a network of paths between them. Paths will need to be at least 30cm (1ft) wide with every other path double this for easy wheelbarrow access. Individual beds should not be longer than 3.5m (12ft) otherwise you can waste a lot of time walking around them when working in the garden. The beds can of course be of any design, from a simple series of parallel rectangles to a more complex design of interlocking shapes.

Raised beds enable weeding, planting, maintenance and ultimately harvesting of crops to take place without ever needing to walk on the soil.

Raised beds have drained upper layers of soil that prevent tender specimens rotting during winter while keeping a water reserve below for them in summer.

Whatever design is chosen, try to follow the same recommended bed and path widths, remembering that narrow angles and very small beds are more difficult to construct and ultimately a less efficient use of both materials and space.

The beds should be marked out on the ground before building them to check the overall effect. Try wheeling a barrow around among them and see if the width to the mid-point in a bed is within easy reach. Once the layout is decided, the beds can then be built up using timber or other suitable materials. Once constructed, the bed must be filled and it is at this stage that it is possible to create a deep, good quality soil. The basis of this should ideally be the same as the original top soil, although this can be further tailored to a particular plant's needs in order to encourage vigorous growth and health. Before filling, remove the top 30cm (1ft), and add at least the same volume again of a mixture of organic materials and stones/grit to improve drainage, before returning the topsoil to improve the drainage and structure. The ultimate aim should always be to create an open friable soil with plenty of oxygen available for strong root growth.

Raised beds also have the advantage of warming up more quickly than the surrounding soil in spring, thereby enabling plants to get a head start in the early part of the year. Furthermore, the loose soil also makes weeding much easier, while the wooden edges are useful for attaching supporting hoops, various crop covers and cloches, if and where these are needed. The edges of the beds are also ideal for fixing barriers for pests such as copper, paper or water traps to prevent slugs or other pests from entering the beds.

Even where soil has been improved, it is important to keep off it to prevent any recurrence of the compaction problem. When planting plants in a wet or wet-prone soil, dig the planting holes carefully to avoid smeared sides, and break the base and sides up with a fork if necessary to ensure that it does not easily fill with water. Always be careful when planting wet-tolerant plants that they are not planted directly into standing water. Unless they are a true aquatic species, capable of growing in open water, most plants that naturally grow in marshy areas would be found on small mounds where the crowns of the plants are above permanent moisture.

Plants for Wet Gardens			
Common name	**Botanical name**	**Common name**	**Botanical name**
Maple	*Acer spp.*	Meadowsweet	*Filipendula spp.*
Black alder	*Alnus glutinosa*	Chameleon plant	*Houttuynia cordata*
Birch	*Betula spp.*	Forget-me-not	*Myosotis scorpioides*
Dogwood	*Cornus spp.*	Yellow flag Iris	*Iris pseudoacorus*
Sweetgum	*Liquidambar styraciflua*	Siberian Iris	*Iris sibirica*
Rose	*Rosa spp.*	Ligularia	*Ligularia spp.*
Currant	*Ribes spp.*	Loosestrife	*Lysimachia spp*
Willow	*Salix spp*	Bergamot or bee-balm	*Monarda didyma*
Spirea	*Spiraea spp.*	Bethlehem sage	*Pulmonaria saccharata*
Snowberry, coralberry	*Symphoricarpos spp.*	Rodgersia	*Rodgersia spp.*
Elderberry	*Sambucus spp.*	Foamflower	*Tiarella spp.*
Viburnum	*Viburnum spp.*	Spiderwort	*Tradescantia virginiana*
Goatsbeard	*Aruncus dioicus*	Chinese globeflower	*Trollius spp.*
Astilbe	*Astilbe spp*	Blue vervain	*Verbena hastata*
Elephant's ear	*Bergenia spp.*	Lady fern	*Athyrium filix-femina*
Siberian bugloss	*Brunnera macrophylla*	Wood fern	*Dryopteris celsa*
Marsh marigold	*Caltha palustris*	Royal fern	*Osmunda regalis*
Bleeding heart	*Dicentra spp.*	Ostrich fern	*Matteuccia struthiopteris*
Joe-Pye weed	*Eupatorium spp.*		

Shaded Gardens

While some gardeners tend to consider shade as a problem, where plants are concerned this is a long way from the truth. Far from limiting plant selection, an area of shade increases greatly what can be grown in the garden. Having said this, there are varying degrees of shade and as all plants need at least some light, the darker the corner, the fewer the options are likely to be. It is important to know how shady a place is in order to best select the plants most suited for those conditions. Many shade-tolerant plants can of course grow across a range of conditions, often also thriving in full sun, although the time of day they are exposed to sun can make a difference. For example, morning sun is less intense and many shade-loving plants are perfectly content, and even depend upon a little morning sun. Others however, dislike morning sun, with camellias being a prime example of this; direct morning sun tends to scorch flowers and buds covered with dew. Locations exposed to the midday sun on the other hand bear the full brunt of its heat and light, a situation that often results in scorch damage to the majority of otherwise shade-tolerant plants.

Permanently shaded places are ideally suited for growing plants such as ferns, which will thrive in the cool moist conditions that tend to prevail there.

Evergreen plants Japanese aralia *(Fatsia japonica)* often perform well in the shade as they compensate for the lack of light by making food all year round.

With a little planning, a shady corner can become a feature in its own right, by using a mixture of shade tolerant shrubs and herbaceous plants.

Shade-loving plants are often also moisture-loving plants, thriving in soil that is moist, but well drained. As the season progresses, many of these cope with steadily drier conditions and higher temperatures by entering a phase of temporary dormancy, due largely to the fact that they cannot replenish moisture from the ground quickly enough to prevent wilting. While some plants tolerate less moisture and are happier in somewhat drier shade, very few readily tolerate an extended drought. While watering can help alleviate drought in the short term, adding plenty of organic matter to the soil and topping it up regularly in the form of a 75mm (3in) deep layer of open organic mulch will help keep most shade-loving plants healthy.

Where shade-loving plants have to grow beneath other taller plants they can experience a more serious problem in the drier summer months due to the effect of root competition. Many trees and shrubs have dense fibrous roots near the soil surface, capable of absorbing most of the available moisture and a good deal of the available nutrient; making it difficult for the plants below to establish and grow. In these situations, it may well be best to select shade-loving but drought-tolerant plants that will tolerate and compete in these conditions. In these situations, however, it is also worth considering the health of the taller, shade-giving plants themselves. The shallow mat of fine roots at or near the soil surface is of course vital for their continued health, growth and ultimately survival. If these roots are damaged as a result of soil preparation and planting, the plant may suffer serious damage. This is especially likely if dealing with specimens such as Rhododendron and Azaleas or Magnolia, which have especially shallow, fibrous root masses. When planting under larger specimens, it pays to carefully dig individual planting holes and avoid trying to cultivate the whole area, as this is very likely to cause extensive, and serious damage to the root system.

A last point to consider where plants are the source of shade is that areas initially in part shade when the trees or bushes were small, may in time become more heavily shaded as these mature. This will of course ultimately lead to plant losses, as those needing more light gradually succumb to the increasing shade. However, far from being a disaster, this can be an opportunity to try new species of plants, better able to thrive in the conditions.

Carefully chosen shade-loving plants can be used to create the effect of a cool shady grotto; the perfect respite from the heat of a hot summer's day.

Root competition can rob soil of moisture and nutrient; notice how the growth of these annuals decreases the nearer to the root-zone of this tree they get.

Plants for Shade

Full sun refers to locations receiving full sun for at least six hours per day. (Depending upon the latitude of a garden – i.e. how far north or south it is from the equator – plants in full sun may be exposed for between thirteen and eighteen hours of sunlight during early to mid-summer.)

Dappled Shade refers to locations receiving partially filtered sunlight, usually as a result of an open or high canopy of a tree (or trees) overhanging them; areas that often receive direct sunlight earlier or late in the day.

Part Shade refers to locations receiving in the region of four or five hours of direct sunlight a day.

Full shade refers to locations receiving no direct sunlight, such as might be found beneath low-limbed trees, or dense evergreens, or in the shadow of a high wall.

KEY   Full Sun ✪   Dappled Shade ○   Part Shade ◗   Full Shade ●

Common Name	Botanical Name	Light	Common Name	Botanical Name	Light
English ivy	Hedera spp	✪●	Bleeding heart	Dicentra spp.	○◗
Yew	Taxus spp.	✪●	Cardinal flower	Lobelia cardinalis	○◗
Purple coneflower	Echinacea purpurea	✪○	Jacob's ladder	Polemonium caeruleum	○◗
Alder	Alnus spp.	✪◗	Columbine meadow rue	Thalictrum aquilegiifolium	○◗
Maple	Acer spp.	✪◗	Barren strawberry	Waldsteinia spp.	○◗
Snowy mespilus	Amelanchier spp.	✪◗	Anemone	Anemone spp	○●
Astilbe	Astilbe spp.	✪◗	Bugleweed	Ajuga reptans	○●
Dogwood	Cornus spp.	✪◗	Jack-in-the-pulpit	Arisaema spp.	○●
Magnolia	Magnolia spp.	✪◗	Sedge	Carex spp.	○●
Box	Buxus spp.	✪◗	Plumbago	Ceratostigma spp.	○●
As species	Hydrangea spp	✪◗	Lily-of-the-valley	Convallaria majalis	○●
Elderberry	Sambucus spp.	✪◗	Barrenwort or Bishop's hat	Epimedium spp.	○●
As species	Viburnum spp.	✪◗	Japanese Winter creeper	Euonymus fortunei	○●
Barberry	Berberis spp.	✪◗	Dog's tooth Violet	Erythronium spp.	○●
Cobnut or Hazel	Corylus spp.	✪◗	Witch-hazel	Hamamelis spp.	○●
Holly	Ilex spp.	✪◗	Plantain lily	Hosta spp.	○●
Mock orange	Philadelphus spp.	✪◗	Dead-nettle	Lamium spp.	○●
As species	Cotoneaster spp.	✪◗	Ostrich fern	Matteuccia struthiopteris	○●
Coral bells	Heuchera spp.	✪◗	Royal fern	Osmunda spp.	○●
St John's wort	Hypericum spp.	✪◗	Pachysandra	Pachysandra terminalis	○●
Siberian iris	Iris sibirica	✪◗	Lungwort	Pulmonaria spp.	○●
Japanese rose	Kerria japonica	✪◗	Foamflower	Tiarella cordifolia	○●
Currant	Ribes spp.	✪◗	Trillium	Trillium spp.	○●
Snowberry	Symphoricarpos spp.	✪◗	Common periwinkle	Vinca minor	○●
Clematis	Clematis spp.	✪◗	Shield fern	Polystichum spp.	◗
Honeysuckle	Lonicera (climbing)	✪◗	As species	Primula spp.	◗
Virgin's bower	Parthenocissus spp.	✪◗	Sweet woodruff	Galium odoratum	◗●
Spiderwort	Tradescantia spp.	✪◗	Japanese painted fern	Athyrium niponicum	◗●
Globeflower	Trollius spp.	✪◗	Shooting star	Dodecatheon spp.	◗●
Columbine	Aquilegia spp	○◗	Shield fern	Dryopteris spp.	◗●
Goat's beard	Aruncus dioica	○◗	Hellebore	Helleborus spp.	◗●
Lady fern	Athyrium filix-femina	○◗	Solomon's seal	Polygonatum spp.	◗●
Elephant's ear	Bergenia spp.	○◗	False Solomon's seal	Smilacina spp.	◗●
Bellflower	Campanula spp.	○◗	Bellwort	Uvularia grandiflora	◗●

Exposed Gardens

Exposed gardens tend to be on a hill or in an open setting but can also be the result of the built landscape in the case of, for example, a roof garden. What they all share is the tendency to be affected periodically by strong winds, and it is this factor that makes them different from other sites. Having said this, they do of course share many characteristics with other gardens, including light or shade, soil types and the overall climate. The method most frequently used to mitigate the effects of wind is to create shelter, usually in areas for patios and seating areas or to create calm growing conditions for less robust specimens.

Barriers can be a mixed blessing where wind is concerned, often creating turbulence and 'eddies' as the wind hits them, sometimes exacerbating rather than relieving the problem. The real trick is to create a filtered barrier that reduces the impact of the wind, such as might be created by a planted hedge or a climber growing over a trellis. Trellises and associated shrubs or climbers can also help to reduce the turbulence caused by wind 'hitting' a wall, thereby limiting its effect on surrounding plants. Any 'shelter belt', hedge or similar feature will of course need to consist of suitably wind-tolerant plants, and this usually means using a relatively high proportion of evergreens as the 'back-bone' of the planting to ensure that the benefits are felt

Where high winds prevail from a particular direction, the plants at the front tend to bear the brunt of the damage, and therefore protect those behind.

all year round. Even then, a newly-planted shelter belt or hedge planted in exposed conditions will normally need protection in the form of temporary windbreaks around them until they are well established.

Another approach that can easily be combined with shelter planting is making sunken areas within the garden to provide even more shelter for patios, seating and planting. The first step in achieving this is to establish where the most sheltered area is, ensuring that this is relative to the year-round prevailing wind and not just that particular day. Ideally, a sunken terrace should be excavated to a depth of 60cm (2ft) and given further protection with a low, wind-filtering shelter belt around the upper edge. The effect of this can be dramatic as even a modest shelter planting can lift the wind for a distance of up to twenty times its height. In other words, a 1m (3¼ft) high screen gives a degree of shelter to an area of up to 20m (65ft) in length. Ultimately, the thickness of the windbreak has a major effect upon its efficiency. For a thicker planting, the windward side needs to start with low growing planting, gradually building up the height.

Whatever method is used to mitigate the effect of wind though, it is unlikely to remove its effects completely, meaning that the choice of plants is always important. Wind causes physical damage to plants, breaking limbs and stems, and drying out foliage. Often it is the top third that bears the brunt of the damage and of course, taller plants become more prone as they grow. In addition, plants growing in containers may be blown over and suffer additional stress due to water loss on account of constant air movement over their leaves. Low growing species and varieties are of course more immune to these problems, making them the preferred choice in many settings. Care must also be taken when positioning fragile structures such as greenhouses, or frames, as these are especially vulnerable to sudden, violent gusts. These must always be positioned in a sheltered spot, with a separate wind break if necessary, in order to ensure that they are kept safe. In addition to this, sheltering a greenhouse will have the additional benefit of stabilizing its internal environment; a glasshouse or frame in an exposed setting being much more liable to temperature fluctuations due to the cooling effect of high winds.

If a garden's structure is carefully planned so as to provide good shelter, particularly if hedges or other planting is used to achieve this, sheltered areas will develop in time, which in turn will enable a greater plant choice for future planting. At the outset though, the style of planting is likely to reflect the degree of exposure experienced, meaning that plants with robust but flexible stems which move with the wind, will be the preferred option. Even low-growing herbaceous plants will benefit from the additional support that twiggy pea sticks or short branches, pushed into the ground around them early on in the season, will give them in the summer months. Ensure that any plants chosen make 'good neighbours.' Plants that lean into the surrounding specimens as gusts occur therefore should spring back and not cause damage or harm when they do this.

Coastal Gardens

While the traditional view of the coast can be one of gentle balmy breezes over calm blue waters, in the main, this is a long way from the truth. Of course, coastal gardens do vary according to their location but as a rule most are very windy, being constantly subject to salt-laden, often quite brisk winds or, worse still, periodically battered and even 'sand blasted' by fine grit in the worst of the yearly storms. As if this were not enough the soil, while often variable, is frequently sandy or stony with higher salt levels than those even just a short way inland, and as a consequence is frequently nutrient poor. All of this would seemingly make gardening in coastal conditions rather difficult but, if carefully planned, it is feasible to have a truly magnificent coastal garden that will be the envy of other gardeners that visit.

Plant selection is, of course, important with suitable candidates needing to be able to tolerate the effects of wind and salt. There are however certain advantages to gardening along the coast, and chief among these is the tendency for coastal areas to be somewhat more frost free than those even a short way inland. If wind damage can be alleviated by using shelter planting to protecting part or even the entire garden from strong winds, this often yields the full benefit of the milder climatic conditions.

For gardens almost right on the coast, salt deposited from spray can build up on the foliage and in the soil around plants that can in turn cause extensive damage to less tolerant specimens. Plants sensitive to salts usually show injury almost immediately and frequently decline quickly after exposure. Air-borne salt-spray draws moisture out of sensitive plant tissue, causing desiccation and burn, a situation that can be exacerbated during summer or hot dry weather, when leaf margins are most likely to show burn or scorch. Salt spray and a build up of soil salt can ultimately result in branch dieback, stunted stem and leaf growth, an overall lack of vigour, and eventually death. These sorts of injury are of course most evident nearest to the sea, and although it does steadily decrease with distance, sensitive plants can still show wind-effected 'salt-burn' for up to one kilometre (0.6 mile) inland. Aerial salt damage is frequently a one-sided thing though, with the seaward portion of the plant primarily affected, often leading to a characteristic windswept effect.

On very exposed situations like this limestone cliff, even this wind tolerant juniper grows in tortuous forms under the relentless effect of the wind.

Plant injury due to soil salt is usually rarer in coastal gardens as the effect of regular rainfall often leaches the salt from the soil more quickly than it can build up. However, problems can occur if the sea inundates land – for example during a storm – or if salt water percolates inland some way, seeping under the ground and thereby causing the soil water to become brackish. Coastal regions often experience saltwater intrusion as groundwater is taken from aquifers via boreholes for example and is replaced by saltwater. Whatever the cause, the net effect is a build-up of sodium and chloride (the breakdown products of salt when dissolved in water), which can damage plants as they absorb them into their

The effects of the wind are often seen in the landscape, where the constant effect of wind can form extensive, shifting sand dunes on some shorelines.

Once the effect of wind has been removed, the range of plants that can be grown in coastal locations is often increased due to the warming influence of the sea.

Even when cool conditions tend to prevail, the effect of coastal warming enables some gardeners to grow unusual or exotic specimens such as this *Banksia*.

roots. These net effects (for all but those species able to tolerate and grow in salt water environments) can be seen in a variety of visible symptoms, including browning along leaf edges; stunted growth; fewer and smaller leaves, flowers and fruit. Essentially, these symptoms are very similar (even identical) to drought, which is hardly surprising, as soil salt damages the roots severely, resulting in rapid and serious root loss.

If attempting to grow plants in areas where soil salt concentrations are high, it is very important to use salt-tolerant plants. Ironically though, the greatest problems caused by salt toxicity rarely occur in coastal regions but are commonly encountered in towns or by roadsides in areas that experience cold winters, this being the result of de-icing salts used to clear snow and ice. While it is possible to choose salt-tolerant plants for these areas, the uncertainty of the levels of salt involved means that trial and error may be the only way to find out exactly which plants tolerate the conditions. One solution to reduce the amount of damage caused following recent inundation with salt water is to irrigate the affected land, in order to help move salts down through the soil. This works most effectively on more freely-draining soils, whereas heavy soils or sites prone to water-logging and high water tables are likely to be more seriously affected. Traditionally, gypsum (calcium sulphate) is applied to clay soils that have been flooded by the sea, or otherwise inundated with salt to mitigate its effects. In general this is applied at a rate of 30g per m^2 (1oz per yd^2) although this may vary according to the soil type and amount of salt involved. Gypsum works by chemically ridding the soil of sodium (the most damaging element of salt as far as plants are concerned) but also improves drainage by causing the soil to break into small, more freely draining aggregates; a process called 'flocculation'.

If the problem exists because of salt percolating into soil water through seepage from the sea itself, such as may be found near the sea in low lying areas, then the easiest solution would of course be to build raised beds or plant on mounds (if growing vegetables) as both of these situations can aid the movement of freshwater up into the soil by capillary action, while leaving more salt-laden water in the lower levels. Any salt that goes with this water would usually be washed back through by irrigation or rainfall.

Salt Spray Tolerant Plants

T = Plants with highest degree of salt tolerance suited for use in most exposed areas
M = Plants with a moderate degree of salt tolerance for use in lower salt areas
* = Plant is tolerant of soil salt

Common Name	Botanical Name	Salt	Common Name	Botanical Name	Salt
Maple	*Acer spp.*	T	Sumac	*Rhus spp.**	T
Horse-chestnut	*Aesculus hippocastanum**	T	Elderberry	*Sambucus spp.*	T
Juneberry	*Amelanchier spp.*	T	As species	*Spiraea spp. (most)*	T
New Zealand cabbage tree	*Cordyline australis*	T	Lilac	*Syringa spp.*	T
As species	*Forsythia spp.**	T	Bald-cypress	*Taxodium distichum**	T
As species	*Fuchsia spp.*	T	Elm	*Ulmus spp.**	T
Honey locust	*Gleditsia triacanthos**	T	Strawberry tree	*Arbutus unedo*	M
As species	*Hydrangea spp.*	T	Birch	*Betula spp.*	M
St John's wort	*Hypericum spp.*	T	Sun rose	*Cistus spp.*	M
Walnut	*Juglans spp.**	T	Ginkgo	*Ginkgo biloba**	M
Larch	*Larix spp.*	T	Crab apple	*Malus spp. (particularly ornamental cultivars)*	M
Sweet gum	*Liquidambar styraciflua**	T	Plane	*Platanus spp.**	M
Russian-sage	*Perovskia atriplicifolia*	T	Cherry	*Prunus spp.*	M
Blue spruce	*Picea pungens**	T	Mock-orange	*Philadelphus coronarius*	M
As species	*Pittosporum spp.*	T	Rowan	*Sorbus aucuparia*	M
Shrubby cinquefoil	*Potentilla fruticosa*	T	Viburnum	*Viburnum spp.*	M

Plants suitable for Windbreaks and Shelter planting

Common Name	Botanical Name	Salt	Common Name	Botanical Name	Salt
Barberry	*Berberis spp.*	T	New Zealand flax	*Phormium spp.*	T
As species	*Cotoneaster spp.**	T	Pine	*Pinus spp.**	T
As species	*Elaeagnus spp.*	T	Firethorn	*Pyracantha coccinea*	T
As species	*Escallonia spp.*	T	Oak	*Quercus spp.*	T
Japanese spindle	*Euonymus japonicus*	T	Rugosa rose	*Rosa spp. (particularly R. rugosa*)*	T
New Zealand privet	*Griselinia littoralis*	T	Snowberry	*Symphoricarpos albus*	T
Shrubby veronica	*Hebe spp.*	T	Tamarisk	*Tamarix tetrandra*	T
Sea-buckthorn	*Hippophae rhamnoides**	T	Broom	*Cytisus x praecox*	M
Juniper	*Juniperus spp.**	T	Shrubby althea	*Hibiscus syriacus*	M
Daisy holly	*Olearia macrodonta*	T	Holly	*Ilex spp.*	M

Cold or Frost-prone Gardens

The range of temperatures that a garden experiences through a complete growing cycle depends mostly upon where it is situated. Most important in all of this is the prevailing climate, and gardeners living in places where the winters are characteristically harsh must accept this as a fact of life. But despite this, local variations in the geography and topography of an area mean that even in relatively mild climates, some places tend to be more prone to cold than others. Often, these places are prone to more frosty days per year than the surrounding land and are often referred to as 'frost pockets' or 'frost hollows'.

While winter frosts can (or at least should) be foreseen in cooler climates and appropriate action be taken, frost in the late spring or early autumn can be more unpredictable, frequently causing much more severe damage when it happens. Early or late frosts usually occur on calm clear nights, where the air near to the ground cools as heat radiates back into space until just after dawn. This results in a situation known as 'temperature inversion' where temperatures increase with height above the ground (as opposed to the more usual decrease with height) that causes what is known as a 'ground frost'. This results in a situation where the temperature near the ground can dip to or even below freezing, damaging

Gardeners living in places where the winters are characteristically harsh must accept frost as a fact of life, and should choose plants able to withstand this.

The palm (TOP RIGHT) is healthy, having withstood the winter cold. Another growing next (BOTTOM RIGHT) to it was severely damaged, as the hedge and wall behind created a frost barrier and therefore colder conditions.

plants before the sunlight warms the ground once more. These ground frosts can form even when air temperatures as little as 1.2m (4ft) above the soil surface remain as high as 4°C (39°F) and in many ways, even if the frost itself does not damage the plants, the wild fluctuation between daytime highs and night- time lows can prove very stressful to vulnerable plants; with even otherwise hardy specimens often being affected by such late frosts.

Frost may also occur in low lying areas as cooler air over the higher ground (perhaps on hills or mountain sides) becomes cooler than the air at the same altitude above the 'valley' beneath. The cold air is more dense and begins to flow down the slope into lower lying areas (cold air drainage) resulting in a phenomenon known as a 'katabatic' wind. These are generally light, and often blow unnoticed, although the resulting temperatures in low-lying areas can be significantly lower than that of the surrounding higher ground. Often they fall low enough for ground frost to form, and in all cases, the surrounding higher ground remains warmer than in the depression. Temperature differences can be as much as 8°C (14°F) between a valley bottom and land at 200m (700ft) above this at the height of the frost, which are often seen in these places both earlier in the autumn and later in the spring than on the surrounding higher ground.

Larger frost hollows (also known as cold pools) are characterized by cold air trapped under an overlying blanket of warmer air during calm winter weather conditions, often seen as a shallow 'lake' of ground fog. The formation of a 'frost hollow' is not always just at the lowest point on a slope though, and can often be enhanced (or even a direct result of) by the flow of cold air being obstructed by obstacles such as hedges or more seriously solid boundaries like walls or fences.

In warm dry areas, frosts occur through heat loss from the ground at night. Here, grass walls trap heat in the day and warm bottles full of water retain warmth, and radiate this through the night.

The bottles, placed next to each tomato plant, radiate heat at night, preventing frost damage and can also be used to provide slow drip irrigation if needed.

Dealing with Early or Late Frosts

While it may at first seem challenging to grow delicate plants in gardens situated in or possessing a frost hollow, there are some things that can be done to prevent damage by light frosts. Water holds heat more effectively than land, as do darker bare soils. This means that moist, firm and bare soils tend to absorb more heat in the day and lose heat more slowly overnight than dry, loose and weed-covered soils. The beneficial effect of water can also be enhanced by keeping a supply of water above the ground, to store up the heat of the day. This can be done by filling clear glass or plastic bottles with water and standing these among plants in order that they can be warmed by the sun. As the sun sets, these bottles will gradually radiate the heat to the surrounding air, and although the water (and ultimately the surrounding air) will slowly cool, it will normally be sufficient to prevent a frost and the resulting damage this could cause, as well as to prevent cold shock and ensure good growth and cropping. It can also be used in conjunction with a fleece covering to further enhance the warming effect.

If cold air flow is obstructed by a barrier, such as a hedge, or particularly a fence or wall, then removing this can of course help prevent frost, although this may not always be in the general interest of the function or design of the garden. In these cases then, planting less sensitive or taller (woody) plants can be the best compromise.

Types of Frost Damage

In colder climates, where frost or frozen ground can persist for days or even weeks at a time, many plants begin to suffer what is effectively a drought stress as roots are unable to harvest water. Most hardy plants get around this by entering a phase of dormancy, usually after a gradual period of acclimatization during the autumn, in which the plants internal chemistry and even their cellular make-up, start to alter in readiness for the coming chill. Despite this ability, a sudden unseasonable frost can be devastating, as hardiest spe-

A severe frost can be very damaging to more tender herbaceous specimens, although these often recover in spring despite their alarming appearance.

A late frost often causes more damage than those of the preceding winter, as young, susceptible growth is more prone to damage than the mature leaves.

cies often show a marked difference in their growth patterns (and indeed, the degree of frost sensitivity) according to the season. Late or early frosts are often only noticed when young, fresh growth is affected, usually browned and blackened as if by fire; often with little or no effect upon the more mature growth surrounding it. The real damage though is often less obvious and, even if a frost does not occur, sudden drops in temperature can cause a severe check in the growth of a plant for weeks to come.

Plants that are frost tender (that is those from warm, perhaps tropical climates), do not have any mechanisms to resist frost and some will quickly die from cell damage as a result of sudden cold or frost. When growing these types of plants, it is important that they are protected from this happening wherever possible. One obvious way of doing this is to establish the average dates of the last spring frost and the first one of the autumn. This is not necessarily an iron-clad guide, but it does cut down the chances of damage. Even after the last frost has seemingly passed or as the first autumn chill approaches, it may still be best to provide additional protection, such as a layer of fleece or cloches to ensure the plants do not become severely chilled at night. Individual plants can be protected from early or late frosts by covering them with recycled plastic bottles.

If a shrub is severely damaged by frost, the result can sometimes be dieback from the tips, something that must be pruned out in spring as growth begins.

Plant Hardiness

Plant hardiness is generally considered to be the lowest temperature that a plant can withstand during the winter. This is the basis of numerous classification systems, including the US Zone system, widely used by American gardeners to determine whether they can grow a particular plant in their area, as well as equivalent systems from the RHS (Royal Horticultural Society) in the United Kingdom and the EGF (European Garden Flora) across mainland Europe.

There is of course more to plant hardiness than an ability to withstand winter temperatures. Indeed, if temperature alone dictated hardiness, gardeners in the British Isles for example might expect to grow numerous tropical plants outside all year round. The fact that this is not the case serves to illustrate that there are other factors which combine to determine where a plant can grow, many of which are much more important than simply the lowest winter temperature a plant can withstand.

Summer temperatures are of course equally important when determining where a plant can survive and in some places, even if it does not get too cold during winter, a plant may still be at risk from prolonged high temperatures. Conversely, some species may not receive sufficient warmth during the summer to ripen or prepare sufficiently to withstand the oncoming winter. Soil type, levels of rainfall (and when this falls) also have a profound effect, as does the degree of shelter or exposure. Lastly, in high or low latitudes, day length, the angle of the sun and ultimately the brightness of the light, can all prove to be as important as the temperature, in determining whether a plant could really be considered hardy. Individual plants will vary in their ability to accept a particular set of circumstances and every garden provides a different environment. Even when a plant's requirements have been researched and matched to a garden, the only way to know if it is truly hardy in that setting is to try it out.

Hardy species, while well adapted to winter cold can benefit from a little help as the season draws to a close. Mulch can help prevent frost damage through the spring and autumn, but it is best not applied late in the autumn, despite much conventional 'wisdom' on the subject. Late mulch, applied in a cold or frost prone area, can actually encourage continued growth; something that will result in extensive damage to immature growth once the frost arrives. In addition, some herbaceous plants are prone to rot if covered by mulch. The other thing to avoid in the autumn is applying fertilizers of any kind. Even after the first frosts, there can be a mild spell from late autumn into early winter, and adding fertilizers will also tend to stimulate late, tender growth. The key then is to mulch and fertilize only in the spring, through the summer and into early autumn, but to let nature take its course through winter.

Container plants are particularly prone to frost damage during the coldest parts of the winter, as their roots are less protected than those of plants growing in open ground. These can often be helped by wrapping both the top-growth and the pots themselves, moving them into a more sheltered spot and applying further cover if a cold snap is forecast.

Plant Hardiness Scales						
Heat Tolerance		Cold Tolerance*				
Total number of Days over 86°F	Zone	°C	Minimum temp	°F	US Zone	EGF Zone**
0	1	-45		-50	1	H1
1-7	2	-40		-40	2	
7 - 14	3	-35		-30	3	
14 - 30	4	-30		-20	4	
30 - 45	5	-25		-10	5	
45 - 60	6	-20		0	6	H2
60 - 90	7	-15		10	7	H3
90 - 120	8	-10		20	8	H4
120 - 150	9	-5		30	9	H5
150 - 180	10	0		40	10	G1
180 - 210	11	5+		50	11	G2
210+	12					

* In the case of cold hardiness, this is generally considered to be the lowest temperature that a plant can withstand during the winter
** EGF= European Garden Flora

Urban Gardens

An urban garden, for many, is a vital oasis of green calm right in the heart of the concrete sprawl; the perfect antidote to the pressures of modern living and a chance to 'commune with nature'. But to create that perfect dream of calm and space often means contending with a range of problems. Done well, an urban garden can be a really exciting place, full of strong architectural shapes and seemingly exotic species, the best of which continue to look good all year round. Whatever the style that is adopted though, the plants growing in them must be chosen carefully if they are to cope with and ultimately thrive within the challenging effects of modern urban life.

Urban Areas and the 'Heat Island Effect'

Urban areas are stressful places for life of almost any description; not just humans but also the plants (and animals) that share this space. Towns and cities are also vastly different from the countryside that surrounds them, often tending to be both warmer and drier than their rural equivalent. This is because buildings and paved surfaces absorb heat during the day, before radiating it back into the air at night, thereby reducing the chances of frost and moderating low temperatures during winter. This temperature difference is usually greatest at night, largely because of the effect of buildings and paved surfaces re-radiating heat built up during the day, this being most obvious when winds are weak. Indeed, many urban areas are essentially a full 'hardiness zone', warmer than rural areas just a few miles away. Conversely, warming effects carry over into the summer, with urban microclimates often trapping heat, which ultimately creates a scorching environment that can damage plants.

Areas with the least bare earth and vegetation tend to be most severely affected, due mainly to the fact that less energy is used up in these places in evaporating water. In addition to the storage capacity of buildings and sealed surfaces, heat is also generated by heating, cooling, transport and so forth; as well as by

the increased potential of the complex three-dimensional structures of landscape to trap solar energy; these all act together to raise the temperature. This can amount to a marked increase both above and below ground, with air temperatures often in excess of 5°C (9°F) higher than the surrounding countryside. Add to this the fact that the average soil temperatures in open, unvegetated areas in cities also tends to be around 3°C (5.5°F) warmer, heavily vegetated or wooded areas and cities suddenly seem both warmer and more variable than the surrounding countryside.

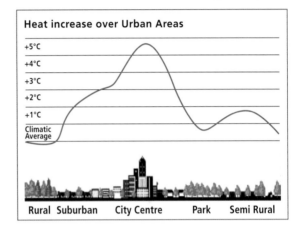

Urban Rainfall and Soil-water

While a built-up area may result in a few less rainy days per year, on average, urban situations get a similar amount of rain as the surrounding countryside. The problem for plants growing in urban locations then is not so much how much rain falls, as how much is retained in the soil. Many towns and cities have, as a result of the necessities of modern living, extensive areas of impervious surfaces, such as roads, car parks or other paved areas that do not allow the free passage of water through them and into the soil below. Add to this the effect of the buildings themselves – rooftops do not allow water to percolate through to the soil either during or immediately after rainfall – and it quickly becomes apparent that much of the rain that falls across highly built-up areas is lost into drains and ultimately rivers. This of course does not directly affect islands of garden greenery, as these do allow the passage of water. Indeed, extra water can be channelled from roofs and paved areas to the growing areas themselves, or be stored in tanks or other containers for later use. The real, perhaps slightly indirect problem occurs when the net effect of all the lost water is felt, causing lowering of the water table (because groundwater recharge is lessened). At the other end of the scale, if rainfall occurs seasonally, or if it is unseasonably heavy, the effect of sudden runoff from sealed surfaces can be to cause flooding or waterlogging, as the amount of infiltration space left for the water to escape into is insufficient for the volume that has fallen.

Pollution in Urban Gardens

Both air and soil in an urban garden can be affected by pollution and this area, like many aspects of urban living, is a complex one. This is because of there being many forms of pollution; fumes generated by traffic emissions or (if the garden borders a road) runoff from the road such as salt used to melt winter ice and frost; as well as dust, dirt and rubbish blown (or thrown) into gardens.

Of all of these pollutants, it is arguably the emissions from burning fossil fuels – mostly car exhausts, heating oil or gas fumes in most modern cities – that result in polluting gases such as sulphur dioxide, carbon monoxide, nitrogen oxides, hydrocarbons (essentially un-burnt fuel), soot and carbon dioxide. The most talked about side effect of all this is of course the growth of illnesses including lung cancer, asthma, circulatory diseases, bronchitis, and various allergies, all of which may either be caused or worsened by the effect of increasing levels of air pollution. If pollutants are harmful to humans, then they are also harmful to plants. Of course, the amount of pollutants floating in the air of a given city at any one time can and does vary, often as a result of climatic conditions, the time of the day, and even time of the week. Some pollutants however form mixtures; the notorious 'urban smog clouds' that often are not apparent in their effects upon either the humans or plants that live in a city due to the invisibility of some injuries in the short term. Pollutants in this mixture often include Nitrogen Oxides (NO_x), Ozone (O_3), the effects of which can be exacerbated by light to form photochemical smog and PAN. If this wasn't enough, various solvents and suchlike from construction materials (occasional and mostly short term in their importance), and particulate emissions that also come out of some exhausts (soot, for want of a better expression!), all add to the poisonous broth that infiltrates the city air.

A visit to any city quickly shows that there are some plants that not only survive, but also thrive in the environment. Pollution is also rarely uniform

Lichens with more filamentous or open growth habits (LEFT) tend to be rare in central areas of large cities, or other places where air pollution levels are high.

across the city (at ground level at least) and some areas are less affected than others. A good indication of the air quality in an area tends to be the lichens found there. Lichens are composite organisms that consist of a symbiotic association of a fungus with a photosynthetic partner, usually either a green algae or cyanobacterium. They are found almost everywhere from the most extreme environments (arctic rocks to hot deserts) as well as often being found abundantly in gardens on branches, bare rocks, walls and roofs. Lichens are not only widespread but may be long-lived; meaning that they are useful indicators of environmental disturbance. Quite simply, the longer and more 'luxuriant' their growth filament patterns are, the cleaner the air they are growing in. If the lichens in your garden are all short, close-hugging encrusting types, then the air may well be polluted. If they are longer and more 'hairy' in their appearance, then the air must be cleaner. Not only that but if the colonies of this latter type are large and extensive, they indicate that the air tends to be clean as a matter of course and has been so for some time.

Problems with Urban Soils

Damaged Soils

Many urban locations have soils that have been damaged by their prior use (or perhaps abuse) or by the effects of recent development work. Often, people taking on a newly built home in an urban setting inherit a whole range of problems that can, if not properly addressed, result in poor plant establishment and growth. The commonest of these problems is the result of soil becoming compacted during development work, this consequentially restricting soil drainage, as well as water infiltration and free exchange of air. The net result of this is a depletion of oxygen within the soil, leading to loss of soil life, disruption of normal cycles, and ultimately a build up of harmful substances.

Soils in urban settings can also be contaminated with various pollutants, the range of which may be vast and usually directly associated with the land's former use. Having said this, toxins that are the result of industrial processes are rarely a problem, as the developer would

Fuel spillages are a frequent cause of soil damage in urban locations; the net result of this is a loss of soil life and disruption of 'normal' natural cycles.

have been required to remove any such contaminated material. There can be instances of localized pollution from chemicals however, chief of which is the effects of localized fuel spillages towards the completion of work, or more occasionally, buried rubble or other inert matter. The latter of these, while not directly toxic to plants, can interfere with rooting, drainage and (in some cases) might make cultivation difficult.

It should never be assumed however, that just because a soil has suffered damage that it cannot be repaired. Many urban soils are inherently rich in most of the major plant nutrients and are infertile only because the natural nutrient cycles have been arrested due to the soil's poor structure or due to the depleted level of organic matter they contain. Of these nutrients, nitrogen shortage is often the most noticeable problem, although digging in organic matter and/or using legumes as a green manure crop often leads to rapid and significant improvements in its availability. The greater problem that must be overcome is the lack of numbers and diversity within the soil's living community of micro-organisms; although these often recover surprisingly quickly if the soil is well managed and maintained.

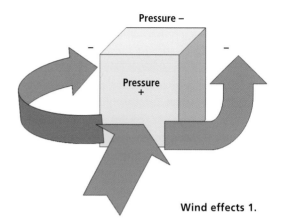

Wind effects 1.

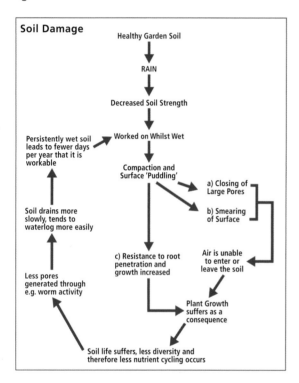

Soil Damage

Healthy Garden Soil
↓
RAIN
↓
Decreased Soil Strength
↓
Worked on Whilst Wet

Persistently wet soil leads to fewer days per year that it is workable

Compaction and Surface 'Puddling'
a) Closing of Large Pores
b) Smearing of Surface

Soil drains more slowly, tends to waterlog more easily

c) Resistance to root penetration and growth increased
Air is unable to enter or leave the soil

Less pores generated through e.g. worm activity

Plant Growth suffers as a consequence

Soil life suffers, less diversity and therefore less nutrient cycling occurs

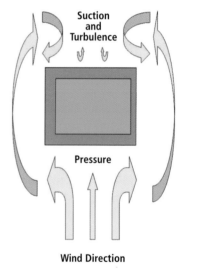

Wind effects 2.

Wind and Urban Locations

Buildings, while they often offer protection from wind in many places, can become problematic in an urban setting, particularly in high density developments where in many cases they tend to exacerbate its effects by causing turbulence. This is of course beyond the scope of most gardeners to counter, as the effects are the result of the surroundings, rather than an internal problem. Having said this, it is useful to be aware of exactly how the wind can be affected by the surrounding town or cityscape, as this may well have a bearing upon which plants will thrive there.

This wind strike effect has three principal outcomes, all of which may make growing plants difficult.

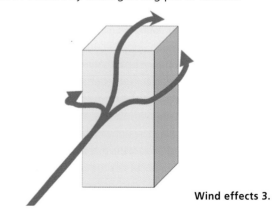

Wind effects 3.

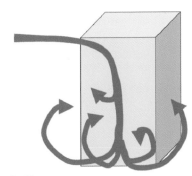

Wind effects 4.

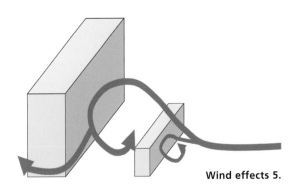

Wind effects 5.

Of course, the direction that the wind is coming from can vary throughout the year meaning that any built-up area will be prone to occasional damage from wind turbulence. Quite simply, the more solid obstacles (buildings, walls and such like) that the wind can encounter, the more wind resistant plants will need to be.

Gardening in a Limited Space

Many urban gardens have only a limited space, often with little or, in some cases, no open soil to grow plants in. This makes careful garden planning all the more important, and despite the limitations that small spaces such as patios, terraces and roof gardens can sometimes impose, there are many ways that these spaces can be transformed into green oases.

Roof gardens vary according to the type of roof involved and can be as varied as any other type of garden. With a little imagination they can easily form an excellent outdoor green-space, which often doubles up as urban wildlife sanctuaries, due to their relative seclusion from people and domestic predators such as cats, dogs or feral predators such as foxes and rats. At their simplest they are described as a green roof, where the roof of a building is partially or completely covered with a growing medium that has been placed over a waterproofing membrane into which the vegetation is established. These can be established on both pitched and flat roofs with many different designs and construction methods

used to make them. They vary in their relative complexity and the work to establish one on a permanent dwelling space is usually best left to a specialist contractor, although a shed or similar may be achievable for a gardener. Green roofs are essentially spaces that use plants as an alternative for tiles or other roof materials and are usually not used as a leisure space. Having said this, they can, if well planned, be extremely ornamental and can greatly improve the environmental credentials of the building.

However, more complex designs are sometimes made which can be used as a space for relaxation and leisure. These may be no more complex than putting a few planted containers onto a roof

Even where space is limited, it is still be possible to create an area of garden that not only provides a space to grow plants but also an outdoor living space.

Even the limited space found at the front of some urban dwellings can be converted into a tiny green oasis, that helps counter harsh urban surroundings.

terrace (or sundeck) to make it more pleasant to sit on. Others, however, may be far more complex and can be very ornately designed. Roof gardens frequently feature plants that are quite tough as they must cope with the dual effect of dry and windy conditions that often prevail there. Anyone interested in creating a roof garden, would be well advised to seek advice from an engineer or specialized firm to check that the structure involved is able to support it as the first priority. The engineering implications can be complex and ensuring its safe completion may well be a legal obligation where a dwelling is concerned. At the very least, a specialist can offer advice and perhaps provide an outline design to help with all of this.

Patios, Walls and Containers

Patios and courtyard gardens can offer similar challenges to a roof, especially when space is limited. Their major advantage is that items placed out onto a patio are not limited in respect of their size or weight by the fear of damage to any building or structures below. The most common addition to a patio would be to build raised planter beds or to place containers in order to grow plants. It is often surprising just how many things will actually grow in a pot and it is perfectly feasible to have a garden full of resplendent blooms using no more than containers.

Remember that the soil in a container is more easily drained than topsoil in the ground and the plants grown will require a rich potting mix to be at their best. A patio can seem rather stark and plants offer the easiest way to remedy this by softening the edges and blending it into the surroundings. The appearance of a new patio can also be artificially 'aged' by planting some smaller creeping plants such as thyme (*Thymus spp.*) in the cracks between individual paving slabs.

If space is especially limited the number of plants grown can always be effectively increased by making use of the surrounding walls. In the most extreme examples of this, architects have actually engineered living walls where plants are rooted in compartments between two sheets of fibrous material anchored to a wall. Water trickles down between the sheets and feeds moss, vines and other plants. While this idea may be too complex for most home gardeners, some of the effect can be captured by placing troughs and hanging baskets on the walls to create this third dimension to your available space. In addition to wall mounted pots, a few annual or smaller perennial climbers planted in large pots near to the wall, will clothe these in greenery and flowers. Twining plants such as a honeysuckle (*Lonicera spp.*) or jasmine (*Jasminum spp.*) rapidly cover a wall-mounted trellis, look great and on warm summer evenings fill the air with their delicious, heady perfume; arguably the perfect antidote for stressful city life.

Window-boxes mean that even people living in properties without a formal garden space can still have some plants growing around them.

In summer, even a modestly sized pot can easily be transformed into a blaze of colour using a nothing more than a few tender annuals and perennials.

GARDENING FOR SUSTAINABLE RESULTS

A sustainable garden usually means a variety of things to different people. However, the methods used are less important at the outset than the goal in mind. If a garden is to be sustainable, the aim should be to create and maintain one that can be used productively over an extended period of time. While there are no hard and fast rules then about the type of garden it should be, there are certain considerations that must be addressed, chiefly concerning the inputs and outputs from the garden space. Essentially, inputs from outside the garden (with the exception of natural things like rain, sunshine and so on) should be reduced, and negative outputs such as waste or pollution from the garden similarly controlled. This seems simple at first glance, but it is important to consider this in the widest sense, 'to think globally while acting locally'.

Environmental Footprints

An 'Environmental Footprint' (EF) is a commonly used method, the aim of which is to measure how much of the planet's resources are required to meet human needs. It represents the amount of land and sea used to live what might seem rather ordinary lives. Land is used for a whole range of resources it can provide, such as food and drink, fuel, building materials – ultimately everything humans buy; to build and live on as well as for its capacity to process the waste produced as a result of all the other activities.

In much of the developed Western World the environmental footprint is 5.6 global hectares (gha) per person per year. In other words, the land needed to support all of our current activities is roughly

OPPOSITE PAGE:
A small productive polytunnel is not only environmentally friendly, but can save on grocery bills too.

RIGHT: Sustainable gardening is only one aspect of what for some is a way of life; this eco-home is aiming for minimal impact on the environment.

equivalent to 56,000m² (66,975yd²) or a square plot of land whose sides are just over 335m (776ft) long for every single person on the planet. Even if a child were half of this then (a debatable point) an 'average' family of four would need at least 16.8 hectares (41.5 acres) to sustain them. To put this really into perspective then, if everyone on the planet lived like this there would need to be 3.5 earths for everyone to live on. Plainly then, living sustainably and within the limits of the planet requires that the available resources be used more efficiently. Of course this needs a sustainable target for any environmental footprint, and this can be calculated by looking at the total area of the earth's productive land and sea and dividing it by the number of people in the world – a calculation that results in a footprint of approximately 1.8 hectares per person.

Every action taken in a garden that makes the use of resources more efficient then will have a direct effect in reducing the environmental footprint for that household. Although this may not be the answer in its own right it is extremely positive; something that is within any individual's control and ultimately an achievable goal.

Inputs and Outputs

In order to understand how a garden can become more sustainable, it is important to look at the inputs necessary and the outputs achieved. Inputs are essentially those which come from (or are introduced) from outside the garden. The major input factors in gardens do of course vary according to the type of garden concerned but most common involve the purchase of tools and various sundry products, use of fossil fuels, structures and, where used, additional fertilizers and chemical products. Of these, tools arguably have the least impact as they (potentially) last a long time if well cared for, especially traditional hand tools. Having established this, their manufacture and the supply chain needed to get them to the point of sale (an often increasingly complex affair in the global economy), do add to their environmental impact. Other sundry products (for example pots, wood, fleece and so on) and larger items such as glasshouses,

sheds or other structures also carry with them this burden of manufacture and transport. The increasing (and in some respects ever more complex) array of garden 'power-machinery' bring the recurring costs of maintenance and fuel inputs.

The story can become even more complex when considering 'traditional' inputs like manure, as these can also have high environmental costs even if sourced locally because of the high volumes and/or quantities used. After all, each horse needs land to live on, stabling, fencing and other containments; veterinary care, additional food and fodder as well as the equipment needed to ride them. This is still true of agricultural animals, although the riding gear could be omitted with these! Indeed, when miscellaneous inputs such as transport, waste and recycling are added to a variety of garden inputs, or the resultant garden output, then these can account for a significant proportion of its ecological footprint.

Fossil Fuels and Transport

Fossil fuels are a finite resource and their consumption to provide for human energy needs has a negative impact upon the planet as a whole. In short, practically everything that is commercially manufactured, and every item that is transported to a point of sale (and indeed from there to the garden) uses fossil fuels during the process. They may also be used to power certain items of garden machinery or to heat glasshouses and so forth and, in this way, they are an input. Often, gardeners buy items from sources nearby, and in this way the transport from the vendor to the garden only represents a small proportion of the overall footprint. The true cost can only be calculated if all the energy that has gone into obtaining and (where appropriate) making the basic materials, their manufacture into the finished item, and after this, the transport from the place of manufacture to the vending site, is taken into account.

Even if plants grown in the garden are considered, the actual fuel requirement of getting to and from the site where they were produced is an input. Even if they are raised in the garden, if pots, compost or other

Green energy generated from wind power is just one example of an alternative to fossil fuel use, and is a source of power that is truly sustainable.

sundries are used, they were made and transported and so constitute an input, albeit much reduced. Having established this then, it quickly becomes clear that the way that a garden is run greatly affects its associated inputs. A new garden, for example, or one that is extensively redesigned, will necessarily have greater inputs at the time of its construction. This of course could be offset against time (provided that the items are well maintained) as the structure may last for a number of years, therefore lessening the impact of the garden into the future. The type of garden, and how this affects other aspects of your lifestyle, can also have an effect. Growing vegetables, for example, will need to factor in the energy costs outlined above although, if crops are raised on site ongoing inputs from other materials tend to be reasonably small, as people generally go to a garden supplier very often. They do however, frequently visit greengrocers; meaning that the transportation costs associated with their vegetable consumption needs are reduced considerably.

Water Other than Rainfall

The cleaning and distribution of water through a mains network has a large environmental cost which, if plants are to be irrigated from a mains source, needs to be taken into account if a full garden environmental footprint is to be established. If water is managed well, with for example rainwater storage, grey-water use or water-wise planting being practised, the footprint associated with water is generally small when compared to 'ordinary' household use. It is quite simple then in this case, as lowering the use (or perhaps, more importantly in the longer term, the dependence) for garden plants on treated water, automatically lowers the environmental footprint of a garden. Rainwater of course has no environmental footprint attached, as it falls naturally; although the collecting and storage devices used to enable its use, do need to be factored into the calculation. Having said this, the longer-term benefits usually outweigh the production costs.

The cleaning and distribution of water has a large environmental cost, which must to be taken into account if plants are to be watered from a mains source.

Embodied Energy and Water

Any product has an embodied energy and/or water cost attached to it. Essentially, these are the amount of either element that was used in the manufacture of a product. Wood, for example, needs cutting (usually with powered saws); metal needs mining, smelting, refining and casting, whereas even a young plant bought from a garden centre has had water applied. These costs may seem invisible and so are said to be 'embodies', either because they are a constituent part, or were essential in the synthesis of the item. This of course could be widened out into the other embodied materials, but for the sake of simplicity, these two have been used as the major focus here.

Compost and Compost Products

Compost can represent a 'challenging area' when calculating a garden's environmental footprint. In the most obvious cases, material obtained from sources external to the garden all come with at least a nominal footprint cost. This is especially true where items such as potting mixtures or ornamental bark mulch are supplied as bagged items for sale in garden suppliers. The term compost also includes recycled kitchen waste or other biodegradable household or garden waste, converted on a heap or in a container. Of this, only that which is the direct result of plants grown on site is not an input, as kitchen scraps could at least in part, be derived from other activities. The real nub of the importance of home composting is that the material involved is not treated as waste, and so needs no transportation away from site for subsequent treatment. This of course saves a considerable environmental footprint associated with waste disposal.

Some critics of home composting have pointed out that its production does produce a small amount of CO_2 and (if not properly managed or aerated) methane. While this of course is true, these by-products are derived from plant material, meaning that over the long term, their use in subsequent soil enrichment and enhanced growth of plants in the next season renders them largely carbon neutral, as this release of gas is a seasonal factor and not permanent.

Ecology and Biodiversity

On the whole, the ecology and subsequent biodiversity found within a garden may seem to be the result of 'natural' processes. Of course while this is true to a point, if the plants are factored in, the picture skews somewhat. Indeed, any garden is a sort of arrested or managed ecosystem, with the life within it constantly responding to a steady stream of somewhat unnatural inputs. Add to this, the fact that imported organic matter, biological control agents, pets and (albeit unintentionally) pests and diseases are all introduced by humans and it is clear that the biodiversity of a garden is almost as much the result of human input as it is natural processes.

The story does not end there though, as gardens may favour unnaturally high populations of species such as birds, particularly if they are fed. While this is no bad thing, it also constitutes a human input; one that of course has an output, as the birds that often visit do not necessarily reside within the garden.

Other outputs occur when species effectively escape the confines of a garden. Garden plants often become naturalized in an area, mostly with minimal impact, although if these become invasive they can be extremely problematic. Pests, diseases and weeds imported on plants, or within the growing media they are in, can also prove troublesome if they escape the garden, as can some of the biological control used to stifle them. The harlequin ladybird, Harmonia axyridis, was introduced into North America in 1988 to control pests. It is now the most abundant ladybird (ladybug) species to be found there, having supplanted and out-competed most of the native species across much of the continent. It was introduced to Continental Europe in the early 1990s, subsequently escaping and finding its way to British shores by 2004. Since then its spread has been rapid.

What all this shows then, is that even an unintentional ecological input can have far reaching ecological outputs.

The harlequin ladybird, *Harmonia axyridis*, is an example of an insect introduced to control pests that has since outcompeted native ladybirds.

Pesticides and Fertilizers

Fertilizers and pesticides obtained through a supplier, whether synthetic or organic in their origin must necessarily be classed as inputs if they are being applied to a garden. This would, of course, not be true of 'home-made' recipes, provided that all the ingredients were produced there in the garden with no imported items added to them.

When any and all pesticides or fertilizers (bought or home-produced) are applied in gardens, they have a natural tendency to become mobile in the environment and as soon as this happens there is a risk of their becoming a garden output; with several factors affecting how these may subsequently move. Ideally, if applied correctly and in the appropriate dosage, any chemical agent would remain in the soil or on the plant, doing its job until broken down into harmless by-products. In reality though, many can and do leave the point of application and are lost. Several things can make this happen. In the case of material applied direct to the leaves or stem (foliar feed, pest control and so on) this can drift away from the target (if sprayed in windy conditions); evaporate or volatilize into the surrounding air (if sprayed in hot sun); or perhaps most commonly runoff or drip from the plant onto the surrounding soil. Chemicals reaching the soil either because they were applied there or got there accidentally generally move via three remaining pathways: variously being dissolved in runoff water; leaching down beyond the root zone and into ground water; or becoming incorporated into other chemical compounds into the soil that are then eroded or removed. Many fertilizers and pesticides may well break-down before they reach ground water or surface water (streams, rivers, or lakes) but the risk is present.

Most manufactured chemicals are supplied with recommendations about how much can be safely used and at what intervals. Unfortunately, the mentality that more of a product will be more effective often leads to these recommended quantities being exceeded; meaning that chemicals which do not reach their intended target saturate the natural capacity of the system to deal with them and free the remainder to move in the environment in other ways. The chemistry of a compound also affects how a material will move in the environment. Unfortunately, most 'organic' fertilizers and pesticides are soluble in water, meaning that they move wherever water moves; while other substances such as plant-based oils volatilize easily, enabling them to move freely with the air. Once airborne, they can move for long distances being deposited only when the air is relatively still or when it rains.

Chemicals that remain in the soil can be removed under the action of micro-organisms, if they are held there for a while, meaning that chemical loss is almost always greatest on sandy or free-draining soils. Soils that are very sandy, for example, allow water to move through them quickly, do not easily hold onto the chemicals added to them, and often do not contain a large population of soil organisms relative to other soil types. However clay soils, or those rich in organic matter, not only slow water movement and loss, but also readily attach to added chemicals, and generally have a greater number and diversity of soil organisms to decompose the chemical.

Of course, no comment upon the use of pesticides would be complete without dealing with the problem of their build-up in living tissue. Many chemicals, and especially those used as pesticides, can accumulate in the tissues of organisms, in a process known as 'bioaccumulation'. As a rule of thumb, bioaccumulation results in higher concentrations of a chemical further up the food chain. Mercifully, most chemicals that have this tendency have been banned from use in gardens, though chemicals, including fertilizers, may be accidentally eaten by animals that feed on treated soil or vegetation, or mistakenly swallowed as grit or food.

Hard Landscape Materials

The term 'hard landscape' describes a whole variety of construction materials used in garden construction and corresponds with the term 'soft landscape,' used to describe plant materials or organic soil additives. Hard landscape necessarily utilizes a wide range of materials, including brick, gravel, rock and stone, concrete, timber, bitumen, glass, metals and so on, all of which can essentially be broken down into two types. First there are the raw materials (stone, wood and others) that, while they may have been made into a product in their own right, consist of naturally occurring substances. The second is the manufactured products (concrete, glass, metal and so forth) where the material basis was first manufactured before further fabrication occurs.

Almost all hard landscape elements in a garden are inputs, and carry a considerable ecological footprint in their wake. There is, of course, the embodied energy costs associated with their manufacturing or processing, packaging and indeed their transportation to consider. This said, there are items that are less damaging than others and, while difficult to generalize, anything made from local materials and manufactured locally tends to be less damaging and less environmentally costly than those imported from further afield.

Hard landscape necessarily utilizes a wide range of materials, including brick, gravel, rock stone, and concrete, and can be environmentally costly if used.

Buildings, Structures and Storage

In many ways, what is true of hard landscape materials is also equally true of buildings and structures, meaning it need not be repeated here. Having said that, things like greenhouses might be heated in colder periods, and while the amount of fuel needed to do this is often low, it is nonetheless an ongoing input. Storage, specifically of home-produced vegetables and fruit, also needs to be considered differently in certain ways. Of course, the environmental footprint of a building erected to do this remains the same as any other equivalent, meaning that most of any footprint comes from fridges and freezers. While these are convenient for the storage of produce, refrigerators do carry a high cost of manufacture and supply, even if they were obtained second hand, and do carry continuous running costs.

Equipment

Equipment is a variable commodity that often includes a bewildering array of manual and automatic tools, pots, propagators, clothing and other allegedly 'essential' items. Most of these are manufactured items that carry a considerable environmental footprint in their own right, and while few are as indispensable to the gardener as advertisers might claim, some are more useful than others. The real trick here is to choose designs and products that have been around for a long time. These are the tried and tested items that have stood the test of time and remain deservedly popular as a consequence. While there is little room for reducing the footprint involved in the manufacture of common manual tools, such as spades, forks, trowels and such, buying good quality tools (and caring for them) can ensure that these last for many years, ensuring that over time their impact is low.

Avoiding power tools is another positive approach, as these are rarely essential and even where they are the best option, the rarity of their use may mean that it is better to hire them and use them for just a short time. Electrical tools are often cited as being more efficient (albeit only slightly) although even the best of these require energy to run; despite this, if renewable sources of energy (wind and solar) can be accessed then that portion of the footprint would be reduced. All of them do, however, need periodic maintenance and the majority of electrical items tend to contain high proportions of non-recyclable materials such as plastics.

Products

This term essentially encompasses a whole host of other items that do not easily fall into preceding categories and are often variable in nature as a result; they largely share the same sorts of ecological impact as the preceding categories. In short, the ecological footprint of a product mostly varies in two areas; those sourced from a long supply chain and those used in large quantities. Some will of course have better credentials than others and the choice as to whether to use them will ultimately depend upon whether they are an important item to use, but perhaps more importantly it depends upon whether there is a home produced or recyclable alternative that could readily be substituted. For instance, liquid feeds can be substituted with plant or compost teas. Bulky items (with high transport costs), such as manure, can be substituted by growing green manures or using home-produced compost. The latter can also be used as an alternative to bought-in compost used for growing media in pots or tubs.

Remember also that most of the ecological footprint 'spent' on each individual's behalf relates to services and infrastructures that operate in society as a whole. Even once personal actions such low-input gardening, household energy saving and other lifestyle choices such as whether or not to fly are exercised, much of the remainder is beyond an individual's own control; a fact that some find hard to believe. However, the activity within a garden is within an individual's control and, if nothing else, is a positive contribution. It is a step in the right direction and, when all is said and done, great fun!

Carbon Emissions

Scarcely a day goes by when there is not some mention of climate change in the news. Central in all of this is a natural phenomenon called the 'greenhouse effect' which, although being a familiar term for many people, is frequently misunderstood. In short then, the greenhouse effect (despite the fact that the name makes it seem like something effected by humans) is not only a naturally occurring phenomenon, but also the mechanism that allows the earth to be warm enough to support life. Without the greenhouse effect the average temperature of the earth would be a cool -18°C; essentially the same temperature as the North Pole!

The greenhouse effect gets its name because the gases in the atmosphere act in a similar way to panes of glass in a greenhouse. Radiation from the sun – consisting mainly of visible and ultraviolet (UV) radiation – can travel through glass into a greenhouse.

When this radiation is absorbed by objects such as the plants, staging or ground in the greenhouse, it is re-radiated as infrared (IR) radiation, or heat. This heat cannot easily escape through the glass, and so warms the air, causing the greenhouse environment to warm-up.

The atmosphere of the earth produces a similar effect, due to the presence of so-called greenhouse gases. The sun's radiation passes through the atmosphere, is absorbed by the surface of the earth, and is re-radiated as infrared radiation. The greenhouse gases then absorb or reflect this heat, prevent it from escaping to space, and so warm the atmosphere.

A number of gases give rise to the natural greenhouse effect including water vapour (clouds), carbon dioxide (CO_2), methane (CH_4), nitrous oxide (N_2O), ozone (O_3), chlorofluorocarbons (CFCs), hydrochlorofluorocarbons (HCFCs) and hydrofluorocarbons (HFCs). Within the past few hundred years human activities have increased the concentrations of some of these greenhouse gases in the atmosphere, which are believed to have thrown the natural greenhouse effect out of balance. Essentially the atmosphere is trapping too much heat and causing the temperature of the earth to rise, a situation known as the 'enhanced' greenhouse effect or (more popularly) as 'global warming'.

Ironically, many greenhouse gases make up a very small percentage of the concentration of the gases in the atmosphere; nitrogen and oxygen make up 99 per cent; whereas carbon dioxide, for example, makes up only 0.037 per cent of the gases in the atmosphere.

What is wrong with Global Warming?

Although global warming may conjure up a picture of warmer weather, it could also lead to many changes in our normal lives. Nobody is sure how severe the effects will be. Sea levels may rise as warmer weather could melt the polar ice caps; water supplies might also be affected with some areas receiving more rain, while other areas might experience drier weather and, eventually, droughts. Needless to say, gardens could well be affected. Warmer climates may well mean

---

WHERE DO GREENHOUSE GASES COME FROM?

- Water vapour is the most important greenhouse gas, and occurs naturally in the atmosphere because of evaporation from the oceans and by a process known as 'transpiration' in plants. Humans have little if any control over the amount of water in the atmosphere.

- Carbon dioxide is the most important greenhouse gas which has man-made sources. Carbon dioxide is released by animals (including humans) when they breathe; by burning fossil-fuels (coal, gas and oil) or wood; and through the cutting down of trees and plants that take in carbon dioxide.

- Methane is an extremely effective absorber of radiated heat, although the amount in the atmosphere is less than carbon dioxide and its lifetime in the atmosphere is brief (ten to twelve years), compared with some other greenhouse gases produced naturally when vegetation is burnt, digested or allowed to rot without oxygen being present. Methane also comes from rice fields, grazing cattle, landfill sites and coal mines.

- Nitrous oxide is produced naturally by the oceans. Human sources of nitrous oxide include the use of synthetic (nitrogen rich) fertilizers and the production of nylon.

- Ozone is a relatively unstable form of oxygen which, unlike the commoner (O_2) molecule that contains two oxygen atoms, has three oxygen atoms (O_3). In the lower atmosphere, ozone is an air pollutant often found in cities with high levels of traffic, and is known to detrimentally affect breathing and will burn sensitive plants. However, the 'ozone layer' in the upper atmosphere is beneficial, preventing potentially damaging ultraviolet (UV) light from reaching the earth's surface.

- CFCs do not exist naturally; they are man-made chemicals used in air conditioning, fridges and polystyrene foam. CFCs are also powerful agents in destroying the ozone layer, leading to a global effort to halt their production. Although levels are now declining, their long lifetimes mean they may remain in the atmosphere for over 100 years.

- HCFCs and HFCs are also man-made chemicals, used to replace CFCs. They are less stable and degrade more rapidly but are still a concern.

longer growing seasons but, on the other hand, plants might be affected by less water, an increase in the number of pests and parasites, and an absence of cold winters meaning that more traditional plant varieties in United Kingdom gardens might no longer thrive.

Tropical diseases could also become a widespread problem at higher latitudes in a warmer world and this could have an effect upon outdoor workers – including those out tending their own gardens.

What Can Gardeners Do to Help Prevent Global Warming?

Despite the multitude of advice available on this subject, it essentially boils down to the need for us all to reduce energy use (for instance energy used to make products which are then bought) which in turn reduces the amount of greenhouse gases released. In addition, recycling garden and kitchen green waste; avoiding

---

OTHER MAJOR CLIMATE CONCERNS RELATED TO TEMPERATURE

Global cooling

During the 1970s, it became evident that estimates regarding global temperatures showed cooling since 1945. At this point, the general public were largely unaware of carbon dioxide's effects with most reported environmental concerns of the time centred upon domestic waste disposal, chemical disposal, smog, particulate pollution, and acid rain. The idea gained a brief spell in the popular and scientific press during the mid-1970s, although this also marked, somewhat ironically, the point where the temperature trend stopped decreasing. The focus moved to carbon dioxide in relation to both natural and man-made effects that could cause variations in global climate.

Despite being largely ignored for a number of years, the theory of global cooling has gained a number of new plaudits recently with current concerns being centred upon the possible cooling effects of a slowdown or even a shutdown of the 'thermohaline circulation' (see below) that supporters of the theory say might be provoked by an increase of fresh water mixing into the North Atlantic due to glacial melting. The probability of this occurring is generally considered to be low among the wider scientific community but it is not without precedent, having last happened some 13,000 years ago, when the rapidly melting glaciers at the end of the last Ice Age led to a sudden reversal in the temperature increase that was being experienced at that time, which led to a return to cold conditions, This lasted for around 1,000 years before warming re-commenced! Despite the fact that all climate models and predictions find the likelihood of this happening in the present day to be low, the idea intrigues the public mind and is often over-hyped; this forming the basis of the popular, if scientifically inaccurate, film, The Day After Tomorrow.

Note: Thermohaline circulation is the term used to describe the global density-driven circulation of the oceans. Derivation is from thermo – for heat and haline – for salt, which together determine the density of sea water. Wind-driven surface currents (such as the Gulf Stream) head polewards from the equatorial Atlantic Ocean, cooling as they go and eventually sinking at high latitudes (forming North Atlantic Deep Water). This dense water then flows downhill into the deep water basins, only resurfacing in the northeast Pacific Ocean somewhere in the region of 1,200 years later.

Global Dimming

The burning of fossil-fuel produces not only greenhouse gases but other by-products, such as sulphur dioxide, soot, and ash. These pollutants can actually change the properties of clouds; quite simply by making clouds with larger numbers of droplets than found in 'unpolluted' clouds. Polluted clouds are more reflective, with the result that more of the sun's heat and energy is reflected back into space, reducing the amount of heat reaching the earth in a phenomenon known as Global Dimming. Climatologists believe that the reflection of heat may have already made waters in the northern hemisphere cooler; a situation that, far from saving the planet from global warming, merely serves to disrupt rainfall patterns.

'Contrails' (the vapour from planes flying high in the sky) are seen as another significant cause of heat reflection. This came to light during the aftermath of the 11 September 2001 terrorist attacks in the United States, when all commercial flights were grounded for the next three days. This allowed climate scientists to look at the effect on the climate when there were no contrails and no heat reflection and they found that the temperature rose by some 1°C during that period. This has led to fears that global dimming has been hiding the true power of global warming.

Sources of Horticultural Carbon Emissions Associated with Gardens	
From outside the garden	**From within the garden**
Fuel, used in e.g. transportation	Decay
Packaging	Burning
Industrialized manufacturing processes	Using fossil fuels for e.g. lawnmowers

the purchase of products which use too much packaging; and only buying wood or wood products grown in sustainable (renewable) forests, can all help.

Reducing the amount of carbon generation associated with a garden is an attempt to make the space 'carbon neutral'; the situation whereby the total carbon generated by all activities associated with the garden is offset by the amount that it absorbs in the year. In the final analysis, adopting a sustainable approach to gardening and growing more food at home both help to make gardens more 'carbon neutral'.

Reducing 'Garden-miles'

The supply chain associated with gardens follows a predictable pattern: it begins with inputs from the manufacturers, moves onto handling between various distributors before goods arrive at shops and other suppliers, and are purchased, used and, in some respect or other, enter what is known as 'the waste chain'. Many of the most popular garden products are obtained through such supply chains, often in a seemingly very long, complex and convoluted way. As a result, many can boast a high number of 'garden miles', in the same way that food travelling long distances or through complex supply chains would have high 'food miles' when compared to home-produced or locally sourced items. Given that food consumption accounts for up to a third of a household's carbon footprint, home food production could reduce not only the carbon footprint of the garden but of the whole household. Indeed, home food production is generally considered to rank as highly as other methods of reducing carbon footprints such as double-glazing, replacing an old boiler or reducing car use. Adding these to the efforts

in the garden, as well as insulating the whole house, can start to make a real and achievable contribution to reducing carbon emissions.

Finally, it is worth pointing out that gardening sustainably, naturally involves ecologically- efficient habits such as saving rainwater, recycling materials and composting biodegradable waste; all of which are likely to reduce overall carbon footprints. Indeed, the positive effect of regular outdoor activity on health ensures that the need to access healthcare is reduced and, believe it or not, this reduces a gardener's carbon footprint even further.

Energy-Efficient Greenhouses

Greenhouses are understandably popular with gardeners offering the opportunity to grow a much wider range of plants; often making these available much earlier or later in the year. Of course, cloches and cold frames offer similar benefits at a fraction of the cost, although neither gives the same amount of dedicated growing space as the true greenhouse. Indeed, the growing space is a major advantage, ensuring that crops are protected the whole time a gardener works on them; a frame or cloche on the other hand must remain open the whole of the time; meaning that the plants endure an icy winter blast while being tended.

Apart from the obvious inputs related to the manufacture and transport of the greenhouse itself, there can be an ongoing environmental cost associated with heating them. On average a greenhouse may need to be heated for 120 days or more during the winter period, often for as much as twelve hours (or more) per day. The amount of fuel this would consume will of course vary, depending upon whether a thermostat is used to regulate temperature, the degree of additional insulation used and of course the external ambient temperature.

What Type of Greenhouse is Best?

Despite the array of designs available, the simplest constructions are usually more than adequate for most gardens. It is more important that one is chosen that fulfils the needs of the garden itself; after all, there is little point in erecting a huge greenhouse if it is only ever half full of plants!

Almost all plants like to grow in reasonably warm conditions with most growing best between about 16–24°C (60–76°F). While winter light levels may

Small greenhouses tend to lose heat quickly once the sun goes down or in cold weather; an ideal way to avoid this is by insulating them with bubble wrap.

For a greenhouse to be efficient, all available space must be utilized properly, with space beneath the staging used for shade loving, or overwintering plants.

still be sufficient to help power growth, the low temperatures at that time of the year can severely limit this. The greenhouse simply raises the temperature by trapping daylight which heats the air and raises the temperature within several degrees above that on the outside. Of course, these temperatures fall during darkness and although insulating the house can help prevent this, it can only really be offset by heating the interior. Temperature fluctuations are not all bad news though and a fall of about 4–6°C lower than that of the day is actually preferable for most plants.

The real trick with a greenhouse is to ensure that the conditions within it do not fluctuate wildly or to extremes. By monitoring the conditions inside the greenhouse, it is possible to exert a considerable amount of control over the internal environment. Limiting the amount of light by shading will cool the greenhouse as will opening the vents and letting the hot air escape. Heating or insulating the greenhouse on the other hand and keeping vents shut will maintain temperatures if they fall outside. This can only really be achieved if a clear picture is established as to how this varies throughout the day; something that is best measured by taking an average temperature reading inside the greenhouse using a maximum and minimum thermometer. This shows two readings, one being the highest temperature achieved in the last twenty four hours, the other showing the lowest. Comparing this to another similar thermometer placed outside the greenhouse can help to establish the difference to the prevailing climate and see if the temperature is fluctuating to extremes.

Before resorting to a heater as night time temperatures begin to dip, remember that it can be both cheaper and more efficient to insulate a greenhouse by providing additional layers within the structure to trap air. Bubble-wrap polythene is a popular method that it is easy to place in position and allows the transmission of light. In addition to this, careful placement and the use of nearby shelter planting can also help to reduce the chilling effects of high winds.

Heat can also be stored by collecting it from entirely natural sources. In a similar way to the method used to counter a radiation frost outdoors, glass or plastic bottles, filled with water and allowed to warm in the sun can act effectively as a sort of storage heater.

Painting the outside of the bottles black increases their efficiency by ensuring that they absorb more light and so become warmer than the surrounding air. As the sun sets, these bottles will gradually radiate the heat to the surrounding air, and although the water (and ultimately the surrounding air) will gradually cool, it will normally be sufficient to keep the temperature raised from that outside the greenhouse, particularly if it is well insulated. Any 'green' heating, supplied by renewable energy systems (such as a solar cell or heat exchanger) could also be used, although these often prove rather costly to buy in the first place.

Of course, young plants are often the most vulnerable specimens where sudden temperature dips are concerned, and it is at this stage of growth where additional heat could prove vital. A potential economy in respect of the energy costs involved in raising these, would be to raise seedlings in spaces that are already heated (or at least likely to be hotter), such as a conservatory, or windowsill in a warm room; only moving them out into a greenhouse or frame once growing strongly.

Making the Best Use of Natural Light

Balanced plant growth is rather dependent upon glasshouse design as well as proper planning for the light requirements of the crop. As a general rule, traditional ridged greenhouse designs should always be orientated with the ridge running east to west to make the best of the available light. Low light in winter can of course limit the growth of plants, but a greater problem can be summer light levels, especially when combined with elevated temperatures, that cause problems for the plants. Shading a greenhouse has the dual benefit of reducing summer temperatures (if excessive) or to protect young plants from very intense sunlight.

TOP RIGHT: **Greenhouses work best when they transmit as much light as possible; and a yearly clean not only helps to do this but also helps prevent disease spread.**

RIGHT: **Angling a mirrored surface on the 'shady' side of the greenhouse means that additional light is reflected back onto the plants to encourage strong growth.**

Polythene Tunnels

These are essentially a layer of heavy-duty polythene stretched over a construction of steel tubular hoops. Polythene tunnels can sometimes prove popular with home gardeners because they are able to cover large areas relatively cheaply in terms of cash cost when

Polythene tunnels have become increasingly popular for home gardeners, as they cover large areas cheaply compared to a similar sized glasshouse.

Modern cloches vary considerably in their designs, complexity and materials used, with some being quite elaborate, and resembling mini greenhouses.

compared to a similar sized glasshouse. In common with glasshouses, they are mostly constructed from materials that have to be obtained through long supply chains, meaning that they have a high ecological footprint associated with them. The materials also tend to consume non-renewable resources, further extending their footprint. Polythene tunnels are also likely to have a shorter lifespan than a glass structure, especially the plastic covering, which is likely to need replacing once every five years or so. While some of this might be reused in other garden projects, most of the waste plastic will need disposing of through the waste chain.

Frames, Cloches and Other Protection

Of course many gardens have either insufficient space or use for a glasshouse or polythene tunnel and in such cases, it may be better to consider a more limited form of protection. A cold frame is a popular item that might best be described as a covered garden; too small and low to accommodate the gardener along with the plants. While they can substitute for a greenhouse in some ways, their commonest use is to shelter seedlings and young plants as they are gradually hardened off, prior to transplanting or planting them into their final position in the garden.

A cold frame also enables early sowings of summer flowers and vegetables some weeks before outdoor sowing leading to early flowering and, in the case of vegetables, sometimes allowing for an extra crop within a season. Once conditions improve, a cold frame often proves useful for rooting cuttings of deciduous and evergreen shrubs and trees; while softwood cuttings of Chrysanthemum, Pelargonium and Fuchsia take root faster in a frame, particularly during the warmer months.

Cold frames are best positioned where they receive direct sun at least half the day, preferably on well-drained soil (if situated at ground level), and are kept free from flooding during heavy rain. A location with adequate wind protection (to prevent rapid chilling) is ideal.

Cloches were traditionally a bell-shaped, movable glass cover, serving as a 'mini-greenhouse' set directly over plants growing in the garden. However, over time many designs have arisen and one of the commonest, the European cloche, is usually built in 60cm (24in) sections that vary in height from 22–60cm (8–24in) and 40–65cm (16–26in) in width. A European cloche is made of four panes of glass held together with heavy galvanized wire fittings, incorporating a handle for ease of carrying, which can be taken apart easily and moved from one spot to another. In this design, several cloches placed end to end will make a long 'miniature greenhouse'. Many variations to the design exist though, some incorporating ventilation and utilizing a huge range of materials. Cloches are used variously to protect newly transplanted or tender plants from spring frosts, but are also very useful in helping to warm up the soil prior to seed sowing or planting.

Of course, it is perfectly feasible to make cloches using recycled materials such as old window frames, recycled pallets and plastic drink bottles. Although these recycled materials will have some ecological footprint associated with them; the real issue is the (often large) ecological footprint associated with their disposal. The more recycled products that are used in the making of any structure, means that those products have been given an 'extended working life' and have been (temporarily) diverted from the waste stream.

Plastic bottles with the bottoms cut out can be used to protect small, individual plants from cold, and will generally last a season or two, before they need to be replaced as they become brittle in sunlight over time. Temporary cloches can also be made by arching black semi-rigid polythene piping over a row of vegetables or a flowerbed and sticking it into the ground on each side. Lay clear plastic (perhaps some saved from an old polythene tunnel cover) over the arches. If using this system on raised beds that are enclosed with timber, attaching brackets to the inside edges of the boxes or sinking short pieces of pipe with a larger inside diameter along the sides will help hold the arches. The arches can be used to support fleece or shade cloth to ward off both frost and bright sunlight. When this cloche is no longer needed, simply remove the plastic sheet and pipe ribs.

Frame cloches are easily made at home using cheap or recycled materials such as here where simple wooden frames have been covered with polythene.

More delicate wall grown shrubs or fruit trees can easily be given additional winter shelter by placing a frame covered in clear polythene over them.

Water Conservation and Storage

Collecting and treating water for domestic use has a high cost; both in respect of the money paid for it and also to the environment. Saving water from rainfall or recycling wastewater (sometimes called 'grey water') can provide a means of overcoming the worst ravages of summer drought, while ensuring that the environmental consequences of using it are minimized.

Rainwater collection is in most cases a reasonably straightforward affair, with the commonest system used being the attachment of one or more rainwater butts to a roof drain where it can be stored inside until needed. These rainwater butts vary greatly in size and design and of course they do carry an environmental footprint, although this can be offset by their longevity and the savings in respect of water use over this time. Rainwater is extremely useful for plants growing in containers, particularly edible plants such as herbs, being naturally acidic and therefore unlikely to contain many harmful bacteria. Its acidity also makes it the ideal choice for misting plants under glass on hot days (as it will not watermark leaves with lime) and suits many species sensitive to domestic water additives. Rainwater is also ideal for topping up the summer pond, being much better than chlorinated tap water although, in dry years, a great deal of stored water may be needed to do this.

Recycled (or grey water) on the other hand, is simply the wastewater that is generated from washing, bathing and other household activities. Much of its suitability depends upon how much waste matter it contains; ordinary bath water for instance can be useful for watering a variety of plants. The main problem however lies with its storage – wastewater always carrying the risk of bacterial infestation. Specialist storage methods and filtration can be employed but the easiest way is to use it immediately (once cooled), and to avoid using it for houseplants or edible crops in containers, although it may be used for ornamental containers outdoors. Ensure that any grey water used is only 'lightly tainted' (usually with soap or even just dirt from washed vegetables).

Using Plants to Modify the Environment

Houseplants as Air-Conditioning

While plant lovers like having them around the house, few ever really think of them as more than simply an ornament. Even devoted gardeners might be surprised to discover that plants make them feel better not only because they look nice in the house but also because they make the environment there healthier. Not only do plants naturally remove carbon dioxide from the air and replace it with oxygen, they have also been proven to remove airborne harmful contaminants. In modern buildings features such as air conditioning, improved insulation or other energy-saving measures, tend to reduce air exchange, meaning that the same air is being breathed again and again. Add to this chemicals released from the construction materials used, synthetic furnishings, computers, electrical equipment and everyday household products such as cleaning material, and the air inside a building rapidly becomes a noxious cocktail of stale air and waste chemicals. This is often the reason why people feel ill while inside; affected by what has become known as 'sick building syndrome', a major cause of headaches, nausea, sore and itchy eyes, loss of concentration and even other symptoms. All the more reason to get outside into the garden you may think, but the simple addition of a range of houseplants in the home is an easy, pleasant and a natural way to help remove these pollutants from the air.

Plants alter the air quality in a home in other ways too. They tend to control humidity, through water lost from their leaves, and the humidity that suits them tends to be within the optimum range for human health. Indeed, humidity is an important and often underestimated factor in human health; when it is too low people are more likely to develop viral infections; when too high, their vulnerability to other disease increases.

It is not just the leafy parts of the plant that play an important role though; soil and roots being central in removing air-borne pollutants. Micro-organisms in the soil become more adept at using trace amounts of

Plants not only filter carbon dioxide and replace it with oxygen, but can also remove many of the harmful airborne contaminants found in modern buildings.

household pollutants as a food source over time. Many common houseplants absorb benzene, formaldehyde and trichloroethylene, although the amounts of these that can be dealt with will vary considerably between plant species. Plants also naturally act as sound baffles, reducing unwanted sound levels, such as 'echoing' and if kept near to windows, naturally absorb light and cool a room in the summer months.

One reasonably-sized houseplant in a 15–20cm (6–8in) pot per 9m^2 (100ft^2) should be enough to improve air quality in a house. Keeping them healthy is of course paramount here, as the more vigorously they grow, the better job they do. For many plants this is relatively easy, provided they are kept at around 10°C or above, in bright (but not direct) sunlight. This is due to the fact that many common houseplants evolved in tropical or sub-tropical forests, where light

filtered through the branches of taller trees before it reached them rendering them well suited for even relatively low light conditions.

Finally, as plants absorb carbon dioxide and emit oxygen, this does have a small impact in respect of reducing your carbon footprint. Add this to the fact that windows need not be opened (on cold days) to get fresh air, nor do air conditioners need turning on (during summer) and the carbon reduction benefits of houseplants improve even more, Not only that, but the increased oxygen level has been shown by various studies to lead to increased concentration, productivity and ultimately better health. Researchers have also found that spaces containing plants tend to prove more attractive to people, often being seen as more relaxing, less stressful and as a consequence of all of this, better for mental well-being.

Windbreaks

Where a garden is exposed or subject to high winds, a windbreak or other shelter planting can be a real benefit in respect of the range of plants that can be grown, or even activities that may take place. In order to be effective though, a windbreak or shelter planting should baffle, filter and drain rather than contain wind. To do this, the barrier must be at least fifty per cent wind permeable, as solid barriers do deflect the wind, but make turbulent 'eddies' on the leeward side.

Windbreaks can be made with plants by planting a shelter belt of trees, hedges or lower, more informal, mini-shelter belts using wind-tolerant shrubs or other plants such as bamboo or tall grasses. Features like this can lift the wind for a distance of up to twenty times their height; meaning that even a metre-high screen affords a 20m-long space a degree of shelter. The thickness of the windbreak also affects its efficiency. On the windward side, start with lower planting and build up the height.

For larger sites a series of barriers will tend to be most effective, with the intervals between each needing to be around ten times their height for maximum protection. Shelter can also be greatly enhanced by sinking, for example, a seating area into the ground and planting hedging or wind-filtering plants around the upper edge.

Planting for Summer Shade and Winter Sun

Gardens in higher or lower latitudes often experience relatively cool or even cold winters, followed by warm or perhaps hot summers. For dwelling areas then, winter sun is a welcome bonus, particularly in the home. During the summer however the situation can be reversed, with shade from the sun's heat being sought after. The more sunlight hitting and entering a building in summer, the warmer (and often more uncomfortable) that building will be; often meaning that residents resort to using fans or even air conditioning, raising the carbon and environmental footprint of their home. Plants offer the possibility of moderating the effect of the sun, not only within the garden, but also as a form of environmental modification for the home. Planting a deciduous tree on the sunny side of a garden means that during the summer, the leaves will shade your garden and house. Conversely during winter, the bare branches allow the warmth of the sun into the garden and/or house.

In order to plant most effectively it is important to plan the position of any trees to be planted very carefully. For the most efficient use of winter sunlight and warmth, it is extremely important to know the direction of and lowest angles of the winter sun. Heat from the winter sunlight is rarely particularly intense until mid-morning and often declines markedly by mid-afternoon. This means that the most important value

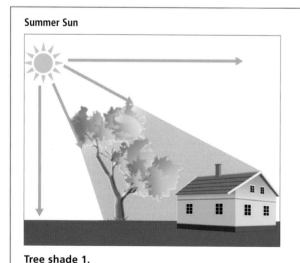

Summer Sun

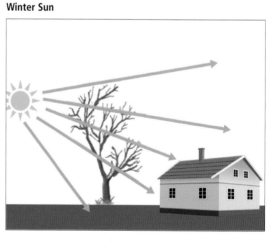

Winter Sun

Tree shade 1.

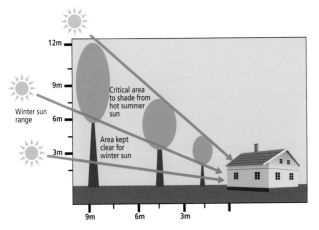

Tree shade 2.

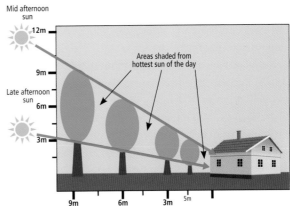

Tree shade 3.

to consider is the height of the sun at around midday. For the summer calculation, however, the low-angled (late-afternoon) western sun, is often the hottest part of the day and so does need consideration.

If a design plans to use evergreen plants on the sunny side to screen or block an unsightly feature or view, this may still be possible, provided that these plants are not allowed to grow so tall that they block the low

winter sun. A 1.5m (5ft) evergreen screen, for example, should be placed no more than 6m (20ft) in front of a wall or window so as to avoid any loss of winter sun. On the shaded side however, where there is never any sun, evergreens of any height may be used. Having said this, some light always enters windows on any side of a house, and very close plantings to a window can render a room both gloomy and claustrophobic.

SEASONALITY AND THE ANGLE OF THE SUN

The relation of earth and sun changes with the seasons; as the planet revolves around the sun in its yearly cycle. During a calendar year, the northern hemisphere of the earth gets the direct rays of the sun during the period between May and August; the southern hemisphere experiencing a similar intensity in the corresponding period between November and February. Summer therefore, is simply the period where either hemisphere is facing towards the sun. In summer the days are longer and the sun is higher in the sky, while in winter the converse is true.

The angle of the sun also varies according to a place's position in either hemisphere. In the northern hemisphere for example, the sun shines from a predominately southern angle, never shining from the north. The further north that is travelled, that is the nearer the pole, the lower the angle is that the sun achieves at its mid-summer or mid-winter maximum. In the tropics therefore, it is nearly directly overhead; whereas at the North Pole it barely crosses the horizon, even at the height of summer. This also leads to the effect of long summer days (with correspond-

ingly short nights) and long winter nights (with short days), this trend becoming more exaggerated the nearer the pole. Of course the same is true of the southern hemisphere, except that the pole involved is the South Pole, and the sun never shines from a southerly angle.

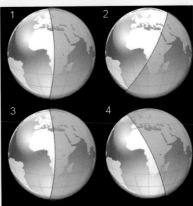

1. Line of sunrise in March

2. Line of sunrise in June – Northern Hemisphere summer

3. Line of sunrise in September

4. Line of sunrise in December – Northern Hemisphere winter

Lines of sunrise.

Ultimately an important consideration when selecting trees or indeed any other plants for use as shade is their mature size and characteristics. Choosing species or varieties which will grow to the required height is just as important as deciding upon where it is to be planted. Trees on the sunny side have to shade only a small angle of high summer sun. For that reason, fast-growing, or columnar trees such as poplars may be considered, although their roots can be problematic. Quick growth, provided this does not lead to overly large specimens, can be important as a tree 15m (49ft) away from a building must be around 30m (98ft) tall to provide shade on the sunny side in summer. If this is the mature height of the tree, this will of course take a long time to achieve. If a smaller tree that reaches only 14m (45ft) tall, it need only be planted 3m (10ft) from the building. If the object of planting includes sheltering the house from western exposure to hot afternoon sun in the summer, remember that in many cases, little effective sun comes from that quarter; meaning that trees or shrubs planted there can be evergreen if additional privacy is required. If space allows, taller trees tend to be better as they can be planted away from the house where their roots will be less problematic and cause less interference to water pipes, foundations and landscape plantings; furthermore branches or leaves are less likely to block or damage roofs or gutters. Avoid planting any trees with invasive roots near a house as the long term damage these can cause outweighs the beneficial effects of shade.

Where tall trees are planted for summer shade, lower branches are often not needed for this purpose, meaning that these specimens can be allowed to grow tall and have their lower branches removed – a process known as crown lifting – essentially leaving a high space under them. This treatment retains a feeling of spaciousness and opens up views beyond if these are attractive. While this can be done once the trees approach maturity, it can prove expensive and it is better if they are pruned to achieve this habit as they grow. A good rule of thumb here is to remove only two or three lower branches in any one year, until the desired clear space is reached. It may take several years to achieve this but results in healthier trees and a lot of money saved.

On a smaller scale, summer shade around a porch or over part of a patio can be achieved with a wire or cord trellis covered with vines. Ideally these should be covered with annual climbers like cup and saucer vine (*Cobea scandens*), morning glory (*Ipomea tricolour*), sweet pea (*Lathyrus odoratus*) or nasturtium/canary creeper (*Tropaeolum spp.*). Set any trellis to the south or west side of the porch or patio, so as to let in the welcome morning warmth, while blocking the hottest afternoon sun. If a cord trellis is made from a biodegradable material, as the first autumn frost arrives or once the vines begin to look shabby later in the season, then this can be disposed of, vines and all, in the compost heap.

Covering Eyesores

Many gardens have unsightly views both inside and beyond their boundaries, although plants provide an excellent and effective way of disguising both. The commonest area needing attention is often along boundaries, such as fences and walls. Climbers are the commonest option for covering these quickly, and the choice of plant will affect the way that the area is prepared for them. For climbers that require support, wire stretched taut between vine-eyes, criss-crossing to make a lattice is an option on solid walls or fences. A trellis is the other commonly used option, fixed directly to the surface and held away from the surface to allow the climber to grow behind as well as in front. As well as covering eyesores on the boundary of a garden, it is also worth creating focal points with interesting features and/or planting inside the garden which will attract the eye and distract from any view beyond.

Inspection covers (manholes) are another common garden 'feature' that most would prefer to be hidden from view. Almost inevitably however, these are sited near the house, in highly visible spaces that are often rather inconvenient to hide with planting; in places such as driveways, patios or paths. In these cases, it is possible to disguise them, using inset covers into which a similar (or preferably identical) paving type and pattern to the surroundings is set. Alternatively, you could turn an inset cover into a more creative solution by transforming it into a pebble mosaic, hiding this from over scrutiny by repeating the design or theme at other points in the surrounding paved area. Where inspection covers are positioned in areas of lawn, or within planted areas, these are best hidden simply by standing pots on them and filling this with low spreading plants. This will hide the cover, but allow relatively easy access should this be needed.

Garden sheds can be screened with shrubs or a hedge although, for smaller gardens, it can be a much more space-saving alternative to plant one or more climbers that will scramble over the walls and roof. Other features such as bins, compost heaps and so on, are best positioned out of sight and away from the house; and can be easily be screened by evergreen shrubs or climbers trained over trellis panels. Vines can also be used to cover the bole of a dead tree making it an ornamental pillar, which not only looks good, but also serves as a habitat for numerous species of garden wildlife.

Using Plants to Reduce Noise in the Garden

Plants not only provide shade and visual screening but can also provide effective noise reduction in a garden from outside sources such as neighbours, traffic, or passers by. Indeed, noise pollution can be a real intrusion to the garden and any planting that helps reduce it can be a welcome addition to the garden. Hedges are the obvious answer to this, acting as baffles that diffuse incoming noise. Their effectiveness in this respect depends upon their height and thickness; doubling the height of a hedge will reduce the incoming noise by thirty per cent and the thicker it is, the more noise it will filter out.

Preventing the entry of noise is only one approach though, and sounds, by their very nature, will always tend to find a way in no matter how high or thick a hedge is. Dealing with the remains of any unwelcome noise therefore, is the job of the remainder of the garden. Plants by their very nature help to absorb and deaden sound; adding to this effect by creating their own 'symphony of botanical sound' that masks the offending noise with more natural, pleasant tones.

Evergreen climbers, grown over a fence or trellis offer a quick and effective option for covering eyesores both within and beyond the garden all year round.

Having a variety of plant height and form throughout the garden will accentuate this, as will sub-dividing the space with further hedging, plant-covered screens or trellises to create a series of 'outdoor rooms.'

Water features are another favourite addition to a garden, useful in their ability to break-up noise by setting themselves against it. Because water is fractal (the patterns never repeat) it counterpoints itself to regular rhythms such as music and traffic. Waterfalls are especially useful in this respect, although even a modest bubble or wall-mounted 'spout' can be sufficient to help hide, and distract attention from, outside noise while providing a calm and restful focus for the ears.

Tall growing grasses can sub-divide the space in a garden, creating a series of 'outdoor rooms,' each filled with their own 'symphony of botanical sound'.

A variety of plant height and form throughout the garden will not only help absorb offending noise but also help mask it with more natural, pleasant tones.

Steep Banks

Slopes and banks, made from loose materials such as soil, are by their very nature somewhat unstable. When material such as sand or soil is piled on a level surface, it will tend to form a pyramid or cone shape, the exact shape of which will vary according to the properties of the particular material. This is because for any given material there is a limit to how steep the sides of the cone can be before the whole pile 'slumps'; with the maximum safe angle for a given material being referred to as its 'angle of repose'. These angles of repose are not only different for every material but also vary depending on whether they are wet or dry.

Maximum angle of repose for some common materials		
Material	Slope ratio	Angle of slope
Wet clay	1:2	23°
Dry clay	1:1½	33°
Dry sand or gravel	1:1¾	39°

It is important that the angles of repose are considered during and when constructing new garden features, as failing to do this can lead to subsequent slippage as the soil becomes wetter and less stable during rain. Where there is any doubt as to the stability of a slope, it is advisable to excavate a series of steps or terraces. This is an effective way of preventing runoff and erosion which would otherwise cause scarring of the surface and gradually lead to the loss of topsoil. If the slope is not to be formed as terraces, then vegetation, particularly grass, is a good stabilizer of surfaces, although this is still vulnerable until the grass or vegetation establishes.

Established steep slopes remain challenging in a garden and the steeper the slope the more difficult they tend to be. If the bank requires a more 'kept' look, then consider planting daylilies (*Hemerocallis spp.*), ornamental grasses, lilyturf (*Liriope muscari*), or low spreading shrubs such as Cotoneaster spp. and

Hypericum calcinum. If the slope is very sunny, then plants such as rosemary (*Rosmarinus officinalis*), sage (*Salvia*), rock rose (*Cistus*) or even alpine plants such as stonecrop (*Sedum spp.*), fleabane (*Erigeron spp.*), pinks (*Dianthus spp.*), Cape daisy (*Osteospermum spp.*) and daisy bush (*Brachyglottis spp.*), all make good candidates.

Living Structures

While hedges and indeed much of the garden constitute a living framework, it is possible to create complex and intricate structures – such as arbours and tunnels, wigwams and children's 'play-dens,' or even living sculptures – by using willow (*Salix spp.*), in their construction. Willow can also be used for soil stabilization and making retaining structures, for instance, on a terraced slope. As a living fence or trellis screen, willow will also help to limit noises coming from outside the garden, blotting this out with a pleasant rustling 'white noise'. Willow is of course a renewable resource, and as it continues to grow during the 'lifetime' of the structure it is essentially carbon-neutral. Of course, if it is harvested some distance away from the garden there are some one-off transportation costs, but these will largely be offset by their subsequent growth. Living willow structures have other environmental benefits, as the plants themselves attract numerous insects and (often as a consequence of these) birds. If allowed to flower, the willow catkins also provide nectar and pollen for early emerging bees, during a period where these would often otherwise be limited.

Willow stems can be woven into these shapes during their dormant season; limiting the time that they are harvested (and ultimately dictating when projects may be carried out) to the period between late autumn through to early spring. The stems can be grown in the garden quite easily, although this takes a good deal of space; meaning that it is usually better to obtain them from a specialist grower. Once live stems have been cut, they should be stored with the bases immersed in water until needed. Most species and varieties can be used for weaving, although the faster growing varieties that produce long straight whips tend to be the best,

especially for larger structures. Osier (*Salix viminalis*) is the species traditionally favoured for weaving but others can be used for varying stem colour, leaf shape or texture, catkin colour or interest; making either single species constructions or using two or more species or varieties within the structure.

The ideal site for a living structure is on a soil that is well-drained but almost permanently moist, in a sunny situation. If attempting to establish them in a grassed or lawn area, the grass should be removed from the base of the structure, leaving around 30cm (12in) between the stems and the remaining grass. This will prevent competition from grass plants while the stems

Living structures like this willow yurt, form eye-catching additions to the garden, and with practice are relatively easy to construct and maintain.

establish, which would otherwise inhibit their growth. On previously uncultivated sites, the ground should be dug over and organic matter added, particularly if the soil has a tendency to dry out in summer. Tree guards or other protection may prove essential where hares, rabbits or deer are present.

The willow stems – or 'staves' as they are often called – should be pushed approximately 15–30cm (6–12in) into the ground. Ensure that these are inserted the correct way – that is base into the ground, as a stem inserted upside down is extremely unlikely to root and subsequently grow. It is usually easy to see which the base of a stave is as it is thicker, but always check that buds (held tight on the stems of willow) are pointing upward as final confirmation. If using thicker stems for a main framework, make holes in advance for these; ideally using a bar or steel pin driven in with a mallet in order to ensure that the surrounding ground remains firm and supportive. The complexity of the design will of course affect whether simple or complicated weaving designs will be used but even the simplest structure can look impressive.

One thing that needs to be remembered when making any structure is that staves planted vertically in the ground will tend to grow only near to the tip, whereas those planted at a 45° to 60° angle tend to grow over their entire length, thereby giving them (and of course any structure they are in) a denser growth. For fences and screens, the main staves need to be angled and in two directions. Start by placing one row spaced about 45cm (18in) apart along the line of the intended barrier before inserting another row leaning in the opposing direction, placing these in between the first staves. Where staves cross, these are simply tied together at that point, although weaving them 'one in front, one behind' will ultimately provide a much more rigid structure. Whichever is used, any point where stems cross will ultimately graft together and strengthen the structure. The finished height at this stage does not of course need to be the final height of the barrier, as once the staves sprout, the new growth can be woven and ultimately it should be possible to double the height.

Arches, tunnels or arbours are similar in many ways but need long sturdy staves to be inserted vertically into the ground to mark the main structure. These are then bent over, to be woven or tied together. After this the diagonals are inserted and interwoven in a similar way to a fence or screen, to add strength. The object here is to create an open lattice interlinked feature where the tension of the willow is the force that holds the structure together.

Once spring arrives, new shoots will sprout from the staves inserted into the ground. The new stems can be trimmed back or woven into the structure as you wish. Trimming for shape can be carried out during summer or left until winter, when some of the new growth can also be woven in to fill gaps in the design or strengthen the structure, as shoots are very brittle in the summer and liable to snap.

Vegetable Gardens

Home-grown produce, harvested when just right, not only tend to be more flavoursome than those bought from shops, but are also free of pesticide residues and have a low or neutral environmental footprint. This not only decreases your environmental impact and helps to save on grocery bills but also gives access to unusual varieties not normally available to buy. The success of a vegetable garden will, however, depend largely upon careful preparation, an understanding of how crops grow as well as the systems and ultimately structures that need to be put in place to ensure a successful harvest. While individual crops do have individual preferences, most grow best where they receive at least six hours of full sunlight a day, in a well-drained soil that is around 6–6.8 pH; meaning that any part of the garden that matches that description is certainly where a vegetable garden should be sited. Knowing these general requirements not only simplifies the choice of crops, but also helps formulate plans regarding any structures and layout that will be needed.

A well-planned vegetable garden will outline not only where the crops will go, but also where all the other things that help to do this need to be put; the shape and structure of the plot exerting a huge influence over what can and cannot be achieved there.

TOP RIGHT: **Home growing of fruit and vegetables is a rewarding hobby that can involve the whole family and often proves especially engaging for children.**

MIDDLE RIGHT: **Home grown produce has the real advantage that it can be left to fully develop before being harvested, thereby enabling its full flavour to develop.**

BOTTOM RIGHT: **A productive vegetable garden is the product of careful planning and a good deal of hard work, although most agree that the rewards outweigh the effort.**

The real trick of any successful vegetable garden is a sound plan. This plan starts with a wish list, containing the things most desired from the garden, which must then be compared against a second list detailing all the things that will be needed in order to achieve them – materials required, activities involved, as well as the time they are likely to take. Even in an established vegetable plot, new thoughts or ideas may mean adapting the layout or yearly plan to achieve revised aims. Make notes on the direction of the prevailing winds, sunny or shady spots (noting if these change during the day), always bearing in mind that even the sunniest plot may have shady pockets created by fences, hedges or trees, and identify the soil type in order to help plan which crops may be grown. Remember to think very carefully how much space each crop will realistically need and how much of a particular crop type is likely to be needed; ensuring that real need is separated from the simple desire to grow something; after all, overproduction generates waste, often at the expense of other more useful crops.

Cost should also be a consideration when planning a vegetable garden, as there is not much sense in coming up with a complex plan without the money to build it. Maintenance is also a key consideration at the planning stage, with the amount of time, effort and – where some crops are concerned – expertise, needing to be thought through before finalizing a plan. The best approach is always to try and fit the maintenance requirements around an existing lifestyle and avoid being too ambitious in the early stages.

Despite a huge array of 'essential,' labour saving items for the vegetable garden, traditional methods usually offer cheap and sustainable solutions.

The fact that crops are mostly short term, and as a consequence can be moved around on a regular basis, means that a vegetable garden is subject in the main to an ongoing yearly planning cycle; these changes making it a dynamic and engaging pastime. While true for the plants however, compost bins, sheds, greenhouses, paths and other structures, are necessarily permanent items, meaning that their position needs to be decided before planning where crops will be grown. Any plan should also consider where certain, longer term (perennial) crops will be sited. Fruit for example, may need support on wires or a trellis, a frame for netting and (arguably above all) sufficient space. Other herbaceous perennial crops such as artichokes, asparagus or rhubarb require little in the way of structures but are, nonetheless permanent, and so require a dedicated space. Finally, in order to get around the vegetable plot easily, there will need to be a network of paths, and it is this that will define how a vegetable plot will look; the point when the chance arises to apply a bit of creativity. Traditional designs, with crops laid out in straight rows, in square or rectangular beds to

Tree ripened fruit is tastier than any shop bought items, but needs a permanent place to grow and careful maintenance to yield the best results.

VEGETABLE GARDEN PLANNING TIPS

- Include a composting area – recycling green waste is the easiest way to ensure a good supply of organic soil conditioner.

- Include paths and access – make main paths wide enough to get a wheelbarrow down; paths between rows can be smaller.

- Consider whether permanent structures are really needed – sheds and greenhouses are certainly a great addition to a garden but is there enough space?

- Site a water butt near to the plot – a long walk to fill a watering can means that planting 'thirsty' crops will mean a lot of effort!

- Visit 'model gardens' for inspiration – many gardens have model vegetable patches that can be a great inspiration for you own garden.

- Work out how much time there is to maintain it – work by the maxim: 'If you can't hoe it, don't sow it!'

accommodate this are perfectly functional, although a more ornamental look may prove equally productive if well thought out.

Potagers (kitchen gardens), gain their name from the French word for a soup or broth made with vegetables (*potage*), with the term generally referring to a vegetable garden in which food, herbs, and medicines are all grown. This 'complete kitchen garden' is usually made up of small geometric plots, each containing a variety of useful herbs, vegetables, and perhaps some flowers for daily use, in a hybrid of styles that rejects the need for neat rows of produce preferring to adopt an architectural style like any other garden.

Developing from this idea, rather than devoting all or even a particular part of a garden to edible crops, the best way to start may well be to consider a 'one-for-one' substitution in which existing (non-edible) specimens are replaced with an edible counterpart. If planning to plant out a small tree for instance, a fruit tree could be used. Equally, when choosing a deciduous shrub, opting for a currant or hazelnut and substituting herbaceous flowers for ones with edible blooms such as daylilies (*Hemerocallis spp*), or chives could be considered. Crops such as peppers have very colourful fruits that can easily be used alongside flowers, whereas lettuce, radishes, chard, ornamental cabbage and other short-lived greens can be tucked into gaps in the flower beds.

This same logic that is applied to the rest of the garden can be equally applied to pots and hanging baskets, ideally suited for smaller plants such as herbs, cherry tomatoes and other summer salad crops. The combinations are endless and with a little imagination even a small courtyard garden can become a fairly productive space. One point to bear in mind is that most common ornamental plants often survive with minimal care, while edible plants on the other hand mostly require a certain amount of attention such as extra watering, pruning, fertilizing, or pest management to do really well. If time is limited then, treat edible plants as a 'hobby' within the garden so that they never become a chore. The best option is almost invariably to start small, and expand from there.

The design of a kitchen garden should consider perennial crops like rhubarb, which need a dedicated growing area for a number of years to be productive.

Climbing crops such as peas and beans while traditionally grown in rows can also be grown into a decorative 'wigwam' or trained over trellis to divide space.

If planned carefully, edible plants can easily form a decorative display that is not only aesthetically pleasing but can also provide fresh food for the table.

The Value of Recycling

For many people, recycling has become a part of the daily routine; the act of separating waste into that which can be reused and items which cannot, having become almost second nature. For these individuals, the benefits of recycling are generally clear. For those that are less familiar with the concepts the three 'pillars' of the recycling philosophy are 'reduce, re-use and recycle', often referred to as the 'three R's'. Using these three R's can help improve the sustainability of your garden, as well as its environmental footprint. Reducing the amount of waste a garden generates involves obvious activities such as composting but can

also be improved by refusing to buy products that are 'heavy' in respect of their packaging. Re-using items includes obvious things like pots and labels, but may also include things whose re-use is entirely different from that for which they were originally intended, such as garden tubs made of old car tyres or pallets, used to make a compost bin. Even when an item reaches the end of its useful life (and no obvious alternative use can be found) an attempt should be made to recycle them, so as to enable them to be processed; their raw materials forming the basis of new products.

Waste that finds its way into landfill or incinerators not only generates a heavy carbon footprint through the transport used to get it there, but can also produce further harmful gas emissions during the degradation or burning of waste. Recycling in the garden is an important activity generally, as garden waste accounts for some-where in the region of a fifth of all household waste. While this is generally biodegradable, it still takes up a large amount of space in transit, which even if bound for a composting centre, greatly adds to the carbon footprint of the compost generated. Composting garden and biodegradable kitchen waste in the garden, then, saves energy, helps to reduce pollution, uses less raw material, reduces the need for landfill and ultimately will probably save money. Even for products with a 'carbon heavy' origin such as plastics, recycling means that the carbon and other raw materials are constantly seques-tered (essentially locked up in them) and re-sequestered each time it is used; keeping them out of the waste chain, even if just temporarily in certain cases.

Purchasing and Using Environmentally Friendly Products

Wood

The seemingly endless demand for wood, while argu-ably a trade in a sustainable product, is also a major cause of illegal and destructive logging in the rain-forests of developing countries such as Brazil and Indonesia. This deforestation is often undertaken in an unsustainable and indiscriminate way; causing the loss of biodiversity, displacing local communities and ultimately contributing to climate change. Indeed, the rate of loss is shocking, with an area the size of a football pitch disappearing every two seconds. More disturbing is the fact that much of this logging is destructive (the fabric of the ecosystem is destroyed, usually through clear felling) and can also be the result of illegal operations.

Despite the high incidence of illegally harvested wood, there are few if any laws in place to prevent its sale, meaning that large quantities of illegally logged timber still make their way onto the market, so it is important that any wood products only use timber obtained from environmentally and socially responsible sources such as those certified by the Forest Stewardship Council (FSC). This certification essentially acts as evidence that the timber, or the products derived, can be traced back to source, through delivery notes and invoices, all of which carry a FSC Chain of Custody (COC) number; acting as a guarantee that it comes from legal and responsibly managed sources. Wood labelled by the FSC comes from forests or plantations that are well managed according to strict environmentally and socially responsible standards. Remember also that just because a company supplying goods is FSC certified does not mean that all of its materials and products necessarily are. FSC-certified companies do sell FSC products but they can also sell non-FSC wood products as well.

Of course, one of the problems with wood is that it tends to rot, meaning that much that is offered for commercial sale has been 'treated' to prevent this happening. Most treated timber over the last twenty years or so has been treated with CCA (chromated copper arsenate) in a process known as pressure treatment or 'tanalization'. Research carried out in the USA however, has shown that CCA-treated timber that has been in place in gardens for around ten years leaches chromium, copper and arsenic (all potentially toxic with arsenic being particularly so) into the soil. The levels of all three elements tend to be highest near the timber, meaning that plants grown there will take this arsenic up (although not the chromium or copper). While these amounts are relatively low, a core idea for most sustainable gardeners is of course to avoid any chemical contamination. When buying timber in, it is best to

Even a small decorative pot can provide space to grow a range of herbs that will provide an eye-catching and tasty addition to the summer garden.

obtain timber treated with an arsenic-free alternative. The most environmentally sound of these is wood treated with a product called 'Tanalith E', a product based on copper triazole; the copper being derived from recycled sources while 'triazoles' are biodegradable biocides. Although triazoles are a synthetic compound (and therefore not organic in the horticultural sense), they are commonly used in pharmaceutical preparations as well as plant fungicides, and degrade in a matter of hours should they escape into the soil.

Environmentally Friendly Furniture

Since the majority of garden furniture is made from wood, it is important that these items carry a Forest Stewardship Council (FSC) logo and are preferably treated with an arsenic-free preservative. As well as this though, the wood type is also important, with wood that is produced locally always being the best

Garden furniture need not be newly bought in order to be attractive; here, recycled planks and barrels have been used to great effect to make a bench.

option where the environmental footprint is concerned. In most cases, tropical hardwoods such as mahogany are best avoided, as they tend to be very expensive, waste huge amounts of fuel in transportation and, despite claims to the contrary, are often logged in an ecologically damaging way – even when grown in plantations.

Ultimately though, if grown locally and harvested in an ecologically sustainable way, wood is almost always the best option where garden furniture is concerned, being environmentally superior to all other manufactured material substitutes such as aluminium, steel or plastic and a renewable resource that is ultimately biodegradable.

As with any products, it is worth asking questions and if the manufacturer is not too far away, it might even be worth visiting the factory or workshop to find out more about it and its environmental credentials.

Patios, Paving, Paths and Walkways

Like so many items within the garden, a good number of paving products claim 'green credentials'. This can be misleading however as the tendency to use the word natural for stone for example, while being true (as stone is a natural material) does not in itself imply any environmental benefit will arise through its use. Indeed, even if the material does reach certain environmental criteria, it is still likely to be heavy, and such items need transportation and are costly in respect of fuel use. In addition to this, sealed surfaces tend to channel any water that falls on them away into a drainage system. In many cases, this flows out into the sewerage system and automatically goes to a treatment plant. The result is that a significant proportion of the 'effluent' treated is little more than rainwater. Indeed, the vast majority of the runoff from roofs and pavements is actually reasonably clean and so doesn't need 'cleaning-up' before being returned to the environment.

Add to this the fact that all this additional water discharge shed from sealed surfaces, both during and immediately after a rain shower, exacerbates the problems of floods and droughts by accelerating the hydrological cycle. It does this by dramatically reducing the time between a raindrop landing and it actually entering a watercourse. While the initial result of this is a highly increased rate of flow in streams and rivers, it also reduces the storage capacity of ground surrounding the rivers, (it has no chance to infiltrate), which in turn can lead to shortages of groundwater (and river flow) later.

If paving is a necessity though, it is worth looking for a type that has a porous nature. Surfaces with high porosity are better than sealed surfaces, letting water flow downward and into the ground below. On 'unpaved' land, rain naturally soaks into the ground, mostly travelling down under the action of gravity until it reaches the underlying rock strata. All of this tends to naturally filter it before it eventually joins the main body of 'groundwater', where it is either stored, or slowly flows toward springs, streams or rivers.

In essence, porous paving mimics this, using the natural environment as a conduit for collected water, mimicking what would happen if buildings and pavements were not there, in what is often referred to as a Sustainable Drainage System or 'SuDS'. There are numerous benefits to the SuDS approach, the chief of which are flood control (better management of storm water at source or 'source control'), pollution control, as well as recharging soil-water and deeper groundwater.

Permeable paving systems usually use some form of block paving, such as concrete blocks, clay pavers or a form of bound aggregate to create the surface layer, but recent advances in technologies now enable asphalt and resinous surfacing to be used. Paths and other surfaces can of course utilize materials like woodchip that composts over time, and although the chipping does use energy, it utilizes a material that is a renewable resource.

Wooden seating can be made from a range of reclaimed materials and can form sculptural features or focal points in their own right in some cases.

Walls

Garden walls are a common landscape feature, used variously to divide space and form boundaries or as retaining barriers for soil. Their true environmental cost is usually measured in the amount of fuel that is used in the quarrying, manufacture and transportation of the often very heavy component parts. Of all of these, it is the use of cement that is arguably

Drystone walls have a relatively low carbon footprint as they are constructed without any mortar (and therefore cement) to bind the stones together.

the most contentious, as its manufacture is estimated to contribute around five per cent of all (human-released) carbon-dioxide emissions. Indeed, the manufacture of cement adds somewhere in the region of 1.25 tonnes of CO_2 to the atmosphere for every one tonne of cement produced. The easiest way then to start making walls more environmentally friendly is to cut out the use (and transportation) of this damaging product. Of course, this does not mean that any wall made without it is automatically 'greener' or more

Drystone walls eventually become colonized with plants and act as a wildlife refuge for insects and animals forming decorative features in their own right.

sustainable. In order to improve it further then, the materials that the wall are to be made of need careful thought. The first step is to obtain materials that are extracted or made locally. This of course can be difficult, but does help considerably in reducing the fuel use associated with their transportation costs that would otherwise occur over a long supply chain.

Stone is a popular, natural and durable material that is understandably popular with gardeners. It is of course a finite resource, although it is worth pointing out here that the planet is made of rock, meaning that there is (from a practical standpoint) an awful lot of it! Having said this, it is not a consistent commodity, and the rocks available in one area vary in their suitability for use in construction to those of others. In addition to this, certain places have extensive tracts of usable rocks occurring as 'outcrops' near to the surface, while in other areas, the rocks are either buried deeply under soil or those that do outcrop are of dubious or unsuitable quality.

If rock is available, it is always the best option to use a locally quarried stone, ideally opting for reclaimed rock if and wherever possible. This means that the transportation costs will be lower, although for newly quarried rock there will be the cost of the energy used to extract it, which must also be considered.

Reclaimed materials, be they stone, bricks or blocks or tiles are always a preferable option where these can be obtained locally. They do of course have an embodied energy cost, although this has to be offset against the fact that their reuse means that they have had their working life effectively extended.

Where a retaining wall is to be made without the use of cement, dry-stone walls are one option. These walls are constructed using stones without any mortar to bind them together, being held together instead by the interlocking of the stones, and can be used to make buildings, boundary walls or to form retaining walls for raised beds or terracing. A free-standing dry-stone wall would be constructed by placing two rows of large flattish stones along the line or perimeter to be walled as a foundation. These can be sunken into a shallow trench to provide added stability, although this is not always necessary. Smaller stones may be used as 'chocks' in places where stones do not fit together snugly or if they are naturally rounded.

The walls are built up to the desired height layer by layer and at intervals large 'tie-stones' or 'through stones' are placed which span both faces of the wall; effectively bonding what would otherwise be two thin walls leaning against each other, greatly increasing the strength of the wall. The wall surface should slope, very slightly so that each side is effectively leaning in; leading to a finished wall, the base of which is a little wider than the top. The commonest and easiest way to ensure that this is done is by using an 'A-shaped' frame known as a 'batter frame', set to the required angle, usually 1:6 – an angle of 15° from vertical. If a double-sided wall was to be 120cm (4ft) in height then, it would need to be 40cm (16in) narrower at the top than at the base.

The gap in the middle of a free-standing wall should not be left empty, but should be filled with stone rubble or earth as each course is laid, ensuring there are no gaps. This ensures tightness between stones; reducing the chance of collapse by limiting the chance that stones will move during settlement. The gaps between stones also need to be bridged, so that above and below each join, there is another stone and not another join – in a staggered, 'bricklike fashion'. Not doing this (that is allowing so called 'running

joints') for more than two courses is essentially a serious weakness in the fabric of the wall. The final layer on the top of the wall also consists of large, coping stones which, as with the tie stones, span the entire width of the wall and prevent it from breaking apart.

If a dry-stone wall is needed as a retaining wall, it can be built as a single skin. The construction is very similar to that of a free-standing one, although the tie stones are used to add stability by setting them into the soil or backfill. It is essential though that the backfill or soil filling is placed as the wall is built, and packed in tightly to ensure that it is properly stable.

DRY STONE WALL QUICK BUILDING CHECKLIST

There are five basic rules regarding the construction of a dry-stone wall.

1 The larger stones should always be placed at the bottom of the wall, except for through stones and top stones.

2 Taper the wall from base to top, following a 'batter' of around 1:6 (an angle of 15° from vertical).

3. Use tie-stones or through stones to span both faces of the wall and improve stability.

4. Stagger the joints and avoid running joints.

5. Keep the middle full.

In addition to these construction rules, when building a dry-stone wall always ensure that:

• The foundation trench is set out using lines to position, ensuring the base is wide enough to encompass the batter needed on the wall face and dig it out.

• Stones are stacked along the length of the trench leaving room to work.

• Foundation stones are placed along the length of the entire trench filling voids as work progresses.

• The face is correctly angled preferably using a pre-constructed batter frame to do so.

• Stones are laid carefully to get a good face to the wall, ensuring that this is smooth and without bumps or bulges.

• The top is finished with a layer of coping stones, which span the entire width of the wall and prevent it from breaking apart.

If a dry stone wall sounds a bit complicated, or the type of stone available is unsuitable for use in this manner, a 'gabion wall' could be the solution. Gabions are essentially rectangular cages or 'baskets' made with heavily galvanized wire, which are filled (usually) with stone and stacked on one another, to form a tiered wall, – that is one that steps back with the slope rather than standing vertically. They do not make good free-standing walls but can be surprisingly decorative in the right context. The fact that they easily stack, and can be made to do so in various shapes and designs; means that they retain great strength and effectiveness; a quality that can often increase with time, as silt and vegetation fill the gaps and reinforce the structure.

Earth is a substance that can easily be made into a walling material which, although it does have limitations, can be a cheap and sustainable option in certain situations. Various uses of earth exist, including 'adobe' – a mixture of sand, clay, and water which is poured into a mould and left in the sun to dry. Once dried, adobe is exceptionally strong but unfortunately not particularly waterproof unless rendered or clad with another material.

'Earth-bag' construction is a development from the adobe approach whereby sturdy sacks are filled with material such as sand, gravel, clay or crushed

Gabions are essentially rectangular, heavily galvanized wire cages or baskets, which can be filled with stone and stacked to form a solid tiered wall.

rock, these then being used to build walls in courses – forming a staggered pattern similar to any other form of bricklaying. Like a dry-stone wall, these need to be sloped or curved to provide improved stability. Any structure made from them would typically be finished with a rendering coat.

'Rammed Earth' is another method used to form walls, whereby soil is packed tightly into a mould where it is rammed down and hardened to form a durable wall. The best raw materials are usually earth that is rich in chalk, lime and gravel, and these are compressed while damp in successive layers of around 10–25cm (4–10in) using a hand held or powered tamper to compact these layers to around fifty per cent of their original thickness. Further layers of material are added and the process is repeated until the wall has reached the desired height. Once compressed the wall frames can be immediately removed; a necessary action if wire brushing to add texture (and remove the imprint of the frame) is to be done. If the walls are left in the frame, they can become too hard to brush after around sixty minutes, although the whole construction needs a good period of warm dry days following construction to allow it to dry and fully harden; ideally allowing up to two years for it to completely 'cure'. While this seems like a long process, the longer it cures the stronger the structure becomes. Walls constructed outside may be sealed to prevent water damage and there are several proprietary products specifically designed to seal earth walls.

Old tyres can also be used to make the framework of a wall, which can then be filled with rammed earth. These are of course not to everyone's taste, although they can be painted and even rendered to 'hide' them. Earth structures do have the advantage of using locally available materials and because of what the basic substance is (earth) they typically have low levels of embodied energy, generate very little waste and so have a low environmental footprint; especially if the soil is taken from the site where construction takes place. If using soil in construction though, only use subsoil, stripping and retaining the darker, living topsoil for growing plants in – the thing it is best at.

Fences, Trellises and Pergolas

Like many other garden products, fences, trellises and pergolas are traditionally made from wood. It is important therefore, that these items carry a Forest Stewardship Council (FSC) logo, or that they are made with wood that is produced locally and are preferably treated with an arsenic-free preservative. Having said this, other products such as willow or hazel can be grown and woven into durable fence panels and trellises, with materials such as reeds, grasses and even thin 'brushwood' being used to make attractive fence panels. Ultimately though, it depends upon where the items were made, as even apparently environmentally sound alternatives become less so if transported over long distances. The best option is often to visit a supplier in the area that makes their own products and find out more about them.

Dead Hedges

While the word hedge naturally conjures an image of a barrier made from living plants, they were originally made from cut branches and deadwood. This might seem to be a strange idea in a modern context but a dead hedge provides an excellent way of dealing

---

THE ADVANTAGES OF A DEAD HEDGE

- It is a way of dealing with awkward branch wood.
- It provides an alternative hibernation area to bonfire piles.
- It can be incorporated into a windbreak.
- It is cheap and easy to make.
- It will help many useful species to survive the winter.

---

with cut branch-wood (following pruning) and is an excellent way of providing shelter for a whole range of beneficial garden species.

Making a dead hedge involves hammering in two rows of upright stakes, one behind the other, or a single row could be placed in front of a freestanding wall. The space between them is now filled with long pruned branches and the smaller gaps filled with more twiggy material. Over time, the timber will begin to rot down and so will need more branches to be added on top as well as replacing any of the upright stakes which rot through. The hedge will ultimately become a habitat for many invertebrates such as insects or spiders and may act as a temporary shelter for even larger creatures.

A dead hedge is an excellent way of dealing with cut branch-wood (following pruning) while providing shelter for a range of beneficial garden species.

Potting Compost

While composting is the perfect way to cut carbon dioxide (CO_2) emissions caused by its disposal, the resulting material is a valuable garden asset that forms a convenient basis to make home-made potting compost (potting soil) for use in pots and containers. This sustainable alternative not only saves money, but also plant needs and eliminates the carbon/ecological footprint associated with the production and transport of bagged mixes offered for sale in garden centres. Indeed, until the late 1930s most gardeners still made their own compost, often based on traditional recipes handed down through generations and occasionally a closely guarded secret. This all changed in 1939, when the recipe for John Innes Compost was perfected and released to the horticulture trade.

Although the ecological footprint of composting is fairly clear, the effects of bought compost can be less so. Recent concerns over the use of moss peat for example, have led many gardeners in the United Kingdom to seek peat-free alternatives. While this is a positive step in the conservation of natural lowland peat bogs, the alternatives are not always as environmentally sound as claims might suggest. Coir for example, a by-product of the coconut industry in tropical regions, is often mooted as an environmentally sound substitute, but needs transporting thousands of kilometres in order to get it to gardeners in cooler climes. While its use may well be praiseworthy in the country of origin, its carbon footprint is very large in comparison to other substitutes. The essential point then regarding a peat substitute is that it must be

Ingredients for Potting Mixtures

Although there are almost countless recipes for potting compost, a commonly accepted ratio of ingredients is three parts loam, three parts organic matter and two parts sand or grit. Often though, the best idea is to experiment and try out mixes until the 'right' blend is discovered, as ultimately, mixes are often most clearly dictated by the availability of materials to hand in the local area. The following then are merely examples.

Potting mixtures	Benefits
Loam	Provides bulk and a fine texture but may become hard and impenetrable to rot if allowed to dry out. Has a high nutrient exchange capacity of loam and is valuable for potting mixes that also include leaf mould.
Garden compost	Well-rotted and sieved garden compost; holds water, contains nutrients and helps bind the growing medium, although it needs to be mixed with a mineral constituent like sand or loam to ensure that it remains open and well aerated.
Leaf mould	Should be made from fully-decomposed leaves (ideally two years old) and sieved. Its coarse, crumbly texture provides drainage and aeration, is moisture retentive, but does not contain many nutrients, rendering it very useful for seed compost.
Shredded bark	Well composted fine, shredded bark takes at least two years to make and, like leaf mould, is not binding enough to use on its own. As an admixture to other organic matter, it ensures the mixture keeps a light, open, 'fluffy' structure.
Worm compost	The high humus content of worm compost not only holds water and helps to bind the mixture, it is also rich in nutrients, especially nitrogen, and phosphates (ideal for roots) are readily available, making it especially good for seed mixtures.
Sand	Sand is essentially the natural form of glass and has no nutrient value. Coarse (sharp) sand or fine washed grit are commonly added to potting mixtures to add weight, help add air spaces, and ultimately improve drainage and aeration.

gathered from a sustainable (renewable) source, and be produced nearby in order to reduce the amount of transport needed. In these respects, home-made compost is ideal due to its (more or less) negligible environmental footprint.

The requirements of any growing medium for pots are simple. It should bind (stick together) sufficiently to support plants, be relatively stable (that is, it won't readily decompose and sink into the pot), should hold enough water (for the plant in question) while allowing sufficient aeration. Many gardeners question why a potting mixture is needed at all; after all, plants grow quite happily in the ground. The simple fact is though, that if soil were used alone, it starts to behave differently when confined in such a small volume. This is because pot walls alter the water balance while tending to dry the soil which in turn hardens. The net result of this is that the normal soil ecology fails to develop normally (affecting nutrient supply), resulting in poor growth, and in turn a greater tendency to be affected by soil-borne diseases. Garden soil however can be used as a constituent of a potting medium when mixed with other components, helping to control and balance nutrient release and adding weight; an important attribute in ensuring pot grown plants do not fall over.

Pots and Containers

A visit to a garden centre will often reveal a seemingly endless array of containers; all purporting to be environmentally friendly, and often with a hefty price tag. Of course, for all of these, the same caveats exist as for any other garden products; make sure they are from a sustainable source, preferably made locally and ultimately with the lowest environmental footprint possible. It is quite straightforward (and more environmentally sound) however, to make pots for the garden using recycled materials, many of which can be everyday items, or things that would otherwise enter the waste chain. Tyres, old bins, even an old Wellington boot can be used; essentially just about anything that has an opening at one end and will allow water to drain from its base.

In essence, there are two types of pots that are used in the garden. Those that are used to raise new plants (growing pots) and those that are used in display settings (showing pots). Both of these uses can be met using recycled items.

Many recyclable items can be used to make growing pots, with perhaps the cheapest, and most readily available of these being newspaper. The process of making these could not be simpler and involves taking a sheet of newspaper and folding this in half so that it is about 4cm (1½in) longer than an aluminium drink can. Place the can in the top corner of one end and roll the paper around until it is all wrapped around the can. Fold one end of the newspaper inward to make the base of the pot. This can then be filled with seed compost and used to raise seeds. Once the seedlings are large enough, the whole pot can be potted on or even planted directly into the ground, where the newspaper will eventually decompose.

Seed pots can also be made from toilet paper rolls and kitchen towels (the cardboard roll in the centre), or similarly from any other thin cardboard tube, such as those used to hold gift wrapping paper. These have the advantage of being ready shaped and are usually much sturdier than paper pots. A base for the pot can be made simply by making four cuts about 1.5cm (½in) long, lengthwise from one end and folding these in, although it is not always necessary to do this. When potted on or planted out cardboard pots, like their paper counterparts, eventually decompose.

If using paper or cardboard pots, ensure that they are at least 7.5cm (3in) long so as to allow sufficient space for root development. Cutting tubes too short often results in too little compost that not only restricts early growth but can also tend to dry out quickly. Set the finished, filled pots within the confines of another container, packing them in just tightly enough to ensure that they support each other. Ideally, this should be watertight, so as to ensure that the pots can be watered by filling the container with water and allowing this to be absorbed by the paper pots.

Perhaps the most ingenious home-made seed growing pots can be made from eggshells. Unlikely as this may seem, empty eggshells that have been carefully

Recycling is a key aspect of any sustainable gardening practice; here, home made grow bags have been made by filling old sacks with garden compost.

Any large container can be used to grow plants in and a collection of these can be grouped together to form a productive, if quirky garden feature.

broken to ensure that the majority of the 'thick end' remains, are rinsed out leaving enough space to hold a small amount of seed compost, and a small hole carefully made in the base. They not only make interesting seed pots, but are surprisingly durable, allow the growing mix to breathe (the shell is naturally porous) and can easily be obtained from a local source. If the eggs were bought in a cardboard carton, then this can be used to hold the eggshell seed pots, as their round bases do make them inherently unstable and liable to tip or roll around. Once seedlings are large enough to pot on or plant out, they can be planted direct as long as the eggshell is lightly crushed so as to enable the young roots to find a way through.

Alternatives to the above pots include plastic cups (such as those used for yoghurt), paper or polystyrene (styrofoam) drinks cups, or any other suitable packaging products, provided that these have holes made in their bases.

If seeds need a more humid environment to germinate, or for those types that need a period of winter chilling to get them started, a large (2 litre) clear plastic drink bottle can provide the perfect growing start. The bottle is first cut in half with several drainage holes punched into the bottom half of the bottle. This bottom end is then filled with about 10-12cm (4-5in) of seed compost and the seeds sown into this as per their requirements. The top half of the bottle (without the screw top) is now 'replaced' by sliding it over the base. Making a small 1cm (½in) cut on the rim of the bottom half should help ease the top section on firmly. The mini- propagator can now be placed on a windowsill (if warmth is needed) or left out in a sheltered, shady part of the garden to allow it to be exposed to the elements. In warm conditions (or once the weather warms up in spring for outdoor propagators), ensure that the compost never dries out and once the seedlings emerge pot them on once large enough to handle.

When it comes to showing pots, there are seemingly endless possibilities aside from those already mentioned. Old shoes and boots make interesting small pots, where the toe can be either left intact or cut out for plants to spill out at both ends. Old bins or pails can be ideal, especially when painted, perhaps with a decorative design. Wicker baskets can also be used, although these must be lined in order to prevent them rotting away too rapidly and can also be painted. An old wheelbarrow can make a somewhat appropriate setting for plants and old wooden crates can be remarkably showy when used to display plants. Old kitchen pots or pans, and leaky watering cans can all play their part as can more natural materials such as hollowed-out stumps and logs. Whatever item is chosen though, the main thing to be sure of is that there is some form of drainage, thereby preventing things from becoming waterlogged following rain or watering.

Buildings

Buildings, like many other garden features, vary greatly in their environmental impact, much of this depending upon the materials they are made from. Garden buildings made of wood, brick, stone and so on, are similar in many ways to other garden structures, and their impact may well be largely similar as a consequence. Having said this, the manner in which they are utilized or finished can have the result of making them a contributory factor to the garden's environmental credentials.

A shed for example, while variable in respect of its environmental cost, can be used to collect rainwater that falls on its roof in order to supply irrigation water. The value of the roof-space can be further enhanced if the shed has a living roof (essentially a carpet of living vegetation), made of stonecrop (*Sedum spp.*), houseleek (*Sempervivum spp.*) or other suitable species. These so-called 'green roofs' are a great cover for a garden building, replacing the grass or foliage taken up when installing it. Green roofs usually feature a thin growing medium, set over an impermeable membrane, thereby ensuring that the roof itself does not leak into the interior. If properly made, they require very little maintenance, and if made from succulent species, particularly stonecrop or houseleek, generally do not require irrigation once established.

Stonecrop is used due to its ability to resist wind, frost and drought, and is usually sold in the form of sedum mats, consisting of a base layer of polyester, hessian, or porous polythene depending on the supplier. A 2cm (¾in) thick growing medium is placed on top of this and sedum cuttings sprinkled on. These

An old sack, filled with compost and used to grow plants in, provides a textural contrast to the foliage above that contrasts well among other pots and containers.

Replacing a felt roof on a shed or garden building with a green, sedum roof instantly improves its green credentials while providing an attractive feature.

grow into the substrate and rapidly form a dense coverage that is around 5–7cm (2–3in) thick, including the depth of the growing medium. These mats are then placed onto the roof, being laid onto a porous moisture retention blanket, such as capillary matting, making this approach a very light-weight option, although in some circumstances the building may have to have additional support to take the extra weight. On a flat roof, the plants simply stay where they are. On a sloping roof though, a maximum pitch of nine degrees is ideal. Any more and you may need to make a batten edge (or even a series of battened 'boxes' across larger roofs, to hold the green mat in place and prevent it sliding off. A green living roof lasts longer than traditional roofing materials due to the additional protection it affords in respect of heat and wind resistance compared to a traditional roof while contributing throughout its life to reducing carbon dioxide in the atmosphere.

This deer sculpture made from driftwood and scrap metal shows that sculpture made using recycled materials can be interesting and eye-catching.

Garden Sculpture

Sculpture, while not strictly the territory of all gardeners is often included in gardens, and as such deserves at least a mention. Not everyone owns a piece of sculpture but most gardeners will have at least a favourite pot or some quirky item. These items, while arguable in terms of their value as 'art', often work in the same way as sculpture, by providing a focal point. Any garden art or sculpture makes a statement within the garden. A well-made piece needs to be shown off to its full potential, sometimes in full view in the middle of a lawn, or in other cases by 'peeping out from foliage'.

While garden sculpture is of course a subject broad enough to merit a volume in its own right, the same simple truths regarding the materials, energy, and any waste resulting from its manufacture apply to sculpture as they would to any other item. To the French sculptor Auguste Rodin, sculpture was simplicity itself. When he famously said; 'I choose a block of marble, and chop off whatever I don't need', he rather ironically portrays an image of wastefulness, the eventual sculpture bearing testimony to the material which was discarded. Indeed, like so many additions to the garden, sculpture often carries a hidden cost in respect of its environmental footprint. In a sustainable context then, the best sculpture necessarily combines the ethics of a low environmental footprint, with the necessity of recycling and wise use of materials. Of course, this should never be an excuse to compromise the art itself and if anything, a renewed, sustainable approach should always seek new solutions and different possibilities.

There is a simple inescapable truth here then. Anything that is included in the garden must be carefully assessed as to its environmental credentials. The lowest impact is almost always achieved when things are made on site, using materials to hand, preferably conducting the work in a way that does not pollute or create waste. The challenge facing the production of sustainable, low impact garden sculpture, and the quirks that this may bestow upon a garden are akin to the whole focus and scope of sustainable gardening. Each should be unique, say something about the personality of the owner, and ultimately provide pleasure for years to come.

Recycled building materials can be used to make a habitat stack to help beneficial garden creatures (*see* Chapter 5), which adds interest and texture to the garden.

This clever roundhouse design using reclaimed timber, logs and construction materials incorporates a novel sculptural quality to this habitat stack.

Old felled or fallen trees can be carved into a variety of interesting shapes and if done carefully seem to spring to life.

Wooden sculpture has unmatched quality in respect of its texture and overall appearance, and if grown on site is a sustainable form of garden adornment.

USEFUL ADDRESSES

ORGANIZATIONS

UK

The Royal Horticultural Society
80 Vincent Square
London, SW1P 2PE
Tel: 0845 260 5000
www.rhs.org.uk

Garden Organic
Coventry, Warwickshire, CV8 3LG
Tel: 024 7630 3517
Email: enquiry@gardenorganic.org.uk
www.gardenorganic.org.uk

Pesticides Action Network (PAN) Europe
Development House
56–64 Leonard Street
London, EC2A 4LT
Tel: 020 7065 0920
www.pan-europe.info

USA

American Horticultural Society
River Farm
7931 East Boulevard Drive
Alexandria, VA 22308
(V) 703.768.5700
Toll Free: 1.800.777.7931
(F) 703.768.8700
www.ahs.org

National Gardening Association
1100 Dorset Street
South Burlington, VT 05403
Tel: (802) 863-5251
www.garden.org

Pesticide Action Network North America
49 Powell St., Suite 500
San Francisco, CA 94102
Tel: (415) 981-1771
www.panna.org

Ecology Action
(USA-based but with an international focus)
5798 Ridgewood Road
Willits, CA 95490
Tel: (707) 459-0150
www.growbiointensive.org

Florida's Online Composting Center
(Online composting tutorials and more)
www.compostinfo.com/main/intro.htm

Canada

Canadian Organic Growers
National Office
323 Chapel Street
Ottawa, Ontario,
K1N 7Z2
Tel: 613-216-0741
Toll-free: 1-888-375-7383
Email: office@cog.ca
www.cog.ca/

The Composting Council of Canada
16 Northumberland Street
Toronto, Ontario M6H 1P7
Tel: (416) 535-0240
Email: ccc@compost.org
www.compost.org/englishoverview.html

Suppliers

UK

Sundries
Harrod Horticultural
Pinbush Road, Lowestoft
Suffolk, NR33 7NL
Tel: 0845 402 5300
www.harrodhorticultural.com

Wormeries and compost bins
Wiggly Wigglers
Lower Blakemere Farm
Blakemere, Herefordshire, HR2 9PX
Tel: 01981 500391
www.wigglywigglers.co.uk

Original Organics Ltd.
Unit 9, Langlands Business Park
Uffculme, Cullompton
Devon E15 3DA
Tel: 0808 1209676
www.originalorganics.co.uk

Biological Control
Just Green
Unit 14
Springfield Road Industrial Estate
Burnham-on-Crouch
Essex CM0 8UA
Tel: 01621 785088
www.just-green.com

Ladybird Plant Care
The Glasshouses
Fletching Common
Newick, Lewes
East Sussex, BN8 4JJ
Tel: 0845 0945 499
www.ladybirdplantcare.co.uk/

Greenhouses, Sheds and Frames
A1 Sheds
Forester's Lane
High Street, Tranent
East Lothian, EH33 1HJ
Tel: 01875 613090
www.simply-sheds.co.uk/

Plants and Seeds
Thompson & Morgan
Poplar Lane
Ipswich, IP8 3BU
Tel: 0844 2485383
www.thompson-morgan.com/

USA

Wormeries and Compost Bins
Compost Bin Supply
Clean Air Gardening
2266 Monitor Street
Dallas, TX 75207
Tel: 214-363-5170
www.compostbinsupply.com/

Happy D Ranch
Environmentally-friendly Worm Farm
PO Box 3001
Visalia
California 93278
www.happydranch.com/

Biological Control
A1 Unique insect Control
5504 Sperry Drive
Citrus Heights, CA 95621
www.a-1unique.com

Biocontrol Network
5116 Williamsburg Rd, Brentwood, TN 37027
(800) 441-BUGS / Tel: (615) 370-4301
Email: info@biconet.com
www.biconet.com

Planet Natural
1612 Gold Ave.
Bozeman, MT 59715
(406) 587-5891
www.planetnatural.com

Plants and Seeds
Thompson & Morgan Seedsmen, Inc.
220 Faraday Avenue
Jackson, NJ 08527-5073
1(800) 274-7333 or 1(732) 363-2225
www.tmseeds.com

Stokes Seeds Ltd
PO Box 548
Buffalo, New York
USA, 14240-0548
Tel: 1-716-695-6980
Email: stokes@stokeseeds.com
www.stokeseeds.com/

Greenhouses and Frames
Frostproof.com
512 North Scenic Highway
Frostproof
FL 33843
Tel: 1-800-635-3621
Email: questions@frostproof.com
www.frostproof.com

Gothic Arch Greenhouses
PO Box 1564, AL 36633
Tel: 1-800-531-4769
www.gothicarchgreenhouses.com

Canada

Wormeries and Compost Bins
Vermiculture Canada
Site 8 Box 23 RR 2
Tofield, Alberta
Canada T0B 4J0
Tel: (780) 662-3309 (Edmonton & vicinity)
TOLL FREE 1-866-225-5036
http://www.vermiculture.ca/store/index.php

Pest Control Tools and Sundries
Contech Enterprises Inc.
Unit 115 - 19 Dallas Road
Victoria, BC V8V 5A6
(250) 413-3250
www.contech-inc.com

Plants and Seeds
Thompson & Morgan
47–220 Wyecroft Road
P.O. Box 306, Oakville, ON L6J5A2
1(877) 545-4386
www.thompsonmorgan.ca

Stokes Seeds Ltd
PO Box 10, Thorold, Ontario
Canada L2V 5E9
Tel: 1-905-688-4300
Email: stokes@stokeseeds.com
www.stokeseeds.com

Greenhouses, Sheds and Frames
Cedarshed Industries
PH: 1-800-830-8033
Email: sales@cedarshed.com
www.cedarshed.com

**Rion Canada Greenhouse Kits
(Greenwall Solutions Inc.)**
Vaughan, Ontario. Canada
Tel: 905 597-5710
www.canada-greenhouse-kits.com

INDEX